For almost 43 years three school notebooks lay in obscurity in the County Armagh home of sixty two-year old James McRoberts. The closely-filled pages recorded just over two years in his life in uniform as he played his part in what was then known as the Great War.

During the Home Rule crisis of 1914, one of several in Ireland's history, James McRoberts, like many other men, joined the Young Citizen Volunteers, an organisation that eventually became the 14th Royal Irish Rifles, a battalion of the 36th (Ulster) Division.

These notebooks, written at the time and with footnotes added some forty years later, record his Army service between 8 January 1915 and 3 April 1917. They tell, with remarkable immediacy, of his time at Randalstown, County Antrim and the move to Seaford in East Sussex. From here, after further training, James moved with his Battalion to the trenches of the Western Front.

Written with a degree of humour and some detail his story covers the mundane routine of camp life, recreation behind the lines, the horrors of enemy shelling, the deaths of good friends and the momentous events of 1 July 1916 on the Somme, when his unit was in the thick of the action.

On 1 November 1917, while acting as a scout for a night patrol at Messines Ridge, James was seriously wounded and evacuated to hospital - for him the War was over. Nevertheless, he continued to record what was happening around him both with humour and in detail. Classed as 80% disabled, he was eventually discharged and returned home to enjoy a post-war career as a surveyor in County Armagh.

This is a remarkable memoir that is, by turns, lively, candid, humorous, poignant, and above all a window into the world of an Ulsterman who found himself both witness and participant to a series of remarkable events. His descriptions of army life, both daily routine and the inferno on the Somme in July 1916, add greatly to our knowledge of this most climactic period of history.

David Truesdale (centre)

David Truesdale opted for early retirement in 1998 and since then has written for films and television and produced two battlefield guides on behalf of the Royal Irish Fusiliers Museum; *The First Eagle: the 87th Foot at the Battle of Barrosa* and *Regulars by God! The 89th Foot at the Battle of Lundy's Lane.*

He is the author of *Brotherhood of the Cauldron: Irishmen in the 1st Airborne Division at Arnhem; Angels and Heroes, the story of a machine gunner with the Royal Irish Fusiliers August 1914 to April 1915* (with Amanda Moreno); *Irish Winners of the Victoria Cross* (with Richard Doherty); Leading the Way to Arnhem, a History of the 21st Independent Parachute Company (with Peter Gijbels) and *Arnhem Their Final Battle, the 11th Parachute Battalion 1943/44* (with Gerrit Pijpers).

With David Orr he has written *The Rifles are There: 1st & 2nd Battalions The Royal Ulster Rifles in the Second World War* and *A New Battlefield; The Royal Ulster Rifles in Korea.* They are currently collaborating on a history of the Ulster Volunteer Force and 36th Ulster Division, 1913-1919.

For relaxation he paints in watercolours following the Kelly school of innovation, photographs wildlife, listens to good music, drinks red wine and finds that Tommaso Albinoni (1671-1750) and his Oboe Concerto in D Minor, Op.9, No.2, has been an inspiration during difficult times in any manuscript.

'YOUNG CITIZEN, OLD SOLDIER'

FROM BOYHOOD IN ANTRIM
TO HELL ON THE SOMME

The Journal of Rifleman James McRoberts,
No.1885, 14th Battalion Royal Irish Rifles (YCV)
January 1915-April 1917

Edited by David Truesdale

Helion & Company Ltd

Helion & Company Limited
26 Willow Road
Solihull
West Midlands
B91 1UE
England
Tel. 0121 705 3393
Fax 0121 711 4075
email: info@helion.co.uk
website: www.helion.co.uk

Published by Helion & Company 2012. Reprinted in paperback 2016

Designed and typeset by Farr out Publications, Wokingham, Berkshire
Cover designed by Farr out Publications, Wokingham, Berkshire
Printed by Lightning Source Limited, Milton Keynes, Buckinghamshire

ISBN 978-1-911096-12-2

British Library Cataloguing-in-Publication Data
A catalogue record for this book is available from the British Library

For details of other military history titles published by Helion & Company Limited contact the above address, or visit our website: http://www.helion.co.uk.

We always welcome receiving book proposals from prospective authors.

To the memory of
Jack L Armstrong and Brian Boyd who, although they survived
1 July 1916 and were both awarded the Military Medal, were
killed in the following year.

The better the soldier, the more limited is his outlook
Siegfried Sassoon

As I sit thinking, the past returns,
Unbidden; with awful clarity
The lid comes off the memory jar.[1]

Contents

List of Maps and Illustrations

Armagh War Memorial, little changed since James McRoberts paid his
     annual tribute. However, an amount of damage was caused to the
     Memorial when a bomb exploded directly outside the Courthouse
     on 3 September 1993, with much greater damage to the Museum of
     the Royal Irish Fusiliers, seen in the background. (Jonathan Maguire, BA)   200
Armagh War Memorial today, there is little damage to be seen, unlike
     Continental memorials, which are not repaired in ensuing conflicts.
     (Jonathan Maguire, BA)   200
Remembrance Day Parade, Armagh November 1953. The men have
     just passed the Orange Hall, about half way along the Mall, James
     McRoberts in the centre wearing a dark suit carrying a raincoat,
     to his left is his friend Richard Bennett, behind him, wearing a
     bowler hat, and with glasses is John Webster JP, while in the centre
     of the second rank with an impressive array of medals is George
     McCartney. On the right hand side are two women looking towards
     the camera - the one wearing the light coloured hat is the late Bessie
     Blocksidge, the bareheaded woman is Sheila Irwin. On the left-hand
     side of the parade the first child is Irene McAnlis, the third Brenda
     Stevenson, while the fourth and fifth are sisters Lynda and Loretta Armstrong. 201

Maps

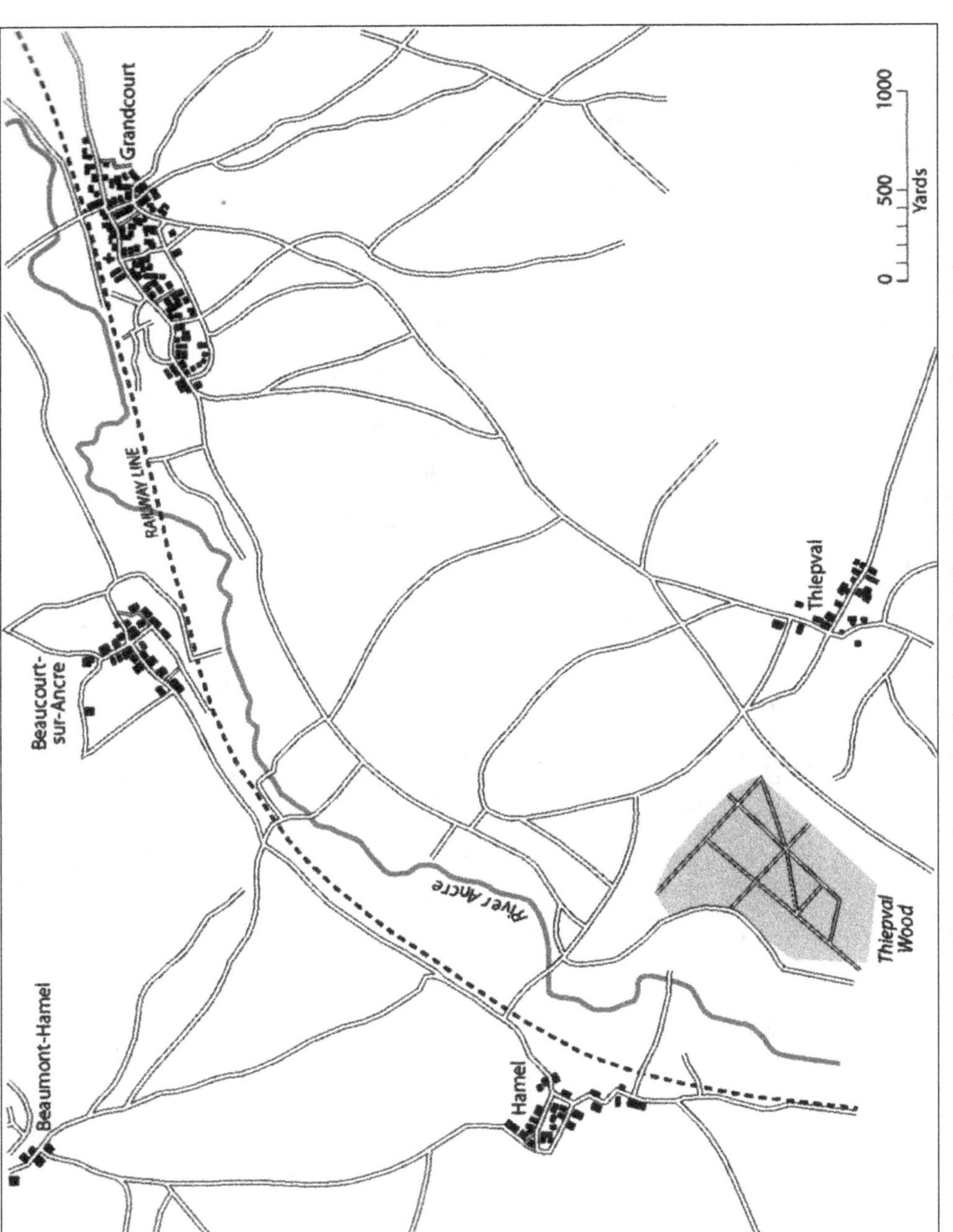

Map 1: The area to be attacked by the 36th (Ulster) Division on 1 July 1916, the advance of the Division was split by the River Ancre.

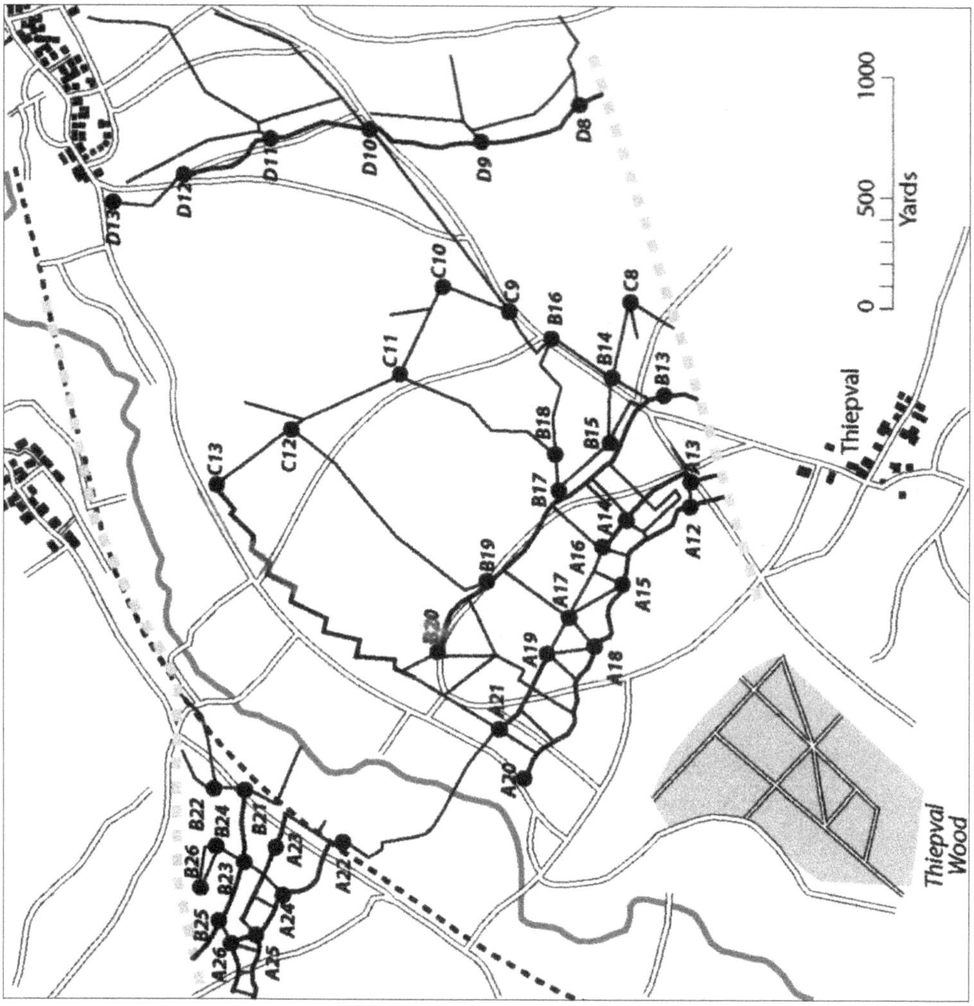

Map 2: German positions plotted on the same map. The dotted lines show the left and right flanks of the Division. On the left was the 29th Division, on the right the 32nd Division.

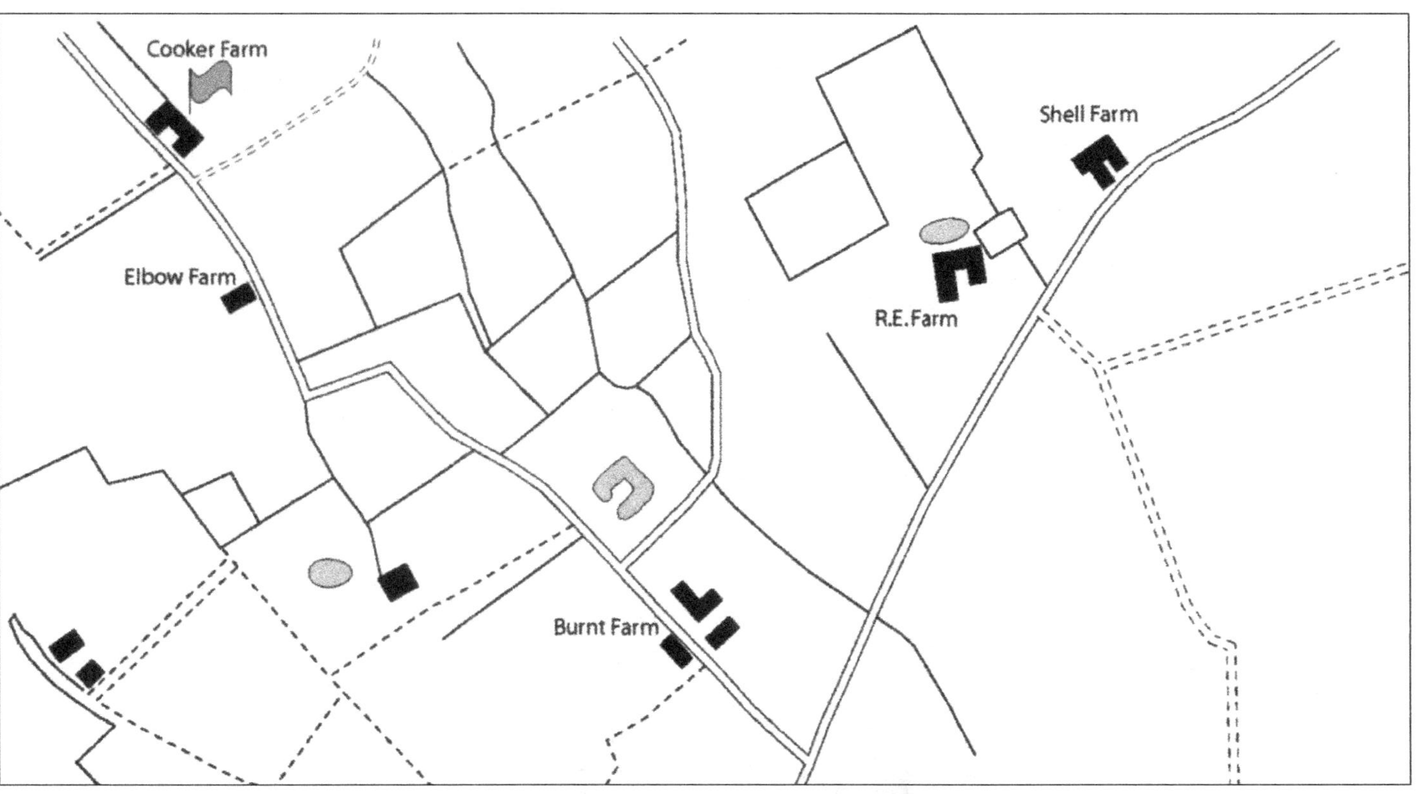

Map 3: A trench map showing Cooker Farm where Private James McRoberts was wounded on the evening of 1 November 1916.

Preface

The succeeding pages have been copied from a diary contained in three notebooks which I kept when I was in the army; footnotes were added forty years later. The only alterations are my having omitted the many repetitions that occurred during my training and some of the more sentimental bits, including several of my criticisms of the British Army; these make somewhat tedious reading nowadays.

My initial remarks on the French people and certain other matters are not to be taken too seriously; they are merely first impressions which are often superseded (by me) further on.

I was born in the County Antrim about five miles from Larne and spent five years at Larne Grammar School. Having decided on Civil Engineering as my future career, I entered Queen's University Belfast and had passed my first year in the summer of 1914. I joined the Army as a Private in November of that year and was posted to Finner Camp near Bundoran in County Donegal.

My Battalion was the 14th Royal Irish Rifles. YCV stands for Young Citizen Volunteers, a body that had existed in Belfast for some years before the War. The YCV along with the 9th, 10th and 11th Inniskilling Fusiliers formed the 109th Brigade of the 36th (Ulster) Division. Explanatory notes on people and places are now inserted into the original text.

I take this opportunity of thanking the 'two Jeans' of the County Surveyor's Office, Armagh, for their patience in deciphering and typing the original manuscript which was often a most untidy mass of writing, generally in pencil and almost illegible.

James McRoberts
Armagh
Northern Ireland
1957

Publisher's Note

The editor and publishers would like to apologise for the poor quality of many of the images in this book. However, it was felt better to includes images of great historical interest, and accept their quality (frequently reflecting the print quality of contemporary newspapers) than to exclude them.

Foreword

Belfast men may have built the *Titanic*, but Ulster was still a province of small farms and market towns, some producing the famous Irish linen. Many of the German rank and file would have been from similar backgrounds, hence the notion that hundreds of thousands of young men were lined up in opposing trenches to confront each other and as it transpired, bombard with shells, mow down with machine gun fire and, and kill and maim with grenades, bayonets and poison gas. The reasons for Great Britain's entry into and, more so, its conduct of the war are questions debated by historians, but here we are merely concerned with commemorating some of those men involved, in particular men of the Somme, two of whom the publication of this diary is dedicated to.

My father loved to see his diaries typed and the extracts published in Ulster newspapers, but, on being persuaded by relatives, and, in particular, my cousin Yvonne McRoberts and her son Major John Schulz of the US Army, to proceed to publication, I realised that a daily record needs editing. Hence, the incorporation of footnotes for ease of reading and, as my father remembered his fellows, I wished to add to the diary something of his own very positive peacetime achievements after the tragedies of war. Highlights of my father's life in the Home Guard and work as County Surveyor of Armagh follow the diary proper.

I have worked at this from the 1950s typed version in my homes in Sussex and Cyprus, greatly assisted by my sister-in-law, Councillor Sylvia McRoberts of Armagh City, and her sons, Bruce and Philip, who helped by checking sources and taking up-to-date photographs in Ulster. Pamela Rea did sterling work retyping all of this and introduced me to the published historian David Truesdale, who has arranged its publication by Helion and added valuable historical detail from various sources with maps and other illustrations. The latter include photographs kindly supplied by the descendants of girls, whom my father, as a French speaker, was able to get to know in villages such as Poulainville and Dranoutre.

My brother Brian was named in honour of Brian Boyd, MM, (killed in action). My niece Flora, Brian's daughter, has a son who also bears this name. I trust that all my father's grandchildren and great grandchildren will find interest and inspiration in reading a record of one whom it may justly be said: "Well done thou good and faithful servant" (Matthew, 25:21)

M. Emerson McRoberts, MA (Dubl) PGCE (Lond)

Acknowledgements

My sincere thanks to all who have assisted me over the last year, but especially to Pamela Rea, who introduced me to the diary in the first place and did a superb job in typing the original manuscript into a workable word document.

Once again, I must thank Dr. Kathy Neoh, who has kept me going long enough to complete another project.
Pamela Agnew, Royal Ulster Rifles Museum, Waring Street, Belfast
Michael Ashmore, National Museums, Northern Ireland
Dr Timothy Bowman, for assistance with discipline and morale within the Battalion
Fanny Caridroit, for assistance with research in France
Hannah Carson, for permission to quote from her poem 'No Man's Land'
Alan Curragh, for photographs
Elaine Davidson, Royal Belfast Academic Institution, Belfast
Patricia Fawcett, for permission to quote from her poem 'The Memory Jar'
Pat Geary, Friends School, Lisburn, County Antrim
Keith Haines, archivist of Campbell College, Belfast
Nigel Henderson, for photographs and newspaper research
Katalin Homonnay, for lots
Noel Kane, Somme Heritage Centre, Newtownards
Bob McKinley, Somme Heritage Centre, Newtownards
Jonathan Maguire BA, for assistance with photographs
Mr C.H. Mawhinney, Ballynure
Karen Mee, Special Collections, Brotherton Library, University of Leeds
Bruce McRoberts, for research
Sylvia McRoberts
Tommy McClimmonds, for acting as proof reader
Roy McCullough, for drawing the maps
Yvonne Hooker McRoberts, for family research
David R. Orr, for assistance with photographs and proof reading
Richard Parkinson, Somme Heritage Centre, Newtownards
Ulysse Perodeau, for assistance with research in France
Mark Ramsey, for allowing me access to his superb collection of Great War letters
Cameron Robinson
Rev. James Rogers, for permission to reproduce the photographs of the memorial plaques at Ballynure Church
Jimmy Taylor, for proof reading
Tsendpurev (Cindy) Tsegmid, Brotherton Library, University of Leeds
Carol Walker, Somme Heritage Centre, for permission to use photographs
Richard Wallace, for assistance with photographs
Alison Weir, Methodist College, Belfast

Kate Willis, for photographs

David Truesdale

Historical background to the 14th Battalion Royal Irish Rifles (YCV)

The 14th Battalion Royal Irish Rifles was formed from the pre-war Young Citizen Volunteers of Belfast. The majority of the YCV was of middle class origin and while it recruited mainly from the greater Belfast area, its members also came from as far afield as Donegal.

The initial meeting of the Volunteers was held in the City Hall, Belfast, on 10 September 1912. The President was Robert James McMordie; the Lord Mayor of the City, on the committee was Major Fred Crawford, a man who would sign the Ulster Covenant in his own blood and as 'Director of Ordnance' be responsible for buying arms for the Ulster Volunteer Force.[1] On enlisting in the YCV each member had to pay 2s 6d and a further 6d each month. Uniformed in a distinctive 'volunteer grey' uniform, he had to attend weekly drills to learn such skills as single stick, rifle and baton exercises, signalling, knot tying, first aid, life saving and modified military and police drill. The YCV Constitution stressed that members should not take part in any political meetings or demonstrations as the organisation was to be non-sectarian and non-political. The development of responsible citizenship and 'municipal patriotism' by means of lectures and discussions was cultivated and the future role of the YCV was seen as 'an organisation, when called upon, would aid the civil powers in the maintenance of the peace.

Anyone between the ages of eighteen and thirty-five was eligible for membership, provided they were over five feet in height and could provide 'credentials of good character'. While recruitment was predominately Protestant a number of Catholics did join, as did Jews and Quakers.[2]

While a report in the *Belfast Newsletter* of 11 September stated that some 2,000 young men turned up at the launch of the YCV later recruiting proved to be difficult. While the formation of the Young Citizen Volunteers was seen as a response to both a German and Home Rule threat the cost of becoming and maintaining membership proved difficult for many.[3] The uniforms were of excellent quality, but expensive and even with the ability of paying for them by monthly instalments were beyond some members. With a refusal by the Government for financial assistance in return for placing the YCV at the Government's disposal, there were many in the organisation who proposed joining with the UVF. Eventually, it was decided that the defence of both the realm and Unionism was of paramount importance and the YCV became a battalion of the Belfast Regiment, UVF. Despite this Lieutenant Colonel Robert Chichester, the first

---

1   It is somewhat ironic that one of the most dependable suppliers of weapons to the UVF was Bruno Spiro, a German arms dealer.

2   In his book *Irish Regiments in the Great War, Discipline and Morale*, Timothy Bowman reveals that in June 1915 there were five officers and ninety eight 'other ranks' who were Catholic.

3   Orr, P., *The Road to The Somme: Men of the Ulster Division Tell Their Story* (Belfast: Blackstaff Press, 2008).

Battalion commander, always addressed his men as 'young citizens'. Those men, who had been NCOs in the YCV, quickly became NCOs in the 14th Rifles, at least until the Division moved to France.

However, the YCV only ever had a field strength of 750 men, and of those who volunteered for service in the 14th Rifles, only 17% came from Ireland, excluding Belfast, while 25% came from England, Scotland and Wales. Among those from England was Rifleman John Patterson from Barrow-in-Furness, who prior to enlisting had been working as a ship's joiner; he was killed on 16 August 1917. There would appear to have been no seamless transmission from YCV battalion to Regular Army battalion.

The fact that the majority of the YCV came from a relatively prosperous background caused a degree of resentment within the remainder of the Division. During the autumn of 1914, the 109th Brigade, consisting of the 9th, 10th 11th Royal Inniskilling Fusiliers and 14th Royal Irish Rifles, was training at Finner Camp in County Donegal. It was a time of unseasonable storms and in October once such storm completely flattened the tented accommodation of the Brigade. As the building of permanent huts had not been completed the Inniskillings had no option but to re-pitch their tents and make do with the sodden conditions for the remainder of the winter. However, the 14th Rifles, with more 'disposable income', simply moved into the various hotels in Ballyshannon and Bundoran.

This diary recounts the service of Private James McRoberts and begins in January 1915, Although he had joined the Army in November 1914 and was posted to Finner Camp in County Donegal, he does not cover that in his diary. While the Commonwealth War Graves Commission refers to the dead of the Royal Irish Rifles as Rifleman, throughout the diary the rank of Private is used. Some footnotes and historical notes have been added to assist in identifying men, locations and certain events.

Training in Ulster

Friday 8 January 1915: Randalstown
We came to Randalstown from Belfast by train and arrived about 3.30pm. We were very comfortable as 'comfort' went in the Army, except for the frightful dirt. As soon as we left the huts we were over the ankles in mud which we carried inside on our boots. We had bed boards to sleep on which at least kept us off the filthy floor. We did nothing except fatigues that day. The demesne was close by so that we could go and look through the fence at the hares and squirrels which seemed to be very plentiful. A special ground-guard had to be appointed at night to prevent poaching.

Randalstown has a population of over a thousand and is located in County Antrim on the north shore of Lough Neagh, about one half-mile from which it is distant. The camp, which was being finished by the builders, was situated in Shane's Park and eventually contained the whole Brigade. We came here, after a belated Christmas leave, from billets in Bundoran, County Donegal.[1]

Sunday 17 January 1915: Antrim
I walked in the evening to Antrim which was four and three-quarter miles distant. The road ran parallel to the Lough and was four to eight hundred yards from the shore. The ground between the O'Neill's of Shane's Castle and heir to all this land was a young boy of about six years.[2] He and his sisters were often seen on their ponies; they were lovely riders. We then had tea in a hotel and came back by rail. I was attached to the second section of Number 1 Platoon, in 'A' Company and I was a Methodist.

Monday 18 January 1915: Antrim
Today the weather was much improved. We had a Battalion march to Antrim accompanied by our three bands, the signallers and the recruits.[3] The morning was frosty and the road white and slippery. We entered Massereene Park at Antrim and passed the Castle where the Royal Engineers were stationed at that time. It seemed a pretty place with some unusual fantastic hedges, tennis courts and rustic arches.

We came out of Massereene Park on to the road, entered Shane's Park and passed right through it without stopping, until we reached our huts. Many parts of the Park were exceptionally well wooded and the tall, Scotch firs seemed to grow out of the water, for parts of the Park were flooded, as the Lough was very full at present.

---

1   Donegal, the county, Donegall, the Square in Belfast.
2   Later Lieutenant Colonel, the Lord Shane Edward Robert O'Neill, DL, Commanding Officer of the North Irish Horse. He was killed in Italy by a German shell on 24 October 1944, age 36 years. He is buried in Coriano Ridge War Cemetery, grave XVII.A.1. His father was Captain the Hon. Arthur Edward Bruce O'Neill, 'A' Squadron Life Guards, killed on 6 November 1914, age 38 years; he has no known grave and is commemorated on the Menin Gate, Ypres, Memorial Panel 3.
3   The 14th Battalion's 'official' march was 'St. Patrick's Day.'

14th Battalion at Randalstown Camp, 1915. (Royal Ulster Rifles Museum)

We passed on our left the old Shane's Castle, a mass of ruins which ran down to the water's edge, and further on we saw the new building on our right. From the top of the tower some people waved a white flag bearing a red hand and a red cross as each party of our marching column passed. I was with the rear-guard the whole time. We saw lots of hares and rabbits which would cross our path, sometimes just in front of our party.

On the 19 January 1915, two Zeppelins attacked Yarmouth and Cromer killing four people, thus causing the first casualties in England from aerial bombardment.

Saturday 23 January 1915: Home

About one thousand of the Battalion, including myself, were given passes from 1pm until 10pm. The weather was fine and frosty so that in the morning we went for a short march, without arms, along the road to Toome. We were intensely proud of our bands, a bugle, a pipe and a flute, which had all been trained by our Regimental Sergeant Major Robert Elphick, who was an old soldier of striking appearance with the South African medals.

After dinner we paraded to the railway station, the new one specifically for the troops, where two special trains were awaiting us. I was given a ticket to Belfast, so I travelled to visit friends on the Shore Road. There I found my friends well, except Meg who had a cold and was 'confined to barracks'. Just like my luck! Meg McRoberts was my second cousin and still lived with her parents. She was a tall, lively, good-looking girl and she and I spent a lot of time together. She married an ex-service man shortly after the war and they lived for several years, during the thirties, near to me in Armagh. He was the local representative of the Shell and BP Company

I went out with her brother Jim to the Hippodrome where the usual tame programme was given. We then proceeded to my Aunt Harriet's. Without children, she was particularly kind to her many nephews and nieces. I had a little chat with Hetty Johnston who lived next door with the result that I came to the conclusion that, should chance give me a suitable opportunity, I might further my acquaintance with this admirable little lady. I reached Larne at 11.30 by the late train and arrived home at 1 am. I entered by the kitchen window and went to bed without anyone suspecting my presence.

Sunday 24 January 1915: Home

No one guessed I was in the house until my brother Matthew went downstairs and spotted my greatcoat. I went with him to Raloo Presbyterian Church afterwards.[4] Matt was about three years younger than me. He possessed a sardonic humour and

---

4   Known locally for its ghost that haunts the old graveyard.

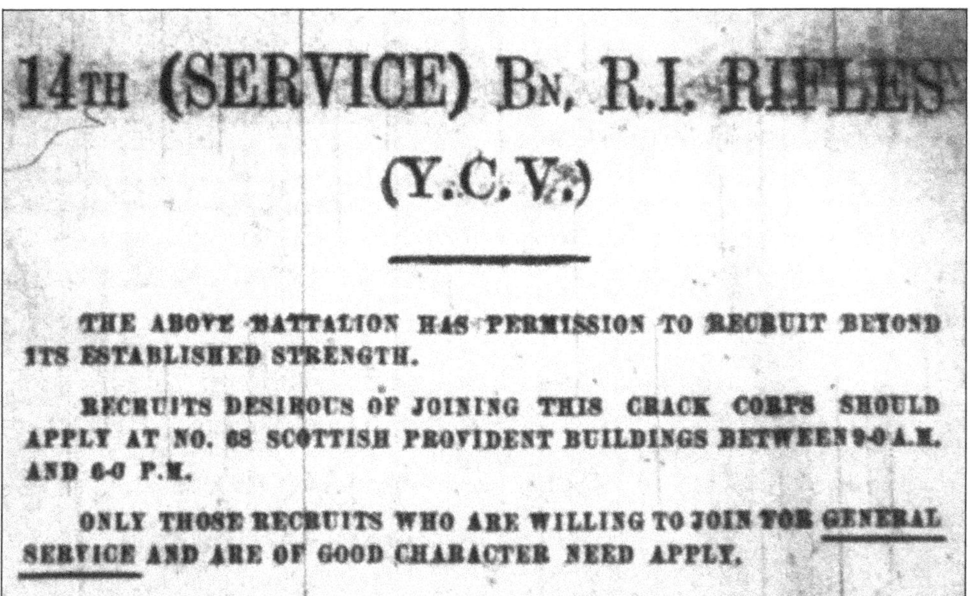

Recruiting poster as it appeared in the *Belfast Newsletter* of 1914 . (Mark Ramsey)

was destined for a farmer's life. After the war he went to Australia and then Canada and wrote what a fine sight it was to see the fur-trappers with their dog teams coming into Edmonton. Matt also liked the heat of Australia where, when ploughing, it was necessary to keep his spare tools buried in the ground so that they would be cool enough to handle when he wished to use them. He loved conducting a team of eleven horses with their load of wool to the railway station. Matt considered it a hard country, covered with the bones of animals that had perished in droughts. So after a few years he came home via Canada, thus completing the circuit of the world.

Matt liked the hospitality of the Canadians but disliked the climate. He gave a graphic description of winter conditions and the layers of clothing he had to don, so that when, for the second time, he saw the electric poles being frozen into Manitoba Lake he decided to return home. But he and my father could not agree and, after a year at home, he left for Australia. I remember the letter he wrote describing how the milk vendor in Naples drove his herd of goats through the streets and supplied his customers with fresh milk drawn from their udders.

Subsequently he married Betty Hall and bought Crookedstone House, Aldergrove. As the poles to the airport crossed his land, his was the only farm to have electricity for the house and milking parlour. He has a family of three children educated at Belfast schools, the eldest becoming an accountant and the youngest a domestic science teacher in Canada. Both sons went to Australia.

After church service at Raloo, the day was keen and frosty, but as the road was slippery and the bicycles uncertain, I walked down to Larne for the 5.50pm train. I reached Belfast at 7pm and went to the Shore Road and had my tea. A tremendous crowd had gathered at the Midland Railway Station to see us off at 9.15pm. We arrived

Clandeboye Camp, County Down. (North Down Museum)

The Battalion on parade. (Royal Ulster Rifles Museum)

at Randalstown about 10pm and immediately tumbled into bed. Everyone I met on my ramble had congratulated me on my good, healthy appearance.

Tuesday 26 January 1915: Randalstown

In the evening a concert was held in the new dining-hall to which everyone was admitted free. The chief artist of the night was Percy French, author of the song 'Mountains of Mourne'. Percy French was born in County Roscommon and educated as a civil engineer in Trinity College, Dublin. Among other well-known songs he wrote were 'Phil the Fluter's Ball', 'Come Back Paddy Reilly' and 'Abdul the Bulbul Ameer'. Until recently there existed a commemorative fountain in Newcastle, Co. Down, between Main Street and the sea, which bore the inscription:

Erected in the festival year 1951 to the memory of
William Percy French
Composer of the famous song
'Where the mountains of Mourne sweep down to the sea'
1854 – 1920

He sang and played on the mandolin, but his most amusing contribution was his series of drawings. French would portray the picture of a baby crying, turn the paper upside down, and the face was distorted with laughter. He made a fine sketch of clumps of pines, growing on a landscape of snow, turned the picture upside down and we looked

James' father and mother. (McRoberts family)

at a number of ships on a beautiful sea. He had quite a number of such entertaining freaks of the pencil.[5]

Thursday 28 January 1915: Ballyscullion

The good weather continued and we set off for a great march at 9.15am with our sandwiches in our pockets. We passed quickly through Toome, crossed the swollen River Bann and travelled on along a narrow road through a poor, boggy district. We stopped for a few minutes once or twice and reached a small village, Ballyscullion, about 3.15pm. We passed through the village which, by the way, contained quite a number of attractive girls and entered the grounds of Colonel Bruce, a cousin of our respected Major. Our respected Major, on the death of his father in 1919, became Sir Hervey Ronald Bruce, DL, JP. (He had formerly been a Captain in the Irish Guards and his home was at Downhill, County Londonderry. He was killed by lightning in 1924 while watching a storm at Eastbourne).

We piled arms in front of the house and 'fell out' for about twenty minutes. The demesne grounds afforded a fine view of Lough Beg and its pretty, little wooded islands, especially the one with the Church known as Church Isle. The islands and their trees were beautifully reflected in the water and made a lovely picture in the evening light

We marched quickly back and in great style. Outside Toome we came on our transport waggons and were served with cups of tea, the worst I ever tasted. It had been

---

5   Unfortunately when the new promenade was built the fountain was buried under the foundations. Part of the actual fountain was recovered and today can be found in Rowallane Gardens, Saintfield, County Down.

No 1 Platoon, D Company, at Randalstown, 1915. (Royal Ulster Rifles Museum)

boiling for several hours at the campfires on the roadside. We reached our huts about 7.45pm and I for one, after devouring my dinner and tea quickly, threw down my bed and got under the blankets. Bertie Cass, my roommate, was out by special permission (so he said) singing in a cantata at the Presbyterian Church and came back at 1.30am, as he told me in the morning.

Friday 5 February 1915: Cookstown Junction
There was an early morning double. At 9.15am the Battalion marched to Cookstown Junction, then on to the Antrim Road and back to the huts. It was a fine, cool, spring like morning, farmers were in the fields, ploughing the lea ground and trimming the hedges. It almost made me sorrowful to look at our long, khaki column with its gleaming rifle butts; it was a strong reminder, among these peaceful fields, that our nation was in a life and death struggle.

After dinner we had more bayonet fighting and at 4.30pm, paraded for pay. I spent the evening inside the hut reading and generally amusing myself. We had two tables, coal for the stove and two oil-lamps, so that we were beginning to recall the little conventions that recall modern good manners and everyone who forgot himself at table now was tossed in a blanket, after having been properly tried and condemned by a special judge and jury. We had quite a number of offenders each night.

Saturday 6 February 1915: Randalstown
We now get our clothes washed, at no personal cost, by the Whitewell Laundry, Belfast, and well cleaned they were. I have had a shower of love letters this week; one from Elsie Graham which I had been expecting for some time and given up hope of receiving. Elsie Graham was a tall, fine-looking girl and was distantly related to me. She was an only child and thought to be rich. She lived with her mother at Ballyclare, County Antrim, her father I never knew. About 1935 I met her, accompanied, of course, by her mother, in Wellington Place, Belfast. By then she had a car and told me she occasionally visited

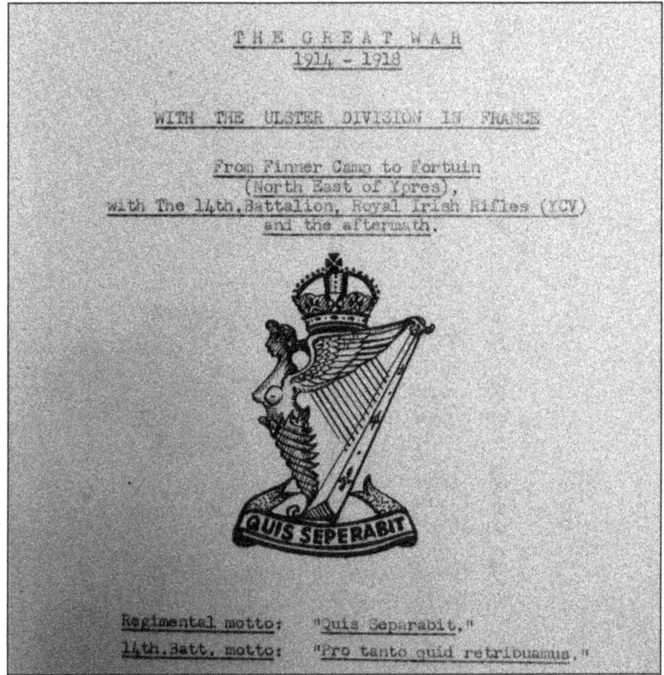

Harp & Crown. (Royal Ulster Rifles Museum)

Armagh. I invited them to call with me but never saw them again. Elsie's mother died during WWII and Elsie shortly afterwards.

Other letters came from Jean McClellan, Polly McClellan and Meg McRoberts. Jean and Polly were sisters of Allan John McClellan who was in the same class with me at the Grammar School, Larne, and we often travelled part of the way home on our bicycles. When I went to Queen's University, Belfast, in 1913, Allan John remained as a master at the Grammar School. He joined the Royal Irish Rifles as a Private but quickly obtained his commission. He visited me in Aveluy Wood in June 1916, and knowing there was to be an advance soon we undertook to see each other again at the Fifth German line but he was killed on the 1 July 1916.[6]

Papa McClellan was very much a Scot and in charge of Ballyboley Hill; their mother was dead. I had some fine holidays there, tramping the moors all morning, where there were two thousand sheep to inspect and lots of hares to shoot. Both girls were slightly older than I and while Jean was always at home, Polly was working in Scotland most of the time.

Shortly after the war the following memorial tablet was unveiled in Ballynure Presbyterian Church by James McQuillan, MA Headmaster of Larne Grammar School:

IN LOVING MEMORY OF
ALLAN JOHN McCLELLAN,

---

6   Second Lieutenant Allan John McClellan, attached 15th Royal Irish Rifles, killed 1 July 1916, age 21 years. He was the son of William and Flora McClellan of Ballyboley, Ballynure, Belfast and has no known grave, commemorated on the Thiepval Memorial Pier and Face 15A and 15B.

Regimental call. (Royal Ulster Rifles Museum)

Second Lieutenant 18 RIR
Killed at Thiepval, France, 1 July 1916. Aged 21 years.
'Greater love hath no man than this, that a man lay down his life for his friends'.
ERECTED BY HIS FATHER Wm. McClellan

Monday 8 February 1915: Antrim

It was a cool, dry day and we had Swedish drill in the morning before breakfast. Afterwards there was a Battalion route march to Antrim and back again. After dinner, instead of going on parade, I dressed in my football kit and ran with the YCV Harriers. There were about twenty of us and we went for a run of about five miles through the Park. I found I could stick the pace quite easily and on return had a cold wash down in the ablution house. I spent the remainder of the evening in the hut.

Wednesday 10 February 1915: Randalstown

After dinner, although it was raining fairly heavily, the Harriers went out for a short run through the Park. It was hard going but I stuck it easily, notwithstanding the fact that the wet grass made the running slippery as I was wearing ordinary shoes. Although there was a concert given that night, I was so tired that I went to bed early in the evening.

Thursday 11 February 1915: Portglenone Road

Bertie Cass and I went out in the evening and struck up with two girls whom we accompanied out the Portglenone Road. My partner, who seemed a rather nice, quiet girl called Miss Jean Brown, refused my ardent advances, maintaining that she was engaged to a chap. I was disappointed and perhaps so was she, but I took her at her word and behaved myself in a worthy manner. I got a postcard from Amy Carthcart beginning 'My dear Curly'. I wrote to her, arranging to see her the following night at 7.30pm if I got away on leave. If not, she was to write back to me.

James in uniform just after joining the Division. (McRoberts family)

Friday 12 February 1915: Belfast

There was no morning parade so I prepared for my week-end leave and eventually got my pass with ticket; the train left at 9.40am with about five hundred of us. I arrived in Belfast where it was a beautiful, cool morning and I went to my aunt's for mid-day dinner.

I made my way to Queen's University, Belfast and spent some time at the Engineering School, seeing Arthur Lovat Higgins and meeting some of the new men. Mr Higgins was an Englishman who, in 1913, was a Lecturer in Civil Engineering subjects at Queen's University. He was a genius in his way and wrote a huge book on Surveying, which was published by Sir Isaac Pitman & Sons Ltd. He also wrote a pamphlet on Transition Curves. In 1918 and 1919 he had a commission in the Royal Engineers but shortly afterwards he went to Manchester University. His death occurred in the early fifties. I learned to my surprise that Joseph Croskery, the last of my class, had responded to the summons and was then a soldier in the Black Watch. (Joseph Croskery is at present (1957) the Borough Surveyor of Bangor, County Down.)

I went down to town again and entering Mr Mullan's bookshop found that out of my class prizes amounting to £3.10.0, I had already purchased books to the value of £3.9.0. A further purchase of *A Tale of Two Cities* (Collins 1/-) easily settled my affairs with that respected firm. After tea at my aunt's I went out to Malone and, just in front of her own house, met Miss Cathcart going to a class in the YMCA She recognised me but explained she had been entered for a Scholarship at the Technical College and could not possibly spend the evening with me. I walked down with her to Wellington Place and was convinced she had an intense admiration for me but on what account I did not guess. I strolled up the Antrim Road but no adventure was awaiting me, so I came back to my Aunt's home where I spent the night.

At the family home in Larne, 1904 – Jane McMinn McRoberts, her son James and her husband Mathew. On her knee daughter Annie and sons Mathew and John. Annie was born in 1902 or early 1903. She never married and died in 1933 from eating apples which were thought to have been sprayed with a toxic chemical. (McRoberts family)

Saturday 13 February 1915: Home – Ballygowan

It was a very bright but cold morning. I travelled down to Larne by the 12.50 train and reached home by the narrow gauge railway. I found everyone well and enjoyed their company for the rest of the evening. Bob Moore, the brother of Sarah Moore who was our housemaid at home for over forty years, had received ten days' furlough and dreaded going back to the trenches when his time was up on Friday evening (having gained a certain respect for German shells and a certain dread of trench living). Bob was a regular soldier in the Highland Light Infantry and had been in France since the beginning of the War. He was eventually sent to Mesopotamia where he was reported missing.[7]

My home address was Ballygowan, Kilwaughter, Larne, where my father, Samuel Matthew, owned a farm of eighty acres. As long as I knew him he was a martyr to asthma, but the only one of his family. Sammie inherited the disease; otherwise he was energetic, inventive and assertive. He lived in the house at Ballygowan, which he greatly improved, until 1931 when he retired to The Grove, Glengormley, Belfast, until his death in 1942.

My mother's maiden name was Jane McMinn and she was born at Ballylagan, Ballynure, the daughter of a farmer. She too was energetic, but also religious and fond of reading. I took her to a trip to London about 1833 and a few years later she visited her son John in Detroit for three months. About the end of World War II she transferred her

---

7   Private Robert Moore, 1st Battalion Highland Light Infantry, died 11 January 1917, buried in Amara War Cemetery, grave XVIII.K.3.

No 12 Platoon, C Company at Randalstown. (Royal Ulster Rifles Museum)

residence from The Grove to Glengormley, to be near her son Matthew of Crookedstone House, Aldergrove, where she died in 1951.

Sunday 14 February 1915: Larne

It was a fine day but cold. I drove mother and my brothers Matt and John to church in Larne. John was five years younger than me and in 1914 he was at the Grammar School, Larne. We were together for the year 1918-19 at Queen's University where he took his degree, BSc (Commerce) in 1921. John had difficulty in finding a suitable job in this country so he went to Canada, eventually becoming a designer in General Motors, Detroit. He married a Canadian girl and has a family of three. His eldest, a girl is a school teacher. His second is a boy, at present doing his training in the American Air Force. The third is a boy also and is called Allan John. John – the father – has been home twice and my mother visited him for three months in Detroit about 1935.

In the evening Matt took me in the trap to Larne again and I travelled to Belfast by the 5.50 train. I reached the City at about 7pm and went to relatives for supper. I found Meg had been seriously ill but was now recovering and had been able to rise from her bed several days previously. There was a tremendous crowd at the Station to see our train off at 9.15pm. We reached Randalstown and got to bed as quickly as possible.

Friday 19 February 1915: Randalstown

YCV Private E. Cobain, the first to die since the outbreak of the War, was buried today.[8] He belonged to 'C' Company and home on leave last weekend, then out on the forced march on Tuesday. On Tuesday night he took ill and the doctor thought fit to send him to hospital in Belfast by the motor ambulance. He died however before he reached

---

8   The first death of a member of the YCV, not of the Division; this was Private W.J. Pritchard of the 13th
    Rifles and occurred on 26 October 1914.

Many members of the YCV served in the Second World War. This is
Thomas Woods, who opted for the Royal Navy! (Mark Ramsey)

Templepatrick, the cause being given as cerebro-spinal meningitis. The three bands and
a firing party went to Belfast to give him a military funeral at Carnmoney.[9]

Sunday 21 February 1915: Randalstown

When in Randalstown, having a few letters to post and no stamps, I asked a man
standing at the door in New Street if he could sell me a few. He could not but pressed
me so warmly to come inside and warm myself that I consented, although I considered
it somewhat cheeky on my part, as I told him. He proved to be a Mr McFadden, owner
of a grocery shop, and had a pleasant lady as wife and a growing family, including an
attractive daughter, Dora, by name. (The McFadden shop was still in Randalstown when
I visited in 1957. The present owner, Norman, was only a boy in 1915. I also met Dora
who is unmarried but blooming and complacent as ever.)

I spent the whole evening there in an agreeable manner, talking about my own
experiences in the Army and getting a fine tea and supper. As I had a pass, I was enabled
to enjoy this company until 10 o'clock when I left with the invitation that I should
come along again. I made up my mind about the matter too definitely to refuse. After I
returned to the hut, the chaps came back by special train from Belfast. They were very
enthusiastic over the manner in which the funeral arrangements of Private E Cobain had
taken place. Everything had turned out perfectly, bands, firing party and the marching,
winning the highest praise from everyone. It had done the YCV more good than any
number marches was the comment everywhere.[10]

---

9   The three bands were a flute band, pipes and drums and a bugle band. In keeping with tradition these
    men would act as stretcher-bearers in time of battle.

10 All did not go as planned. The firing party had paraded under the command of Sergeant Powell and
    after being inspected by the Orderly Officer, had proceeded to Belfast by train. Sergeant Powell had
    been instructed to return to camp immediately after the funeral so that the firing party could return
    their rifles to the armoury, men not being permitted to take their weapons home. The Sergeant and
    his party had been issued with weekend leave passes expiring on the Sunday night, so that they could
    enjoy leave along with the remainder of the Battalion. However, at noon on the Saturday Battalion
    Headquarters received a Brigade Order rescinding all leave. Sergeant Powell had then to collect all the
    leave passes from the firing party. He did not notice that the leave pass handed in by Private Hawthorne
    was an old expired pass. Hawthorne was then able to proceed on leave along with those men who had
    already left the Camp prior to noon by presenting his genuine pass to the gate guard. Private McIllroy

YCV Finner Camp, County Donegal. (Mark Ramsey)

Friday 26 February 1915: Randalstown

In the evening I went down to McFadden's where a number of other chaps had gathered and three young ladies. We had tea, played blind man's bluff and a few other diversions. Only one of us had a pass to stay behind after 8.45pm. How he fared I do not know.

Sunday 28 February 1915: Antrim

Today there were several inches of snow on the ground. I went to church with the Presbyterians and the pipe band. After mid-day dinner, I walked into Antrim and called at Mr Malseed's of the Belfast Bank. My former school friends, Jack and Wallace with their two sons were also with Mr and Mrs Malseed, and a sister of the latter. They had a lovely home and offered a fine high tea. Afterwards we chatted while eating oranges, apples and sweets. I left at 9.30pm and met three other chaps outside the Post Office and, together, we started for Randalstown. It was a fine walk and a good, frosty, moonlit night with showers of snow.

Saturday 6 March 1915: Randalstown

After dinner I went out with the harriers and had a fine run round the park of about seven miles. I held my pace well and in the sprint at the end, came in next to William Scott who was our organiser. As a harrier he was unsurpassed, a fine chap and a wonderful runner.

did hand in his leave pass, but went home anyway, slipping out of the Camp unnoticed. At roll call on the Saturday evening Corporal Woodside reported to Sergeant Powell that McIllroy was absent from parade, Hawthorne's absence not being noticed. In theory Private McIllroy should have been Court Martialed, absence being a very serious crime in the Army. After a prolonged period in the guard room McIllroy was released and no charges pressed. It was assumed that Colonel Chichester had sufficient influence with Brigadier Hickman to have the charges withdrawn. A short time later Captain Bentley, the Adjutant, addressed the Battalion and told them that he was tired of saving them from Counts Martial and that he was not going to do it any longer. However, there were no Courts Martial in the 14th Battalion during his period of Adjutancy.

A PARTY OF THE Y.C.V.'s (14TH R. I. R.) AT FINNER CAMP. NAMES (FROM LEFT TO RIGHT)—Lance-Corporal T. M'KNIGHT, Private A. BROWNE, Lance-Corporal D. T. BOYD, Private E. HENRY, Private B. MARTIN, Lance-Corporal H. MORROW, Sergeant E. POWELL. SITTING—Private J. M'CLURE, Private S. J. JOHNSTON, Private B. JAMIESON, Private D. MARSHALL, Private V. CORRY.

YCV in uniform. (Mark Ramsey)

(William Scott's name appears several times in this diary. He was appointed Sergeant but was missing after the 1 July 1916.[11]) In the evening I went to a concert and cinematograph entertainment held in the reading room but is was not of the best.

Sunday 7 March 1915: Roguery

It was a fine, sunny, warm day, the best weather we have seen since we came to this place of mist and rain. I went to Church Parade with the Methodists at 10.30am. The Church was very small and a local man conducted the service.

In the evening, having a pass, I went out with another chap, Alec Jardine, to have a bit of fun, if possible. We walked quickly away from the town, along the Craigmore Road. While resting at a lonely crossroads, in a land of bog and waste, listening to the bleating of the snipe, a crowd of girls came past, arm in arm. We ran after them and soon started a conversation. Two of the girls went with another chap whom we met and we were left with the other three. Alec Jardine appears frequently in the early part of this diary and I believe he went to France. He survived the War as I met him in the train near Enniskillen in the early twenties. I am told afterwards he went abroad as a Baptist missionary.

I had the oldest girl who was small and quite pretty and I should say about twenty-two years of age. I walked home with her and had quite an exciting time. She had been a lot in Belfast and could speak quite nicely and correctly.

---

11   Sergeant William John Scott, No 15937, served in 'A' Company, killed on 1 July 1916, age 27 years. The husband of Charlotte Scott of Sunnyside Street, Belfast, he has no known grave and is commemorated on the Thiepval Memorial.

Group of Belfastmen in camp with the 14th Battalion (Y.C.V.) Royal Irish Rifles. Names (left to right)—Privates H. Loye, E. M'Kinley, R. Hanley, T. Martin, J. Skolly, J. Magee, Corporal J. M'Clean. Sitting—Privates G. Brannigan W. J. Anderson (late of Linfield F.C.), E. Cathcart.

YCV in uniform. (Mark Ramsey)

Alec Jardine was with this girl's little sister and another girl, who took him to her home where she introduced him to her mother. We intended both of us, to go back some time. Alec Jardine had no pass and we had a most awful rush to reach Camp in time for staff parade at 9.30pm but we managed it all right for him.

Monday 8 March 1915: Randalstown

Peter Kerr-Smiley, who was now our Captain, made a good impression on this, his first appearance amongst us. He spoke few words; he was a cavalry officer, as most knew, and had little experience with infantry and therefore was bound to make mistakes, but we were to do the right thing, to support him loyally and he would do his best so we would get along well together. He had a good voice and seemed to be very cool and collected. Peter Kerr-Smiley was a son of Sir Hugh Houston Smiley who owned a large estate and residence at Larne called Drumalis. Of interest to me was that Sir Hugh had also provided Larne Grammar School with its chemical laboratory and its first scholarship. In 1908 I won this scholarship. Shortly afterwards Sir Hugh died and I, along with the rest of the pupils of the Grammar School, attended his funeral. Captain Peter Kerr-Smiley was promoted to the rank of Major, but about May 1916 left us on sick leave. He served as Member of Parliament for North Antrim from 1910 to 1922.[12]

12　Peter Kerr-Smiley was born in Larne on 22 February 1879, the second son of Sir Hugh Smiley, 1st Baronet. Educated at Eton College and Trinity Hall, Cambridge, he was commissioned into the 21st Lancers and served in the South African War (1901-02) on the General Staff. He resigned his commission with the Lancers in 1905, the year he married Maud, the daughter of E.L. Simpson of New York. He was chairman of the *Northern Whig*, a Belfast newspaper and entered politics in 1906. He

Finner Camp, County Donegal. (McRoberts family)

Tuesday 9 March 1915: Roguery

At night Alec Jardine and I went out our old way and met our two girls amusing themselves on the road. It was a cool, dry night after a warm day, and I, for my part, had a fair time. The young lady proved herself to be very sporting and chummy. We had a good walk back to reach the Camp in time for the First Post.

Thursday 11 March 1915: Roguery

In the evening Alec Jardine and I, both having passes, walked to Roguery and sure enough, met our girls. We went into a small shop to buy them sweets and spent most of the evening sitting at the kitchen fire, talking nonsense. We then left them home and returned to the Camp. Alec Jardine's girl had not been allowed out this evening by her brother, who forbade her to have anything to do with the soldiers, and his companion was little Miss B ... aged sixteen.

Friday 12 March 1915: Ballyscullion

The Brigade marched to Ballyscullion. We had our equipment on with rucksacks containing some clothing to fill the space. I had a blanket inside mine. 'B' and 'C' Companies left at 8.30am as the vanguard and, on reaching Ballyscullion House, formed pickets and outposts round the Park, in which it was supposed the Brigade intended to

---

represented North Antrim in 1910 and continued to hold this position until 1922. His lack of infantry experience in these early days seems to be reflected in a letter written by Captain H.B. Spender to his wife on 22 November 1915; "He [Smiley] was running an outpost scheme of the 14 RIR when the GOC went out and watched. After five minutes the battalion was ordered to march home. The General said he was not out to watch children's play." The reason for Kerr-Smiley's sick leave was a stomach infection. He returned to the Division, served on the Staff and in May 1917 General Nugent sent him to London as the Division's representative in the 'secret sessions' held between Government and the House of Commons. Kerr-Smiley was the author of *The Peril of Home Rule*, published by Cassell & Co. in 1911. He died on 23 June 1945.

An unnamed young soldier at Finner Camp, County Donegal. (Royal Ulster Rifles Museum)

bivouac. The rest of us left at 9am and we had a fine, quick march through Toome, right to our destination, arriving at about 1.30pm.

I had a pair of new boots on, which proved rather large for me; my heels sagging up and down inside them, and marching on the outside of me section of fours I contracted sore feet. During our halt in the demesne I removed my boots and socks and found one heel blistered and the other bleeding. I washed my sores with water from my water bottle, stuffed the inside of my boots with paper and soon we started on our return home. A and D Companies acted as rearguard.

Saturday 13 March 1915: Randalstown

There was only a rifle and clothes inspection, also a bit of general lecturing this morning. After dinner we paraded for vaccination, but my turn was near the last and I did not get away until after 4 o'clock. The operation was practically painless. Turner's father and mother came up on the motor-bike to see their son so I was asked to go down town with them and us four had tea together. Mrs Turner seemed a fine woman, but Mr Turner was a rather small man. Hugh N Turner was a student at Queen's University, Belfast, who joined the Army the same day I did. His father was a Unitarian minister at Templepatrick, County Antrim. He became one of our Transport men, but left the battalion in October 1916, to get a commission. He was wounded at Passchendaele in 1917 and when the War was over he rejoined the University. He qualified as a Doctor and went to Kenya. He has one son who is a Dental Officer for the Belfast Education

Great Northern Hotel and strand, Bundoran, County Donegal. (McRoberts family)

committee and has quite a reputation as a rugby player. That night I went to a gratis entertainment, held in the dining hall; good pictures and interesting songs constituted the programme.

Wednesday 17 March 1915: Randalstown

This was St Patrick's Day so we had roll call only in the morning and a little fatigue work. It was a cold day with outbreaks of sunshine and several showers, but was for most part dry. Regimental sports commenced at 1.30pm. The programme did not suit me too well for there was no jumping and all the races were short, so I only took part in a single event, the one mile race. About ten started and I easily got second place, it being hopeless to try and outrun W Scott, the winner. The race did not fatigue me in the slightest and, when it was over, I would have been quite fit to continue for a few more miles further. The sports were over about 6 o'clock and Mrs Chichester presented the prizes to the winners and I had the satisfaction of receiving, from her hand, my prize of ten shillings.

Mrs Chichester was the wife of our Commanding Officer, Lieutenant-Colonel Robert Peel Dawson Spenser Chichester of Moyola Park, Castledawson, Co. Londonderry, who had been formerly in the Irish Guards and had served in the South African War. He left us in France, early in 1916, and died in 1921. Mrs Chichester then married Admiral Henry Wise Parker in 1928. She is now known as the Right Honourable Dame Dehra Parker, OBE, JP, and was a member of the original House of Commons for Northern Ireland. She was named Dehra because she was born in India. She later became a cabinet member in the new Northern Irish Parliament, formed after the War.[13]

---

13   Dehradun lies in the Doon Valley in the foothills of the Himalayas. During British rule it was where the British would have spent the summer months. Dame Dehra Parker, Minister of Health and Local

An unnamed Army padre with members of the McRoberts family, sadly also unnamed.
The two boys are wearing blazers of Methodist College, Belfast. (McRoberts family)

'A' Company carried away practically all the trophies of the day; the hundred yards, the four hundred and forty yards, the three-legged race, the sack race and the mile.

Wednesday 24 March 1915:
Donegore Hill

The Brigade left about 9.15am on a long route march. We passed through Antrim and took the Greystone Road. Afterwards we went along an elevated highway, round the base of Donegore Hill, and piled arms in the grounds of Sir William Adair. Many of this family are commemorated in the Parish Church of Donegore. The way was through a good, agricultural district which looked very pleasant in the March sunlight. Donegore Hill has a peculiar appearance and interesting history. Donegore Hill figured in the 1798 Rebellion in Ireland. It was the meeting place of the insurgents for the purpose of attacking Antrim. After midday they arrived within sight of the town where they met the British troops whom they forced to take refuge in Massereene Demesne. But afterwards some confusion arose; they were seized with panic and dispersed quickly. Their leader, Henry Joy McCracken was captured a little later on the shores of Belfast Laugh, tried and executed.

Coming back we passed through Dunadry, then along the fine highway to Antrim and reached the camp about 5.30pm. The distance was twenty-one miles on a warm, dull day but I did not mind. I wrote some letters, went down town to post them and came back to rest.

Government resigned on grounds of ill health in March 1957.

The Percy French memorial at Newcastle County Down. (Author's photograph)

Private James Walker was a former member of the YCV and pre-war had played for Linfield Football Club. He came from Dunadry, County Antrim and was one of those who died on 6 May 1916. (Mark Ramsey)

Saturday 27 March 1915: Randalstown

Anyone who wanted to see the Irish Cup Final between Linfield and Celtic was allowed to go to Belfast. Nearly all the Battalion left in two special trains at 11am. I stayed behind as I was not very enthusiastic about the match. The fare was only 1/3d and they were allowed to stay in Belfast until 11pm. We had a short parade about 9.30am, in walking out order to practice saluting. At 3.30pm there was a rugby match with the North Irish Horse who came over a in a brake[14] and were an excellent lot of big, hefty chaps. We took the field with only fourteen men and early in the match one of our side was laid out. It was a rough, tight match and our opponents, being much the heavier team, won eventually by fifteen points to nil. I was playing on the left wing and had my share of rough tackling. After the match the North Irish Horse had tea in the Sergeants' Mess, while our team was given a fine tea of ham and eggs in the canteen.

Thursday 1 April 1915: Ballygowan

There were fatigue duties in the morning, the afternoon free. All the chaps for Belfast were leaving in two special trains at 12.40pm and 1.10pm. I asked to get away earlier and was allowed to do so, thus I left Randalstown at 10.40am and reached Larne at 1.45pm having had to pass some time at Whitehead which was not at all unpleasant, the weather being ideal. I departed from Larne for Kilwaughter Halt in the narrow gauge railway at 1.40pm and reached home where things were busy as usual. All the oats had been sown and many of the potatoes planted. I had a lovely ride on the pony, for about three miles, and I enjoyed it very much although I was not used to being in the saddle. The evening passed quietly.

Friday 2 April 1915: Ballylaggan

I spent most of the day at home reading, or trying to play the piano and practicing 'Poor Old Joe' which shows my knowledge of music. At night I went out for a ride on the

---

14 A 'brake', also known as a shooting brake was a vehicle fitted with longitudinal seating in rows with either side or rear doors; it had originally been designed to take gentlemen, their guns and dogs out hunting. Today they are known as estate cars.

bike through Ballynure, Ballyeaston, Ballyclare and Straid but without any romantic encounters. I finished up at my grandfather's in Ballyleggan.

My mother's father was James McMinn and the person after whom I was named. He was a farmer in Ballylaggan, Ballynure and was the only grandparent I had left at this time. His disposition was kind, quiet and gentle. He lived with my Aunt Martha and her son, Bob, but died in the winter of 1916 when I was in hospital in Leeds. After the war, Bob who was then married, and my aunt went to Mackay in Queensland where they were visited by my brother Matt when he was in Australia. They seemed very pleased to see me and spoke warmly of my healthy appearance. My weight, standing in my walking out uniform, tunic and belt, was exactly eleven stones. A quick ride through the murky darkness at the hour of 10pm, a good supper of oatcake and sweet milk, a read of the newspaper and then up to bed. [15]

Saturday 3 April 1915: Kilwaughter

I passed the morning at home. In the afternoon I mounted my pony and trotted over to my Uncle James' new farm at Kilwaughter. He was a mason as well as a farmer and fond of conversation and good fellowship. He had a large family including several beautiful girls possessing musical and literary abilities. Thus Mary, the eldest, had the facility of producing poems which were published in the local newspaper, the *Larne Times*. Willie was the first born of the family and he and I went to Ballyrickard National School together. He was a local bandmaster but afterwards became religious, joined the Plymouth Brethren and devoted his literary skill to composing theological tracts and verses. Recently he became interested in the publication of *The Ancestry of the Irish-American Thoburns* by C. Stanley Thoburn of Massachusetts, USA, for the Thoburns, McWilliams, Crawfords and McRoberts are all interrelated. After getting the pony tethered up, my uncle's son, Willie, showed me round the place.

The outhouses were in bad repair but there were fine, big fields. There was a water-wheel that drove the thresher and plunge-churn, but might also work a dynamo and corn-grinder. Kilwaughter Castle was nearby and the Park with its lake, swans and an old rotten boat. Kilwaughter Castle was closed up but the outbuildings were accessible and I saw the well-sprung coach that had travelled the rough roads to the Parliament in Dublin before the Act of Union. I stayed there until about 9 in the evening and had a good ride home on the pony, although that required some management as the animal seemed inclined to be nervous in the dark.

Sunday 4 April 1915: Ballyboley

The weather, which has been getting colder for the last few days, now broke out in showers of hail. Matt and I walked to the Methodist Church in Ballynure for the morning service. We sat in the seat used by my Uncle John, behind us sat little Miss Victoria Wilson, dressed in black and with a rosy red, blooming face. Miss Wilson resided at The Mill, Straid, near Ballynure. She became a student at Trinity College, Dublin, and afterwards married Dr. Geoffrey Bewley of that City. An older sister was the wife of the Rev. J.R. Wesley Roddie, Methodist Minister and a younger brother is Hugh Wilson, FRCS, Larne. We had mid-day dinner at my uncle's and then came away. We walked

---

15 Sweet milk – buttermilk.

through Ballynure, turning down past the Parish Church, then along the Ballyboley line, but the roads were silent and solitary.

We agreed to go up to Mr McClellan's on Ballyboley Hill. There we met the father and Jean and had tea. Allen was getting on well and was orderly-sergeant that week so was coming home for Easter. I arose to go and as the father went out of the door, I slipped a kiss to Jean. Then I went out also and away we went, home.

Monday 5 April 1915: Larne

It was Easter Monday and I did my best to attract romance my way but failed miserably. In the morning I went up to the Forth, on my bicycle, and met Willie Knox. William E Knox was my own age and was born t the Fourth within a mile of me. He cycled to the grammar school with me and was apprenticed to a chemist in Shaftesbury Square, Belfast, when I started Queen's University, he was cheerful, talkative and one of the most amusing chaps I ever met.

Willie obtained a commission in 1915 and was wounded in the Battle of the Somme. After coming home he was for a time, on the East Coast Defences. Eventually he was sent to Salonica and contracted fever in the Struma Valley. For years after the War he attended a succession of medical boards. He had a month's free holiday in Portrush and when asked to describe the symptoms of malaria, the doctor said his was the best description he had ever heard of the disease.

About 11 o'clock we both left on our bikes, and went to Larne, leaving our machines with my Aunt Mary Buchanan. Mrs Buchanan was a widow who owned a furniture shop in Larne. She had a large family of whom one boy, John Buchanan, is a few years older than me. Later in life his son would succeed me as County Surveyor of Armagh. We passed the remainder of the day wandering together in quest of girls who might be pleased to go with us. But alas, we found no one sweet and pretty or fascinated by khaki, who might ramble with us round the Cliffs of Waterloo or stroll with us on the grassy slopes of Islandmagee. At nightfall, about 9.30pm, we, at last gave up hope and, sick and sad, left the town. It was certainly a most unkind Easter.

At Larne the weather was showery and the crowd in the streets was not big. There were a few soldiers about, for the local men, who were training in Newtownards were not allowed home for Easter. However there was a flotilla of trawlers in the harbour which was engaged in mine-sweeping: like fishing smacks they were, and each carried one gun. The officers and men were down the town and lots of them were quartered in the Olderfleet Hotel.

Tuesday 6 April 1915: Kilwaughter

Acting on the knowledge that Meg was staying with my Uncle James, I trotted over on the pony about 10 o'clock. Right enough she was and a fine time of fun we had. Meg, my girl cousins and I went towards the park when a heavy shower came on and we took shelter in the old ice-house. We explored the place, indulging in many pranks and friendly caresses. After dinner we continued our amusements in the parlour until with dusty, sweaty faces, tossed clothes and dishevelled hair we had to take leave of one another, I to report myself at home and Meg to stay for her train to Belfast.

I remained at home unto about 6.45pm when I took leave of my own family, and went to Larne by bicycle and to Belfast by the 7.25pm train. At Belfast Station I again saw Meg, as she had arranged to meet me there. We talked a little while and then the time came for the special trains to go to Randalstown.

Saturday 10 April 1915: Lisnalinchy

I put in for a pass to Doagh, to see the horse racing at Lisnalinchy and was granted it. At 10.40am a big company of us got on the train at Randalstown. The carriage in which I found myself did not stop between Antrim and Greenisland with the result that, having arrived at Greenisland; I determined to go on to Belfast. The compartment I was in had a lavatory attached so I remained in there while the tickets were being inspected. Thus I came to Belfast.

First I visited Willie Knox in Shaftesbury Square and arranged to go with him to the races. Not having anything very definite to do in the next hour, I went along the Malone Road and reaching Frederick Terrace rang the bell. Amy Cathcart answered it herself, dressed in a rig that suggested the washing of floors. We talked for a while and then I left, without any feeling of elation or embarrassment, only a little of surprise at my foolhardiness.

I met Willie Knox at the Midland Station and together we went by a special excursion train to Lisnalinchy. It was my first actual experience of how things are done at a racecourse. The ground was wet and it rained constantly for almost the whole day. There was a large crowd and the races were exciting, although I knew nothing about the horses or riders, or betting. I met lots of friends, including Polly McClennan, who was home on three weeks' leave, and Corporal McClellan. There was also a little dame there; accompanied by a girl friend that I used to see on the train going to Victoria College and who showed by her smile that she recognised me. Willie Knox and I met them several times about the field and every time the smile came off but when we spoke to them at the time of leaving we received blank faces and few words. My little witch had, however, the impudence to wave to me from the railway carriage as I was standing on the platform waiting for another train to Belfast.

On my arrival there I went along to Meg's and had tea. Afterwards we went down town and had a right merry time, taking the dark side streets and pretending to be drunk. She came to the railway station which I left at 9.30pm. I had a high time in the carriage with a company of boisterous, singing, merry chaps, many under the influence of good, strong beverages. I reached the Camp at nearly midnight, after an exciting day.

Wednesday 14 April 1915: Ballymena

Today there was a Brigade recruiting march to Ballymena. We left at 9.15am and reached Ballymena at about 2pm, marching through Ahoghill, which made the distance about twelve miles. The day was ideal, cool, dull and threatening rain but keeping dry for the most part. It was great sport, people came out in crowds to see us and the schoolchildren cheered us singing patriotic songs for all their worth. Everyone seemed to enjoy it and our Captain, P Kerr-Smiley, at the head of our company, gave the glad eye all around while we laughed, shouted and sang. We piled arms in the market square and broke off for a short time. General Hickman had spoken a few words about recruiting I dare say, but we could not hear any of this. Brigadier General T.E. Hickman, CB, DSO, MP, was Commander of the 109th Brigade from its foundation in 1914 until 27th May 1916 when he was succeeded by Brigadier General R.J. Shuter, DSO

Great Northern Hotel, Bundoran, County Donegal, one of the hotels
used by the Battalion in the winter of 1914. (McRoberts family)

I now had a few words with my father, mother and my brother Sam whom I had
seen, while marching along the street and who, having found from the newspapers that
we would be in Ballymena, had come up to see me and the rest of us. My younger brother
Samuel later married a business girl, Eileen, and built a house in the Malone District
of Belfast from where he invested in property. Being advised to seek a more congenial
climate for his asthma, selling his fine house in Malone, he moved with his wife and
daughter, Yvonne, to America intending to live in Arizona or some such dry climate.

I was amused at my father who, always trying to make the most of his opportunities,
introduced himself to Captain P. Kerr-Smiley and afterwards started a conversation with
Sergeant Major Carson, putting in, I am certain, a good word for me. He seemed to
be of the opinion that I had been a Private quite long enough and was of the opinion
that the Captain, knowing who I was and a university student would feel entitled to do
something for me.

The march home was by the more direct route, through Magherabeg and only
amounted to about ten miles. I never came through a long march more easily and was
feeling very fresh at the end. We arrived at the Camp about 6 o'clock. All the fellows
were well pleased with the town of Ballymena and the narrow streets teeming with lots
of sturdy laughing girls.

Friday 16 April 1915: Portglenone Road

There was no parade until 2.15pm when the whole Brigade went out. We were to hold
a line outside Randalstown so as to keep back the advance of the two Inniskilling
Battalions, coming from the direction of Portglenone. David Paterson and I were sent
out as a pair of scouts. David was a cheerful and energetic drummer boy. (On 1 July
1916, he was severely wounded and lay helpless for four days in the captured trenches.
His photo appeared in the press in Belfast with the statement that he had been killed.

No 15 Platoon, C Company, at Randalstown. In this photograph only some of the men are identified – Corporal Woodside, G.H.M., Hawthorne, Smith, Russell (in shorts), Patterson, McIlroy, Running, McFarland, Sergeant Powell, Lewis, Ellis, Culbert, Dowdy, Johnston (with dog), P.P., Brown, Lance Corporal McKnight. (Royal Ulster Rifles Museum)

Eventually he was picked up by some Royal Engineers and after a long spell in hospital and numerous operations, was eventually discharged.)

We experienced a bit of adventure. We had covered about three miles, without having seen any trace of the enemy, and were resting on the top of a high hill when quite suddenly their vanguard appeared, coming rapidly out of an old, deep hidden lane. As we were making a quick retreat we were sighted and, only by using our utmost speed and my making a big detour, we escaped.

However we almost ran into their scouts and only missed capture by using speed once more. At last we got back to our company who had taken up two natural lines of defence between thick, high, thorn hedges with the reserve placed in an old quarry. We remained with the reserve who, when it became dark, took up a position at the back of a farmhouse, close to the firing-line. There we lay a long time, at the base of a haystack. The volleys of blank[16] kept crackling all the time and sometimes close at hand, other times away on the flank.

The signallers kept the whole line in touch with headquarters by telephone. I was asleep I think, when I was awakened by Sergeant Major W.J.W. Carson summoning out the reserve. There was a tremendous roll of musquetry, but just then the bugles called, and soon we were back in the Camp. We had tea and then got to bed about midnight.[17]

We all had a laugh against Alec Flynn. He was sent out after the scouts to tell them about the changed position of the company. He did not see us so it seemed he

---

16   Blank – blank firing cartridges.

17   Sergeant Major Carson was later commissioned as a Second Lieutenant and was killed on 1 July 1916. He was the only son of William McRobert and Sarah Carson of Old Cavehill Road, Belfast, commemorated on the Thiepval Memorial, Pier and Face 15A and 15B.

YCV Camp Finner, Donegal, (Somme Museum, Newtownards)

had a good sleep, and then getting up refreshed he struck up with two girls, whom he observed going along a road. He was getting along well when an Inniskilling, putting a rifle through the hedge, ordered him to surrender. Flynn tried to make his escape but only ran into the hands of about fifty more of the enemy. He was caught, the bolt taken from his rifle, his ammunition confiscated and a sentry with loaded rifle and bayonet fixed, placed over him. He arrived in the hut about twenty minutes after us. Alec Flynn was a tall and generally good-natured fellow who reached the rank of Corporal while he was with us. He was beside me when I was wounded the second time and was himself wounded. Afterwards he was commissioned, but at Kemmel Hill in April 1918, he was taken prisoner by the Germans. I used to meet him frequently in Portadown during the 1930s.

Saturday 17 April 1915 – Home
In the morning I was on pioneer fatigues. From it I was called away to be interviewed by Captain P. Kerr-Smiley who questioned me about my parentage, education, etc., and asked me if I desired a stripe, but when I replied I was not particularly anxious he remarked that plenty of others were.

The first two platoons of each company were allowed to go on leave from 1pm that day until 12pm on Sunday. I arrived in Belfast and had tea at my Aunt's, at 350 Shankill Road.[18] I then went to Larne by the 6pm train and up to Headwood on the narrow gauge, travelling with my mother who had been down in Larne; I found all well at home.

---

18   Today 350 Shankill Road is a grocery shop.

YOUNG CITIZEN VOLUNTEERS.

14TH (SERVICE) BATTALION ROYAL IRISH RIFLES.

RECRUITS DESIROUS OF JOINING THIS WELL-KNOWN AND CRACK CORPS FOR FOREIGN AND ACTIVE SERVICE (NOW STATIONED AT RANDALSTOWN) SHOULD APPLY AT NO. 68 SCOTTISH PROVIDENT BUILDINGS BETWEEN 9 A.M. AND 6 P.M., OR AT RANDALSTOWN.
MEN OF GOOD CHARACTER ONLY NEED APPLY.

Newspaper advertisement for the YCV/14th Battalion. These appeared on frequent occasions in order to attempt to bring the various battalions up to full strength, which was not as easy as many today imagine. (Mark Ramsey)

Sunday 18 April 1915: – Belfast
I spent the whole morning about the house at home. In the afternoon I walked down to Larne and travelled up to Belfast on the 5.55pm train. I went to the Shore Road but only found the old people there, the rest being at church. I took the train to the Camp at 9.15pm. Altogether it was a very unexciting holiday.

Tuesday 20 April 1915: Randalstown
In the morning I had a letter from Amy Cathcart asking why I was not writing to her. She finished with these pretty lines:

(1) If you but knew
How just a kindly word or two,
A thought or smile from you,
Would set my heart a singing on its way,
Would ease the burden of the day,
If you but knew.
(2) If you but knew
How great would be the bliss
To wear though toiling hours the memory of a kiss,
Oh, surely you'd consent to bless
Me with that coveted caress,
If you but knew

There really must have been something original in this little girl's head.

Wednesday 21 April 1915: Castleldawson
We had a Brigade march to Castledawson, leaving Randalstown at 8.40am. The weather was cool and dull and the roads easy to walk on. It was a very quick march to Castledawson, with only two stops on the way, each five minutes. Castledawson was a town like Randalstown, only it was bigger and had a factory employing a lot of girls. We fell out for about an hour in Moyala Park. On coming back through the town we were

14th Bn. Royal Irish Rifles.

Bundoran, 5th Jany '15.

Please note that the Battalion moves to Randalstown on the 6th January. You are hereby notified to report yourself at the Midland Rly, York Road Station at 1.p.m. on the 6th inst, for entraining by special train at 2-15 p.m. NO EXCUSE FOR ABSENCE.

R Spencer Chichester   Lt.Col.
Commanding 14th Bn. Royal Irish Rifles.

Movement order received by all members of the Battalion for the
move to Randalstown. (Royal Ulster Rifles Museum)

halted for a considerable time, on the streets, while Brigadier Hickman made a speech from the Fair Hill. We returned quickly, reaching the Camp about 6.15pm.

Saturday 24 April 1915: Belfast

I obtained a pass to Belfast for the evening and left Randalstown by the 1.30pm. I had a troublesome tooth stopped[19] by Mr Morrison of Duncairn Gardens, bought a pair of running shoes for 6/6 and went to have tea at my aunt's. Afterwards I proceeded to call on Miss Amy Cathcart, but was received with such ill grace, she refused to come out, pleading that she was not allowed to, and I had to take myself away. I spent most of the remainder of the time at my disposal walking about the Antrim Road. The evening was mild and dry so I thought what a nice time I might have had with sweet cousin Meg, if I had not wasted time on that little minx Amy Cathcart but we only learn by experience. The train left Belfast at 11pm. The following day we heard of the landing in Gallipoli.[20]

Saturday 1 May 1915: Belfast

Two scouts were required from each company, so I put in my name and got a place, to my pleasure and satisfaction. At 1pm I travelled on a special train to Belfast to spend the evening there. I met Meg along the Shore Road and went for a walk up the Old Cave Hill Road, where we enjoyed each other's company away up on the hill overlooking Belfast. We walked back and I had tea at her home. We went out again together and I took her out the tow-path, beside the River Lagan. Then I accompanied her home, sought my train and eventually came back to Randalstown. I had a bothersome race up to the guard-room with my pass and enjoyed an onion with some dry bread for supper before going to rest.

Wednesday 5 May 1915: Belfast

It was an ideal morning, cool and misty, when the Battalion set off for Belfast at 7.45am. The route was through Antrim and Muckamore, and then off to the right along that terrible, hilly road, straight as an arrow, that leads over the mountain down to Ligoniel on the outskirts of Belfast. The day gradually got warmer and the sun came out in

---

19 Filled.
20 The Allied invasion of western Turkey began as a purely naval attempt to break through the Dardanelles Straits in February 1915; this was followed by the landing of British Imperial and French troops on the Gallipoli Peninsula in April, including the 10th (Irish) Division.

full force after noon. We rested about two and a half hours at Carnavy where we were supplied with good tea and refreshments by a Bloomfield Bakery party. Climbing the mountain had apparently fatigued the chaps as they turned into Captain C.O. Slacke's fields at Wheatfield for a thirty minute repose. They appeared very hot and much done for. Rough looking Charles Slacke became the Commanding Officer of our Company. He was killed on 1 July 1916.[21]

The rest, although only of thirty minutes duration, worked wonders and the march through the city was spoken of as very fine. Enjoying the special freedom of movement allowed by shorts, I was very little upset by the exertion. We stored our rifles in Davidson's Yard and I went to spend the weekend with my aunt at 350 Shankill Road.

Thursday 6 May 1915: Belfast
I passed the morning down town and at night proceeded to the Shore Road.

Friday 7 May 1915: Belfast
I fell in with some YCVs and went to the Ormeau Baths for a plunge. After dinner we went to Windsor Park where the final in the football cup was won by 'B' Company who beat 'A' Company one goal to nil. It was a good match. My mother came up to stay the night with my aunt; also Elsie Graham arrived on the scene, all to have a look at the soldiers on the following day.

The 7th May was the day that RMS *Lusitania* was torpedoed by a German submarine within sight of Kinsale, south-west Ireland. Of the 1959 souls who sailed in her from New York, 1198 perished. Of the dead 124 were citizens of the United States.[22]

Saturday 8 May 1915: Belfast
Today there was a great military display in Belfast. Seventeen thousand men took part in a review of the Ulster Division in the Malone District at 11.45am, and marched past the City Hall at 2 o'clock. It proved to be a successful day and the weather was in a most encouraging mood, only it was a little warm. The YCV paraded at Davidson's Yard at 7.45am and marched by the Ravenhill Road and over the New Bridge, to the ground selected for the review.

The place was a number of large fields, adjoining the Queen's Grounds, on the City side. Here the Division had refreshments; tea, soda cake, and tinned meat, all prepared by the field kitchens on the spot. These arrangements were very well handled. Then we formed up in our battalions and the Inspecting General Sir Hugh McCalmont arrived.[23]

A gun was fired as a signal and an immense Union Jack, the largest in the world, was hoisted at the saluting base, the Battalions presented arms and our bugle-band played the general salute. The march past in columns of platoons commenced; the Inniskilling Dragoons leading, then the Cyclists etc. followed by the Infantry Brigades, the 107th,

---

21 Captain Charles Owen Slacke ("…a round faced fat-bellied gentleman with a cynical smile", Orr, P., *op. cit.,* (Belfast: Blackstaff Press, 2008) p. 73), 14th Battalion Royal Irish Rifles, killed 1 July 1916, age 44 years. He was the son of Sir Owen Randal Slacke and husband of Catherine Anne (nee Lanyon). Buried in Connaught Cemetery, Thiepval, Grave IV.A.9.
22 The Battalion was billeted at Wheatfield House in north Belfast.
23 Major General Sir Hugh McCalmont, KCB, DL, was the MP for North Antrim from 1895 to 1899. He died in 1924.

The Young Citizens did indeed come from privileged backgrounds - R.N. Kennedy and
Graham Allen, both prominent members of Balmoral Golf Club. (Nigel Henderson)

108th and 109th. Thus we were near the rear of the whole parade. The scouts marched
past by themselves, behind the Battalion.

In the parade through the City, the scouts preceded the bands and the short pants
with bare knees, evoking much prattling from a certain section of the City's fair ones
who have no reputation for blushing shyness. Going through the terribly crowded streets
we could scarcely get space to walk properly and the atmosphere was often stifling. We
marched past the General again at the City Hall, through High Street and Royal Avenue
and then to Davidson's Yard. The whole thing was a big festival of fun as far as I was
concerned. After tea at my aunt's, Meg came up to see me and we had a fine evening's
fun. Mother, Matt, John and Elsie Graham all saw me on parade but were gone to their
homes when I came back.

Sunday 9 May 1915: Belfast

While the rest were at church I went for a stroll up the Cave Hill in the morning, it
being a lovely day. At 2 o'clock the YCV's paraded at St George's Market and went to
Divine Service in the Ulster Hall. There was a short sermon by Rev. George Wedgwood
and good singing by the choir which came from Donegall Road Church. The Rev.
George R Wedgwood was a Methodist Minister who had two sons with commissions
in our Battalion but they were both killed on 1 July 1916.[24] After the service we were
immediately dismissed. In the evening I went to Falls Road Church.

---

24 Second Lieutenant P.E. Wedgwood, 16th Rifles, killed 1 July 1916, buried in Mill Road Cemetery,
    Thiepval, grave IV.A.4. Lieutenant Gilbert Colclough Wedgwood, 109th Company, Machine Gun

Battalion pets at Randalstown, Back row, Company Quartermaster Sergeant White, Private Joe Wright, Private William McBurney, Sergeant A. Patton (killed on 27 June 1917), Company Sergeant Major White. Seated, Sergeant Smyth, Sergeant Cole, Cook H. Bingham with Sammy the drake, Company Sergeant Major Griffiths, Sergeant R.J. Elliott with Mick the fox terrier and Sergeant Diamond. (Nigel Henderson)

Monday 10 May 1915: Dunadry

The YCVs paraded in Davidson's Yard at 11.30am and marched to the Midland Station. We were taken by two special trains to Dunadry, where we got off. After WWII, Dunadry became known for a restaurant with posh nosh!

A big fight had been arranged to occupy us through the night. 'C' and 'D' Companies of the 14th and the North Irish Horse were to be the rear-guard of an army which had retreated over the Six Mile Water, after destroying the bridges on its way to Ballymena.

I was with this side and we were to prevent the crossing of the river at any point between Dunadry and Lough Neagh of the hostile army, which was composed of Royal Engineers, Royal Inniskilling Fusiliers, Cyclists and Inniskilling Dragoons. The Royal Engineers were to build the bridges for the pursuing army.

My party had dinner at Dunadry which consisted of boiled potatoes, tinned meat and pickles. Then we marched to Muckamore and had high tea at about 6 o'clock. Meanwhile, the North Irish Horse had been patrolling the river bank and had sighted the enemy at one point. As it was now growing dark we went to relieve them. I was attached to a party of 'C' Company and we had to patrol the river from Muckamore to

Corps, age 22 years, no known grave, commemorated on the Thiepval Memorial, Pier and Face 3C and 12C.

Unknown member of the YCV/14th Rifles. (Mark Ramsey)

the cemetery outside Antrim. I spent the whole night on my feet, running messages and finding out things for my Lieutenant who impressed me as an incompetent man.

The enemy was discovered towards Antrim and I lay on a high bank listening to their movements for a long time; hoarse coughing, rustling among the trees, voices and splashing in the water. Our picket opened fire on them but after a time the disturbance ceased, probably it was only a feint. Far up the river, beyond my part, there was a great deal of firing. There, as I learned in the morning, the enemy started the construction of two bridges, a heavy one and a light one, but they were fired on intensely. In the morning these bridges could be seen, only half-constructed.

Thus the night passed and very still it was, but there was the intermittent chorus of the corncrake and towards dawn, the call of the cuckoo. At 5.30am the action stopped and we set out, a number of weary lads, on our march to Randalstown, six miles away.

Saturday 15 May 1915: Home
I got a weekend pass and went to see my father and mother, arriving home at about 8.30am. They still like to hint that I have greatly disappointed them by enlisting as a Private in His Majesty's Forces. A rather amusing incident occurred in the train as I was going from Belfast to Larne. Two female gypsies, distinguished by their peculiar dress and faces, entered the carriage, at a station. One was carrying a tiny, yellow baby who, for such a mite, had a droll look on his face and both ladies were laden with several baskets which impeded them very much on entering the compartment. These baskets were full of brown paper bags which seemingly contained fruit. As soon as they had settled down in their seats the more jolly looking of the ladies, the one with no child, opened up several brown parcels and commenced to hand out figs, round the

Unknown member of the YCV/14th Rifles. (Mark Ramsey)

compartment. I seemed to merit a special share and then she spoke. She was a gypsy, a very clever woman who knew a great many things and could tell the character and fortunes of people by looking at their faces.

I, that young soldier, was going out to fight in a foreign land but he would not be exposed to danger and would come back unhurt. Would this transpire to be an accurate prognosis? That young lady, she was tall and good looking, liked music and was fond of kissing. That lady, she was dark and modest and was very loyal and true. That chap who was pale and unhealthy looking was very fond of girls. That man, who was a rowdy, careless farmer, was very fond of women also but he was married and his wife need have no doubt of his loyalty. Thus we each and all were dealt with in the space of a few minutes, for the gypsies their baskets and the baby left us at the next station on the line.

Sunday 16 May 1915: Belfast

This was a fine day lending the quiet countryside an almost mysterious atmosphere. I spent the morning in the fields at home until tea-time when my brother Matthew drove me down to Larne to catch the 5.50pm train. On arriving in Belfast, I went to Glenarm Terrace, where I found the family in a state of agitation. A nephew of Mrs McRoberts had died and his young wife and child were staying with her until after the funeral. It was a sad tale and an example of the fierce, stubborn pride and drive for money born in a certain class of the North of Ireland farmer.

The deceased's father, a farmer, had amassed a lot of money by hard work and thrift. The eldest son of the family laboured hard at home for three years, then married the daughter of a neighbouring farmer whom his father held in deep contempt. The older man was enraged at this and bade his son never darken his door again. The young man, with his wife, went to Belfast where he had trouble obtaining constant employment, so that the worry brought about his premature death. I was talking to Meg for a few minutes only.

Wednesday 19 May 1915: Randalstown
The 10th Royal Inniskilling Fusiliers arrived from Castledawson at 10am. They had marched the whole way from Finner Camp, County Donegal, spending the nights in the open fields.

Saturday 22 May 1915: Belfast
While the Brigade was being inspected by the new Lord Lieutenant Lord Wimborne, and the YCVs were earning fresh glory and praise for their steady behaviour, I travelled to Belfast to take part in the Linfield sports, held in Windsor Park. I had entered for the two mile, invitation team race. Seven teams of five men, ours to count, were entered in for this and some of Ireland's best harriers were there from the different camps of the Ulster Division, to which the race was confined.

Meg and her companion, Miss Edith Nichol, were at the grounds and I spent most of the time from 2.30pm to 5.30pm in their company, waiting for my own event. Edith Nichol is married and as Mrs McCord now lives in Sydenham, Belfast. She lost a brother in World War I and her only son was killed in World War II.

Meanwhile several other races were run and very good exhibitions of skill were given by youthful dancers, girl physical culturists, bayonet fighters, boy blue-jackets and boy scouts. The day was very hot, the sun pouring from a cloudless heaven.

At last I was on the cinder path, waiting for the gunshot. I ran easily and eventually came in second, next to the winner, William Scott, also YCV. The third was YCV, as was the fifth, so that our team won easily. In place of Lady Carson, the prizes were distributed by Lady Richardson, the wife of Lieutenant General Sir George Richardson, Commander of the Ulster Volunteer Force. Sir George Richardson, an Englishman and a retired Indian Army officer who, at the suggestion of Lord Roberts, had assumed command of the Ulster Volunteer Force. Owing to the seniority of his rank he was unable to command the Division, which was taken by Major General C.H. Powell. Just before our arrival in France General Powell was succeeded by Major General O.S.W. Nugent, DSO, who commanded the Division until May 1918.

I must say that a rather decent gold medal came my way. I was well pleased with my performance and spent the night at the home of my Aunt Lennon's.

Sunday 23 May 1915: Belfast
I attended Falls Road Church in the morning, took a walk in the afternoon and went to Agnes Street Church in the evening. I had a rather serious talk with Miss Eliza McMinn in the drawing room, where we were alone. Elizabeth McMinn was a distant relation of my own who lived with my aunt, Mrs Lennon, at 350 Shankill Road, during the time the former had an office job in the City. She afterwards married and had two sons. I found her to be easy company. She was sisterly, frank and not easily offended. Taking a rather unusual course for a maiden with a soldier she asked me if I were a Christian and what were my hopes of the future if I lost my life in this war?

I told her candidly my belief, for she would not drop the subject, that I held absolute trust in the teaching of no single religion, nor could I understand how a liberal thinking mind could. We knew not what would happen tomorrow, but if we lived clean, manly lives I did not believe why we should worry or fear. She seemed interested in what I said and did not fling such terms as 'wicked' and 'awful' at me as I could well have imagined many people doing. This spirit of interest, sympathy and intelligence showed her in a new light. My train left for Randalstown at 9pm. Eliza became Mrs Barron with two sons, one of whom lectured at Manchester University. This transpired to be the day that Italy declared War on Austria.[25]

Friday 28 May 1915: Home
At 1.20pm and 1.40pm two trains conveyed the whole Battalion, recruits excepted, to Belfast for a few days, the last in Ireland we were given to understand. I reached home without anything amusing happening, where I found everyone well and my mother especially maintained a good heart and did not in the least upbraid me. ·

Monday 29 May 1915: Ballyclare
I rambled about home all morning and in the afternoon went to take leave of some of my friends about Ballyclare such as Mr Douther and Uncle John. I had tea at Elsie Graham's and on leaving, her mother asked me to write to them and let them know how I was keeping.

Sunday 30 May 1915: Larne
I went to church in Larne, dressed in mufti, my civilian coat and waistcoat were too large for me, but, judging by the hang of my trousers, I must be a bit taller. I was about home for the remainder of the day.

Monday 31 May 1915: Ballylaggan
In the afternoon I cycled to Ballylaggan to say bye-bye to my old grandfather. To meet him I had to find my way to Keown's Moss where he and his grandson Bob were cutting peat. I went to Larne afterwards and was speaking to Lieutenant W.J. McClellan who was home on holiday. I stayed in Mrs Buchanan's until about half past eleven. Everyone spoke enthusiastically of my pluck and good, healthy, athletic appearance. Of course they were oblivious of what the War would do to us all.

Tuesday 1 June 1915: Larne
Father and mother drove me down to Larne to catch the 12.55pm Belfast train. I could say 'Boys, take my advice and stick to your father and mother while they live. Then you will never know the sickening, horrible feeling that comes over you when, shaking hands with your mother, she turns her back on you, her face red and running with tears.' At Belfast I went to take leave of Meg, saw all my Shore Road friends, and left for Randalstown by the 9.15pm train. There was a terrible crush at the station and girls got such attentions in public as they had never received in their lives before. This was a foretaste of the effects of war on social behaviour.

---

25 Italy fought on the Allied side in the Great War, but did not declare war on Germany until 28 August 1916.

Saturday 5 June 1915: Roguery
I spent the evening in the company of Miss Nellie Bankhead. I took her to the pictures and then to a hobby-horse entertainment where we had a swing together. I had been out with her on the Thursday night previously and walked about the road with her. She told me I was teasing her, but I wonder did she know how much she teased me and with what pain and difficulty I walked the four miles back to the Camp.

Wednesday 9 June 1915: Randalstown
We had a half-holiday and two special trains came from Belfast full of mothers, sisters and sweethearts so that the Camp looked like a huge picnic. I had my own surprise. My father and mother had gone to Antrim by pony and taken a car over to Randalstown. I showed them round the Camp as well as the Park, which seemed to interest them.

Thursday 10 June 1915: Things Get Serious At Ballyeston
Two days' Brigade work in the mountains was on the syllabus. The Battalion marched away about 6am, each man carrying a blanket, waterproof sheet and greatcoat. It was a hot day as we made our way to Kells for the first halt. Then we marched to Glenwherry, until we came in front of Brae Hill, where the 10th Inniskillings had entrenched themselves, having gone out to this position the previous day.

Our Battalion lay in reserve while the 9th and 11th proceeded to attack the hill. A squadron of North Irish Horse was working on each side. The Inniskillings advanced in a great number of extended lines, one behind the other, and were just coming into contact with the enemy when the bugle blew the 'Stand Fast'. Why the operations were thus nipped we could not surmise and did not hear explained.

The 14th then marched over Big Collin, a terrible, heavy, cruel march to many of the lads, and halted at the foot of Drumadarragh Hill, close to Dixon's place. The owner of Drumadarragh was Sir Thomas Dixon who also possessed another place at Ballygally, on the coast road near Larne. This residence was handed over to the Hospitals Authority and is now known as the Sir Thomas and Lady Edith Dixon Hospital. The present owner of Drumadarragh House lives there and is a son of Sir Thomas; he is Lieutenant Colonel Lord H.M.L. Glentoran, Minister of Commerce for Northern Ireland. We had dinner at the foot of Drumadarragh Hill. Feeling quite fresh, and being only two miles from Ballyclare, I made my way there and had supper at the home of my aunt, Mrs Agnes Bell. Then I walked to Ballyeaston and, making enquiries, learned that Miss Kitty Gault was at home. I shall always remember Kitty Gault whom I had met at a picnic in Ballyboley two years earlier. These were private picnics to which a dozen or two people were asked to come by special invitation. I had walked with her the whole way back to her home in Ballyeaston and kissed her goodnight; she did not resist and returned the kiss. She was the first girl in my experience to do so and I shall never forget her.

Now, sending a little chap to deliver my card, a very impromptu one, however a very serviceable one, for my little lassie soon appeared accompanied by a fine-looking sister, to whom I was immediately introduced. We proceeded to walk quietly towards the camp reliving much of the fun we had had at picnics in Ballyboley on two certain occasions in the past. Last Post was sounding when we came away from the Camp with its smouldering fires and lines of dark, filed rifles. I walked back with the girls, towards their home, when we met their only brother who had come out to find them. I shook hands with the three and came back to the Camp. It was nearly midnight as I spread my sheet and rolled myself in my blanket and greatcoat. A dull, close night it was as I lay warm and tossing, unable to sleep.

Friday 11 June 1915: Drumdarragh Hill

I do not think I had much rest but rose fairly fresh, just before the bugle sounded the reveille at 4.15am. At 5am we had breakfast and by 6am were on our way to the top of Drumadarragh Hill, a toilsome climb in the early, morning sun. Today we were to be the defenders of the hill against the 9th and 10th with the 11th in reserve. The North Irish Horse was again acting on both sides. We dug a trench right across the top of the hill, a little back from its summit. The front of the hill, looking towards Big Collin, from where the assault was expected, was our screen. Our right flank was very strong, but our left was allowed to remain weak, as the enemy was not expected to come that way. This left was, however, surprised at about 11.30am by a patrol of horsemen and one of our pickets was put out of action, the patrol making good its escape.

At about 2pm the enemy's infantry were seen advancing over Big Collin in great numbers. They attacked our hill in long, extended lines, one behind the other. Our screen opened fire on them but was forced to retire by weight of opposing numbers. The retirement was carried out in a fashion that earned great praise and the control of fire was wonderfully good. The whole scene, with its human lines advancing or retreating looked like the well-ordered pictures of the cinema. The rattle of musquetry did not cease until about 4.30pm when the 'Stand Fast' sounded. Brian Boyd and I spent the whole time to the front and left of the fight. We marched to a certain point by compass and remained in that neighbourhood, watching the roads there. We lay in the back garden of a farmhouse where we were objects of curiosity to several small children. These must have told their mother about us, for she sent out a plateful of newly baked, potato bread, dripping with butter. There were probably cups of tea also, however I have forgotten about them but forty years afterwards I can still smell that hot potato cake. It was sumptuous. It is strange the acts of kindness that become embedded in the memory. We perceived little of the drama that was going on. Away to our right we could hear only the intermittent crash of the rifle fire. On the top of the hill the Battalion had dinner and then tea, after which we marched to Doagh Station and returned to the Camp by train.[26]

Brian Boyd was a good-looking and exceptionally decent fellow. He had knowledge of French and was a Lance Corporal in the Permanent Patrol. For his part in the action of 1 July 1916, he was awarded the Military Medal. Shortly after I was wounded for the second time, he came home and was commissioned to his old Battalion. He returned to Belgium and was one of our few fatal casualties in the Battle of Messines, on 7 June 1917. He is one of the dedicatees of this published version of the diaries.[27]

---

26 'Returned to the Camp by train' was the result of a mutiny within the Battalion. The men refused to march back to their Camp and insisted that a train be provided. The Battalion's Commanding Officer, Lieutenant Colonel Robert Chichester, defused the situation by agreeing to the demand and chartering a train at his own expense. No man in the Battalion received any punishment, but henceforth the 14th Rifles were known as the 'Chocolate Soldiers' to the other units in the Division. Bowman, T., *Irish Regiments in the Great War, Discipline and Morale*, (Manchester: University Press, 2003).

27 Second Lieutenant Brian Boyd, MM, 14th Royal Irish Rifles, killed on 7 June 1917, age 19 years. The son of William A. and Lizzie M. Boys, Cyprus Gardens, Belfast. Bailleul Communal Cemetery (Nord) grave III.C.4.

Just after our arrival in Randalstown, the Inniskillings began to come back and they had the bounce on the chocolate soldiers for they had walked the whole way. They did not remember that they had experienced two days of much lighter work than we, also that while we carried our own blankets on our back, theirs were carried by their transport.

Tuesday and Wednesday 15 and 16 June 1915: Drumdarragh Hill
The brilliant weather continued and at 5.30pm the Battalion set off in full marching order. We went through Antrim, Dunadry and Parkgate and after a toilsome march reached the summit of Drumadarragh Hill. We had hot cocoa served out before we lay down to rest.

Early in the morning we were up and had tea and biscuits, after which we marched over to where our old trenches were, filled them in and came back for breakfast. At 9am we set off for the Camp by the direct route which leads through Cookstown Junction. The morning was exceptionally hot and dusty so that the baked roads were very trying on the feet. Many were the aching toes and heels that entered Randalstown at about 1pm. We had proved however, that we could march to Drumdarragh Hill and come back the following day without the help of a train and thus we won back some of our lost reputation.

Friday to Sunday 18-20 June 1915: Home
This was the centenary of the Battle of Waterloo so we had a half-holiday with Brigade sports. Most of the laurels fell to the athletes of the 14th. I ran in the one mile and came second, very close to the winner my old friend, William Scott. I received my prize of ten shillings from the hand of Brigadier T.E. Hickman.

I cycled away from Randalstown about one o'clock on Saturday with J. Coulter who stopped at Whitepark, and I proceeded home. Johnny Coulter was afterwards injured in an accident in Thiepval Wood. He was assisting in the haulage of a trench mortar gun, when he slipped and the wheel ran over his leg, severely crushing it.

I went to a picnic at Straid in the evening but the affair was as mild as milk and I came home in a quick and circumspect manner. On a Saturday afternoon during the summer, each National School would hold its picnic, or school fete as it was sometimes called. The children would assemble about 3pm in the schoolroom where they were treated to a fancy tea. The band then arrived, playing a lively tune before they were given tea and refreshments. The band leading, all marched to the field. Soon crowds of boys and girls began to arrive, and afterwards perhaps mothers and fathers. For the older ones there was dancing on the grass but for the younger there was 'hindmost of three'. A circle of standing couples was formed while several other pairs started playing 'tig'. The pursued would then take refuge in front of a standing couple when the chaser had then to run after the 'hindmost of three'. When it began to get dark the band played the (National Anthem) *God Save the King* and the picnic broke up, leaving the nice question of who was to accompany who home!

I travelled to the Church in Larne on Sunday and heard a sermon from my Uncle John. I cycled back to Randalstown and on the way Johnny Coulter introduced me to an uncle in Muckamore, an old gentleman connected with the Mill there and father of a

Captain Willis in his YCV uniform. (Nigel Henderson)

grown up family who have all gone from home, except the youngest boy. He was a sporty old chap who made the most of his means.

Friday 25 June 1915: Home
Today I got away on leave at 6 o'clock when I travelled to Larne and cycled home on John Buchanan's bike. This parting was supposed to be the 'last of all the last'.

Saturday 26 June 1915: Ballynure
I went to a picnic in Ballynure in the evening and accompanied Miss Jean McClelland most of the way home.

Sunday 27 June 1915: Randalstown
I returned to Randalstown in the evening.

Monday 5 July 1915: Randalstown
We were told to pack everything we possessed into our kit bags or in our rucksacks. The huts were then cleared out of everything that remained, the bed-boards and mattresses lifted so we were only left with one blanket to carry. We paraded with all our kit and the Battalion left Randalstown, County Antrim, in two special trains starting at 11.15am and 11.45am. I was in the first and the train went through Lisburn and quickly on towards Dublin.

There is a page missing from the original diary which described our arrival in Dublin, the embarkation at Kingstown (now Dun Laoghaire) and our journey across the sea, but I chiefly remember as we passed through the suburbs of Dublin being cheered by the women standing at their doors.

Training in Seaford, Sussex

Tuesday 6 July 1915: Holyhead to Seaford

We reached Holyhead at 12.25am local time but 12.55pm English time and changed our watches accordingly.[1] A special train, capable of taking the whole Battalion, was awaiting us at the harbour, and soon we were on the move again. I fell asleep and when I awoke it was quite clear and we were approaching Crewe, where we had a short stop.

Then we travelled right through the Midlands of England, the fine fields looking somewhat yellow from the recent spell of hot weather and the green woods and the towns appeared, some bright and pretty, some black and crowded. At Rugby we again stopped and were speedily served out with buttered loaf and tea and then we continued on towards London. There were now several parallel lines on each side of us and trains hurried past us laden with business people going to their day's work in the great city.

We passed through suburbs with the familiar names of Hammersmith, Kensington and Chelsea, and crossed the filthy Thames with glimpses of the dome of St Paul's, the Houses of Parliament and Tower Bridge. Then we proceeded through Battersea and the suburbs of infinite London, and finally travelled over the rolling Downs and into our home beside the waves. We reached Seaford about 10.30am. Our huts were all built of wood and not of corrugated iron. They were not quite as well finished as those at Randalstown but they were very fine all the same. The scouts all went into a hut by themselves. The camp was about ten minutes walk from the centre of the town and about fifteen minutes from the sea. On our arrival we had high tea with salmon and in the evening several of us went for a walk round the town. It was very stormy and the sea was running high. We noticed the numerous pretty villas, all built of red brick and roofed with red tiles. There were many soldiers about, we being practically the last of the Division to arrive. The people were very kind to us and eager to do their best to make our sojourn as pleasant and comfortable as possible. Everywhere we met with sympathetic and quick attention and, although their speech was tinged with a peculiar English flavour, we had not the least difficulty in understanding each other. We learned afterwards that people here had been terrified at the prospect of twenty thousand, wild Irishmen coming amongst them. Youth is ever adaptable and naively optimistic we returned to our camp, congratulating ourselves on our interesting and pleasant quarters and looking forward to the prospect of a most enjoyable and instructive summer.

Wednesday 7 July 1915: Seaford

It rained here the whole day, so Ireland is not the only place it could rain; although we had been led to believe so, but rain it did, with a dismal and callous persistency. We remained most of the day about the Camp and had a hut inspection by our Commanding

---

1   In 1880 Greenwich Mean Time was legally adopted throughout Great Britain, being adopted by the Isle of Man in 1883, Guernsey in 1913 and in Ireland in 1916. Prior to this Ireland had operated under Dublin Mean Time.

LOL 862, the Official Orange Lodge of the Battalion. (Nigel Henderson)

Officer, Colonel Chichester, for which we had a lot of general cleaning up to do. There were many recreation halls about the camp belonging to the YMCA, the Salvation Army and the Church Army. There were lots of books and magazines in most of them, also the YMCA hut had a lending library and supplies of free notepaper, ink, pens and blotting paper. During the day we saw sea planes several times and we were given to understand that aircraft were a common sight. In the evening we heard the noise of the guns over in France, and lying in our beds, in the quietness that comes after lights out, we heard the sullen reports even more distinctly, it was a continual, dull thudding din with just the least trace of vibration in the sound.

Thursday 8 July to Wednesday 14 July 1915: Seaford
There was a 'double' in the morning and after breakfast a rout march along the coast towards Newhaven where we piled arms and indulged in a dip in the sea. The water seemed very buoyant and I had not the least difficulty in swimming. Route marches and bathing parades continued daily.

Thursday 15 July 1915: Seaford
There was an inspection of the Brigade by the Chief Deputy, Sir Archibald Murray, of The General Imperial Staff. It was wet in the afternoon and the sea was rough, as it often was, so we stayed in the Camp. On Battalion orders, the words of Sir A Murray were communicated, expressing his great satisfaction with the steady bearing of the men on parade.

No 5 Platoon of B Company at Seaford, 1915. This photograph is taken from an album that featured the entire Battalion. A copy could be purchased by the men and then posted to their homes. (Somme Museum, Newtownards)

Saturday 17 July 1915: Seaford

A number of us went by train to Brighton, arriving there at about 2.45pm. The town had a very imposing appearance on approaching it by the London Railway. There were high, well-build houses, straight streets and the wonderful Marine Parade. The blue sea in the background was broken into by beautiful piers and a wholesome feeling of beauty, health and grandeur filled the air. We spent the entire evening wandering about, directed only by our changing fancy. We paid two pence each and found ourselves on the magnificent Palace Pier, where we listened to a band playing for some time. Then we walked around the restaurant rooms and watched the patient anglers for some time.

The great Marine Parade was filled with a dense crowd, officers and their wives, visitors from London, ordinary soldiers like myself and everywhere the flashing eyes of winsome girls. We talked with many of these females, walked with some but got weary of their flippant manners and their evident consciousness of their own superiority and right to have their own heartless way. A visit to a picture palace, which was disappointing, filled several hours.

Wounded Indian soldiers were noticed with interest in the Pavilion, great, tall fellows, regularly featured they were, and their skin was not nearly as dark as I had imagined.[2] At about 11pm I began to look for a bed for the night and easily found one in

---

2   On the Western Front an Indian Corps consisting of two infantry division and a cavalry brigade served from September 1914. They suffered enormous casualties before the infantry were withdrawn to other theatres in later 1915. Pope, S. & Wheal E-A., *The Macmillan Dictionary of the First World War*, (London: Macmillan, 1995)

Battalion Drum, Pipe and Bugle Band at Seaford. (Somme Museum, Newtownards)

a boarding house in a side street. I had a comfortable room and a good breakfast in the morning, all for two shillings.

Sunday 18 July 1915: Brighton

It was a brilliant morning, giving promise of a still more brilliant day. Just after rising, I went down to the Parade for a stroll, waiting until my breakfast should be ready. I found two YCV's who had spent the whole night in a field outside the town and had been walking around since 4am. I passed the day in strolling about, sometimes with girls, more often alone. I went along the seafront past Hove, then walked back until I came to a station from which I returned to the Palace Pier by the electric railway. I came back to the Camp by train, arriving at 9pm and although I had no pass, my absence had not been reported.

Tuesday 20 to Thursday 22 July 1915: Seaford

This was a good day in which the whole Ulster Division marched past Lord Kitchener in Review Order. The different Battalions were marshalled in several fields, to the north of our Camp, where the arrival of the Chief Secretary of War was awaited. The cheering in the town told us of his arrival at the railway station, after which the march past commenced and continued for about one and a half hours. I had a glimpse of the War Lord as I passed him, taking full advantage of the 'eyes right'. He was seated on horseback and was laughing and asking questions of the Brigadier, T.E. Hickman, CB, and DSO

I spent most of the evening pursuing books, with an occasional attempt to master the Morse Code. Sherlock Holmes I read for the first time, finding it a real lucky bag of information as well as interesting adventure. The weather was unsettled some days were lovely while others were stormy, with heavy rainfall. Bathing parades were not permitted

Battalion officers at Seaford, October 1915, just prior to embarking
for France. (Somme Museum, Newtownards)

for the time being, by a Divisional Order, two poor fellows from another Battalion of the
Royal Irish Rifles having lost their lives the previous Sunday.[3]

Friday 23 July 1915: Seaford

There were Divisional manoeuvres today. We left the Camp at 6.45am and did not return
until about 4pm. The day was fresh and breezy, with a little rain in the morning, but the
manoeuvres could not be followed by us. The Battalion marched slowly forward for a
while, first in columns, then in extended order and finally our whole Brigade entrenched
itself at the foot of a steep hill. These manoeuvres took place in the country to the north
west of Alfriston.

Sunday 25 July 1915: Alfriston

I was orderly today. In the evening we went for a walk through Alfriston and on to
Berwick Station. It was an interesting countryside. The big hillsides of wheat were ready
for harvest and on some the binder had already started work. I had my supper from a
single field of beans but I saw very few potatoes growing and any pigs that I observed
were black. The red, sleepy farmhouses, the country churches, the inns by the roadway,
made me think of the England portrayed by novelists and I realised how thoroughly true
they were to their country and how faithfully they had passed on this picture of it to me
in the glens of Ireland. *Adam Bede* was especially in my mind and, as I saw the families
moving through the fields to the Parish Church, I thought of Mr and Mrs Peyser on that
Sunday so tragically connected with Hetty's career.

---

3   The men who drowned on 18 July 1915, were from the Army Service Corps attached to the 36th
     Division. Driver Robert Wilson, No T3/030917 and Driver Thomas Pollock, No T3/030101, age 36,
     husband of Margaret Pollock of Dromore, County Down. Both men are buried in Seaford Cemetery.

A cartoon that well reflects James and the women he met before
and during the War. (Somme Museum, Newtownards)

Monday 26 to Saturday 31 July 1915: Seaford

I was shooting at the rifle range almost every single day. It lay at the mouth of the
Cuckmere River, along its left bank, on ideal ground. There were hills to the right and
left with the sea in front to receive our shots. We were fortunate in the weather and many
a lazy, voluptuous hour I passed in the grass there, with Sappho or Sherlock Holmes as
my companions. We could never fire more than ten rounds in a day, but I did the best
shooting of my life and particularly found my eyesight immensely stronger.

Sunday 1 August 1915: Seaford

I passed the time in a leisurely manner as I intended going in for sports at Hayward's
Heath the next day. I went down town for a stroll and made the acquaintance of a certain
interesting, little girl, whose weak spot was khaki.

Monday 2 August 1915: Haywards Heath

I had the best and the most enjoyable day since my arrival in England. I left Seaford
at 10.30am and reached Hayward's Heath at about 11.45am. From Lewes to our
destination, Sergeant E. Camlin and I had the agreeable company of two young ladies
to ourselves. Hayward's Heath we found to be a small, clean, well-build town such as
was typical of this part of the country.

Alfred Holland and I went out on a bit of exploration and, finding ourselves in
a recreation park, made bold to speak to several girls who seemed to be watching our
movements with interest. We were rather floored for a little by the cool reception we
experienced so that we took our leave of the group, bidding them good day and saluting.
Our party, sixteen in number, had tea afterwards and then Alfie and I ventured forth

The band on the march at Seaford, still having some difficulty
in keeping step. (Royal Ulster Rifles Museum)

together once more. Outside a door, down a street, we spied two of the girls again. We pointed to the recreation grounds and started to walk towards them. The girls pointed to their bare heads and hurried into their houses. At the park entrance we awaited them and soon they came along, both reading. We joined them and quickly made friends. Aflie's girl was in her teens, beautiful, soft and plump but my lady who was called Nellie Bowland was older, taller and slender; not so beautiful but still she was a good-looking, well-developed girl with fine teeth. We then had to take leave of them, for our sports commenced at 3pm.

The events were nearly all confined to the military and there were representatives from many Battalions. They were held in connection with the local Flower Show, in the same field, and our achievements were watched by many pretty eyes, gathered in from the country around. The crowd, the hobby-horses, the swing-boats, the brass band, the tea-tents, the rifle-shooting and the big marquees all helped to make an animated scene. Our friends had arrived and stayed loyal to us the whole day, walking about with us and waiting patiently while we took part in the different events. The YCV carried off twenty-two medals out of a total of twenty-eight. I gained second in the mile and was in the winning team race of three miles. My running was hampered by a stiff leg, the result of a quick spurt a few days before, but I was not moving with my usual freedom. I remember my leg paining me considerably on the three mile race, but I was enabled to finish by repeating over and over the lines from Kipling's 'Gunga Din'.[4]

> He would dot and carry one,
> Till the longest day was done

Our friends delighted us by going down to the station where they waited, cheering and waving good-bye, until we departed from sight. Truly a day when it was good to be alive: to be athletic and in khaki. Our day did not end there, for we met more girls in our carriage. We got out at Lewes and remained in the town until 10.35pm. We boarded the train again, where we met still more girls of a sort it is not delicate to describe, and so we came into Seaford, refusing the advances of the aforementioned wenches.

---

4   The poem 'Gunga Din', written by Rudyard Kipling, recounts the actions and heroism of an Indian water carrier with the British Army in India. Despite what many people assume, it is far from a racist poem.

No 1 Platoon at Seaford. James McRoberts can be seen seventh from the left in the third row. (Somme Museum, Newtownards)

Tuesday to Saturday 3 to 7 August 1915: Seaford

Bathing parades were frequent but the sea was often rough, making it difficult and dangerous to any but good swimmers. I practiced signalling and sat an examination for our scout badges, in which I did pretty well. I wrote to Nellie in Hayward's Heath and had a letter which showed my love was not too scholastic'. Her name was Miss Nellie Bowland and she soon afterwards moved to London where her address was 99 Churchill Road, South Croydon. I had a letter from her about six months later, in which she gave an alarming description of an air-raid by Zeppelins near her residence. I also received a long, interesting letter from Elsie Graham who stated she was sorry she could not send me one of her photos but they had all been given out and it was too bad, but wouldn't her visage be a poor mascot to have? A fine girl was Elsie and I still chose to think, quite interested in me.

On the 5th, Sir Edward Carson and his winsome lady visited our lines and were heartily cheered; the Attorney-General looked rather pale. With hindsight, perhaps he was just more aware of the enormity of what was happening than we were at the time. In 1917, he became First Lord of the Admiralty and a Member without Portfolio of the War Cabinet, 1917-1918. He achieved part of his aim with the establishment of Northern Ireland in 1921. The 4th of August was the anniversary of the declaration of War. That night a Zeppelin raid was simulated and all lights in the camp had to be screened. On 6 August 1915, General Sir Ian Hamilton landed in Suvla Bay and Anzac in an attempt to divide the Gallipoli Peninsula.

I saw my first mole one day when we were trench-digging and was amazed at the speed with which it tunnelled a path for itself. The lads also found a snake and brought it into the hut. It was about eighteen inches long and apparently harmless.

The entire Battalion on parade. (Royal Ulster Rifles Museum)

Sunday 8 August 1915: Eastbourne

I had a bathe in the morning and in the afternoon Andrew Neely and I set off to walk to Eastbourne.

(Andrew Neely, MM, came from Sion Mills, County Tyrone, and was wounded at the Battle of the Somme on 1 July 1916. He was transferred to the Machine Gun Corps when it was formed and saw service in Italy. He was billeted with the populace in the Alps and I recollect him describing their extreme poverty. The climate was extremely cold in the winter and country people lived and slept in a single room, above the cows in the byre, with the tiniest of stoves to do the cooking. He is married but is now retired and lives in Belfast.)

The day was very warm and the road was toilsome but we were in sight of the town after about ninety minutes hard walking. Very inviting it looked basking in the sunshine, clear and clean, with no mill chimneys or dockyards. There were lovely red villas amidst parks of trees and stretches of sweeping sand with a shimmering, silver sea. As a holiday site, I much preferred it to Brighton; its open, tree-shaded streets were far superior to the narrow roads of Brighton, although its sea and promenade were not so dazzling or fascinating as Marine Parade. We stayed from 4pm to 7pm walking around and taking in all we could.

Many disabled Tommies were about, as there was a camp outside the town, which must have contained at least two thousand wounded. Fine, handsome active lads they all looked, though some were limping and many were pale. We walked back, round by Beach Head and the rocks called the 'Seven Sisters', to our Camp, arriving just in time for Last Post at 10pm.

Monday to Sunday 9-15 August 1915: Seaford

The weather was improving and it became warmer and less stormy. Bathing parades and signalling chiefly occupied the day while at night I wrote letters to Meg, Elsie and to Hayward's Heath.

Monday to Saturday 15-20 August 1915: Seaford

The weather was now very warm, the sea was beautiful and our time was occupied in signalling, scout-games and bathing parades. Brian Boyd and I hired a boat for one shilling an hour and rowed out in it. I was a poor hand with the oars at that moment, but hoped to improve. We each had a dip from the boat, a new and heroic sensation for me.

Cartoon that reflects a certain viewpoint of Army training. (Somme Museum, Newtownards)

Every week we spent one or two nights out trench-digging. Generally the scouts did not work but threw down their blankets and got to sleep. We cooked our meals in our own billy-cans over little fires of old furze stalks and the Irish stew tasted delicious and wonderful was the flavour of the cocoa. On Friday night the field-kitchen first did service for us and well pleased we were with the food provided by them. This night work was a delicate and intricate bit of business that required special gifts of perception and organization.

Sunday 22 August 1915: Brighton
I went to Brighton and had a rather alarming experience. The day was brilliantly beautiful and Brighton poured forth her wealth and scum.

Another YCV and I made friends with two girls who said they were sisters. Mine seemed a fine, little madam of about eighteen summers. She started off a conversation to which I was an interested listener. She discussed the problem of the soldier in billets, telling me of naughty lads in khaki and girls who had been led wrong. She related to the story of her own engagement to a certain chap and how the rupture between them took place two years previously. Then she explained the full story of a local scandal, how a girl friends of hers, who committed herself, had performed an illegal operation on her body; how a rusty hairpin, which had been employed in the operation, led to blood poisoning and eventually death, and how she was suspected of being an accessory in the crime but how she cleared her character before the detective.

Details of different, suggestive post cards she explained with calm, impartial clearness. At first I was slightly flabbergasted by her conversation but, brought round by her fluency and coolness, I helped her on with her stories. My soldier friend and I took leave of our charges about 10pm and returned by a quiet road to the north of the railway station. There was an underworld in Brighton which was appalling and disgusting. About midnight we arrived at the Camp.

No 2 Platoon at Seaford in England. (Somme Museum, Newtownards)

Monday to Saturday 23-28 August 1915: Seaford

We had a week of lovely weather. A cross-country race of four miles was to be run on Saturday and teams of twenty were to start, the result of the race being judged from the tenth man of each team. I was picked for the YCV team and the whole side was excused all parades, except the musquetry, for the week. I was at the range on two occasions and passed my tests, although not particularly distinguishing myself. In the matter of training, I went out only on two runs, both of about three miles. The remainder of the time, I along with another team man, Alan Montgomery, spent down at the sea front, revelling in the sunshine. We took a great interest in the mixed bathing, the forms of the different girls evoking various comments. Both of us, when we resorted to the water ourselves, tried to improve our diving accomplishments, rather than swimming and possibly injuring our legs. Alan Montgomery was a Ballymena man and my rival, and sometimes superior in the mile race. He was killed at the Battle of Messines in June 1917.[5]

Saturday 28 August 1915: Seaford

I felt in good form for the raced which started at 4pm from the barn on the top of the hill, north-east of Seaford. Twenty-two teams had entered and we started first, the others began, one after the other, at intervals of three minutes. The day was very sultry, while the course had not a yard of level ground but led us over hills, through hedges and across ploughed fields, being fully five miles in length. I stuck the first three miles fairly easily but the wind was collecting in my tummy and beginning to cause me considerable agony. I was with the first eleven, right to the foot of the last hill, but had then to stop

---

5   Lance Corporal Allan Montgomery, No 15634, killed on 16 August 1917, age 24 years. The son of
     Robert and Annie E. Montgomery of Castle Street, Ballymena, County Antrim, he has no known grave
     and is commemorated on the Tyne Cot Memorial.

running and walked in, arriving about twelfth. I felt vexed with myself for not being in the first ten, but I felt sure that our team would get a place, although I would have no share in the medals. It eventually proved that our tenth man had come in best of all the teams, his time being thirty-one minutes, forty-five seconds, beating the 8th Royal Irish Rifles by forty-nine seconds. At first there was an understanding that this Battalion had beaten us, and the virulent ridicule the 'Young Canadians' had to listen to for a time, was amusing rather than otherwise. When we reached our Camp we were loudly cheered and all had our tea in the Sergeants' Mess. Afterwards I went down to the promenade.

Sunday 29 August 1915: Seaford
I felt nothing the worse for my exertions of the previous day and had a swim before breakfast and another after dinner.

Monday to Thursday 30 August to 2 September 1915: Seaford
The weather was getting colder. I had a satisfactory day when we scouts attacked two snipers hidden in Peacock Barn, a place beyond the pumping station at Norton. One sniper was concealed in a hay stack, with the outhouses as a retreat; the other had placed himself behind some piled wood, in front of the barn, and stood in the shade, unobserved by the attacking party until they closed in on his position. I spent the evenings writing, playing chess and reading magazines. *Nash's, My Magazine, Billet Notes* and *Athletic*, appealed to me. I gathered up several soldiers' badges down town and posted them to Elsie Graham, at the same time enclosing a letter asking for an appointment should I get leave home. In the evenings I went out rowing and bathing. I never had such easy soldiering or spent such an enjoyable summer. At that time we expected to move to Aldershot, to visit Ireland, and to go to France within the next eight weeks. Would it be true? Wait and see was the only answer I could find. This life was certainly diverting and healthy, but oh to be back at my old work.

Friday 3 September 1915: Seaford
The Battalion, after cleaning up the huts and grounds, paraded in marching order with their kits and went by train, in the night, to Bramshott Camp, Hants. 'B' and 'D' Companies departed about 9.30am, and 'A' and 'C' left at 12.30pm. After our last dinner in Seaford we had our final bathing parade and I enjoyed it.

Saturday 4 September 1915: Bramshott
I fell asleep in the train and did not awake until we stopped at Liphook Station at about 4.30 in the morning, just when it was getting clear. We marched through the small town of Liphook and about two miles, along towards London, until we reached Bramshott Camp. The huts were old and in a very filthy condition. The Battalion before us, the West Riding Regiment, had left at two hours' notice for France and all the old, superfluous clothing and their books and magazines were lying around while even their letters were scattered about and accumulating dust. The grease was still on their plates from their last dinner.

Sunday 5 September 1915: Haslemere
The weather was very beautiful and the air cool and refreshing, amid this fine land of heaths and pine woods. I did not go on Church Parade but went out for a walk. I travelled along the railway in the direction of London, going through a lovely, wooded valley; there were lots of sturdy cottages and orchards of ripening apples but hazel nuts and blackberries were however our lot. I passed through Haslemere, a pretty village with a railway station and quite a number of shops with a variety of female figures on display. In the evening each man was allocated a Lee Enfield rifle.

Monday and Tuesday 6-7 September 1915: Longmoor
We were up early, at about 4 o'clock, and left for Longmoor Range, about five miles distant, where we remained all day and made preparations for another overnight's stay.

The beautiful, sunny weather continued. There were four ranges here; several of them had been built by German prisoners. Firing was going on, simultaneously on all these and during the day the noise never ceased. The country around was very beautiful, wild and grand. It was a sandy soil, covered with heather and huge woods of pine.

A big cavalry camp was quite close, occupied by Hussars and the Staffordshire Horse, while a Camp of Canadian Engineers was not far away. At night, Alec Jardine and I visited the cavalry camp. We noticed the big, clean stables and particularly we remarked on the comfortable, home-like huts in which the men lived. Veritable cottages they were, with porches and built-in fireplaces and having gardens of roses and flowers around them.

Sleeping on the heath was comfortable but awakening in the early morning was very chilly and a dense mist hid everything from view. After a breakfast of loaf, tea and salmon, we took up our positions at the range, waiting until the mist should rise. That day we finished our Recruits' Course and in the evening marched back to our huts.

Wednesday 8 September 1915: Bloodshott
In the morning we proceeded over to Bloodshott Heath and examined the trenches there: they were quite huge, complicated and elaborate affairs. In the evening we marched back to Longmoor. That night we visited the Camp again and listened to a concert entertainment in the YMCA marquee there, several of our fellows contributed to the amusement and were well received. The English troopers were very friendly and gave us all an encouraging welcome.

Thursday to Sunday 9-12 September 1915: Longmoor
The rest of the week we remained at Longmoor and finished our Trained Soldiers' Course on Sunday morning. The weather kept brilliantly warm. We arose about 4.30am each morning and had our breakfast. Then we marched to the range and came back for dinner at about 2.30pm. A rifle inspection followed and then we had tea. Next we went to the YMCA marquee and returned to spread our blankets and so to dream. On Saturday our football team played a match with the Canadian Royal Engineers, and beat them 5-0.

One evening a rumour reached us from the huts that no leave was going to be granted before going to the Front, and that several of the Battalions had – to use the only possible word – mutinied. That night we were paraded and addressed by Major B--, at that moment in a lamentable, intoxicated state. Was it so bad at the Front? If we did not

The 'Merry Mauves Melodies' who put on such a great show at Dranoutre. Sergeant Tom A. Burrows, Corporal A. Sharp, Lance Corporals P.A. Branson and J. Tully, Privates J. Finlay, J. Turkington, W. Pierpoint, D. Wainwright, W. Pendlebury and F. Blair. Centre photograph is Sergeant Robert Chamberlain, (Nigel Henderson)

get leave he said, we were not to mutiny, no matter what other Battalions might do and what they might say about us. We had joined the Army for King and Country and had undertaken to obey its rules and commands. This was the first war most of us had been in and probably it would be the last, thus it behoved us to abide by the rules like men. So let us play the game and to hell with the Pope! The proceedings were a scandal and a shame to the British Army, but the reckless, dare-all manner of the Major had a great influence with the troops.[6]

In the shooting I did fairly well, qualifying for a Second Class Shot, my score being seventy-eight out of a possible one hundred and eighty. Coming back to the huts at Bramshott on Sunday I learned that four days' leave was being given to the whole Division and that 'A' and 'B' Companies of the 14th would go on Tuesday.

Tuesday and Wednesday 14-15 September 1915: Bramshott to Home
'A' and 'B' Companies left Bramshott, marching to Liphook Station, where we boarded our train at about 5 o'clock. I had forwarded a postcard home telling them about my coming. The train carried us through Guilford, Reading and Birmingham. Here I fell asleep and on waking I was still travelling, through the North of Wales. I put my head out of the carriage window, the smell of salt water was in my nostrils and I could see we were passing Llandudno, the Naples of the North. Past Conway Castle we continued and over the shining thread of water called the Menai Strait. We proceeded then through the small fields of Anglesey and arrived in Holyhead at about 3.30am. The Transportation Officer was standing silently at the side of our ship, an old cattle boat named the *Slieve Gullion*. We huddled together on deck and watched the cool dawning of the new day. *Slieve Gullion* is a mountain in the south of the country I was to come to know well. It

---

6   Possibly Major Bruce?

Football Team, with two members wearing YCV uniform
in the background. (Nigel Henderson)

was about 7am Irish Time, when we drew in at the North Wall, Dublin. Soon we were on our second train journey, away north to our happy fields in Ulster. At 11.30am we were streaming into Great Victoria Station and speeding away, each in his own direction. I tramped through the town, got into the Northern Counties Committee Railway at 1.55pm and about 3 o'clock I was in Larne. Another train journey in the little narrow gauge and I was at Kilwaughter Halt. A walk of a mile and I was home and on entering the house, found my father and mother at home.

No change could be observed in their boy, although dusty and drowsy he must have looked after his journey. That evening I spent in the house where I discovered that my people were taking it much to heart because I would probably be going to the Front and seemed almost inclined to be angry with me for showing no great unwillingness to go there. I was told that if the past year could be lived over again, I would never have got their consent to enlist as a Private soldier. They proved prescient of the horrors to come but, in fact, fatalities were greater among the officers than the men. As a matter of fact I would not have had the slightest objection to a commission but, considering how young I was and long the War seemed likely to last, there was no need to hurry. At present I was bent on having a glimpse of the Front just as I was.

Thursday 16 September 1915: Larne
I went to Larne after dinner and had a bathe. The day was fairly warm – very warm it was called here – but the water felt chilly to my limbs, to say the least of it. I stayed late in the town and spent a few hours with Nellie Buchanan out on the Bank Heads where we behaved as cousins properly ought to behave.

Friday and Saturday 17-18 September 1915: 'Home' to Bramshott

I left home after dinner: my mother restrained herself very well. To my eternal discredit or mere naivety let judge who will, but I state the truth when I say that no feelings of the slightest emotion stirred in me, leaving my home and people to go to the line of battle. My father took me down, in the trap to Larne, to meet the train at the broad gauge station. We talked principally of local changes and happenings and his only advice was to mind my health, to which all other things come secondary. The train for Dublin left Belfast at 7 o'clock. Very few people were allowed into the station and there was little demonstration there but as we left our city, thundering cheers followed our way through the suburbs. Bye-bye girls! We travelled quickly to Dublin and were soon aboard our boat. But the journey was slow and it was nearly 6 o'clock in the morning when we touched Holyhead. The train onwards was very slow. As if to try our patience to the very limit, we were eventually stranded at Bordon and had no choice but tramp the remaining eight miles to our Camp. At about 8 o'clock in the evening, we at last were permitted, by the grace of heaven, to lay ourselves down in our own huts. Considering the shortness of the leave, and the inconvenience of the long journey by sea and rail, everyone declared that it was not worth it.

Sunday to Saturday 19-25 September 1915: Bramshott

At the beginning of the week, while 'C' and 'D' Companies were still on leave, there was a tremendous lot of fatigue work left for the others. I was twice marking at Longmoor range, and I fired Part IV of the Musquetry.

Several evenings I went to Grayshott and Haslemere to spy out the richness of the country. Girls invariably responded to our wish to accompany them for a walk and talked in a friendly and interesting manner, but they were very much on their guard against any intimacies. "Will you come for a walk with me through the wood?" "Yes I will if you keep on walking." And with that we had to be satisfied. We were served with the first of our Special requisites for Foreign Service: we received each his pair of trench-boots, fine sturdy and warm they were. The Webb equipment of the latest pattern replaced our old Ulster Volunteer Force fittings; it was no more handy or comfortable, but it was stouter and more suitable to withstand the wet and mud. Big supplies of new underclothing were given out with no stingy hand and each man received his first-aid packet which was fixed in a pocket in the inside of his tunic. Also each man had a few square inches of cloth of a distinctive shape and colour, sewn on to the shoulders of his tunic. In our Battalion it was triangular-shaped and the colour was light blue. As well, each man obtained his 'identification disc'. This was composed of a stiff red, fibrous material about the size of a penny and was worn suspended from the neck by a string. It was stamped with the owner's name, his rank, his regimental number, his religion and the unit to which he belonged. I also received Army Book 64, the soldier's active service record where I signed my last Will and Testament. Another thing we then were issued with was a woollen comforter shaped like a long jelly-bag. It could be used as a scarf round the neck or a covering for the head. Later on I found it quite the thing for patrol work at night.

Sergeant Waring with his pet jackdaw. Pets seem to have been an important inclusion within the Battalion. (Nigel Henderson)

Sunday 26 September 1915: London

I went to London, on pass, arriving about 10 o'clock in the morning. I walked about with some other fellows and saw most of the places the visitor ought to see, but my own expectations were hardly realised. All the sights fancied from afar seemed familiar to me they so resembled (naturally enough) the pictures I had so often seen of them and, if anything, they lost in comparison with their photos. In the evening, however, we were in Hyde Park and the huge ground was thronging with people and soldiers from every part of the world and every corner of the Empire. Many Belgians were abroad and French was heard as often as English. The cosmopolitan crowd and the congestion of vehicular traffic were the most impressive sights about London. Horse-drawn traffic was still predominant and I was fascinated by the agility of the crossing-sweeper youths, who were employed at road junctions, in running to pick up the horse droppings with a scoop and brush and then deposit them in a metal box on the footpath. The houses, monuments and great buildings however, all wore depressing, sombre greyness that covered everything and worried anyone who had formed glowing pictures of tinted palaces, flashing in a dazzling sun.

I was, however, on the lookout for something with a touch of romance about it. While gazing into a shop window, where books of a spicy flavour were displayed, I found a little lady by my side who appeared to be untroubled by any companion. I asked some questions about Waterloo Station, which I could have answered myself, but no matter. She answered plainly and quietly, that I went straight to the point; would she keep me

Lieutenant R.V. Gracey from Helen's Bay, County Down. (Nigel Henderson)

company until train time? She came away on my arm, and soon we had gone round several streets, over Blackfriars Bridge, and then stopped under a pillar on the Thames Embankment. She was small, but with an alarmingly, neat and generous, little figure. She had a fine-featured face with ringlets and a mischievous smile with good teeth. She talked frankly about the books in the shop where we had met and discussed the ones she had read. She was very companionable and for my edification instructed me in the intricacies of her underwear. A poet with the pen of Burns would be required to do justice to the beauty of the figure she showed me. She said her father was a Frenchman and suggested that this might account for her being a little bit different from the other girls one met.

She accompanied me to the station and we exchanged addresses. The train left Waterloo at 10.40pm and I reached Bramshott in the early hours of Monday morning. For some reason I have no record of the ensuing week, although I remember the following events:

Thursday 30 September 1915: Bramshott
It was a dry cold day and the whole Division, including our Artillery, was reviewed by His Majesty King George the Fifth, accompanied by Lord Kitchener, Major General Sir Oliver Nugent the new Commander of the Division and by Sir George Richardson. We marched past in double companies, with greatly reduced intervals, and it was stated that His Majesty had said this was the quickest inspection he had made since the War started.

Friday 1 October 1915: Bramshott
This was my twentieth birthday. About this time the whole Battalion was photographed, and pictures were also taken of each platoon, the officers, the sergeants, the bands, the

signallers, the machine-gun section, the transport, etc. The whole was subsequently printed in a book and, if we paid for it, a copy was sent to our homes.

Sunday 3 October 1915: Liphook

In the forenoon every man was paraded in full marching order and each received one hundred and twenty rounds of live ammunition. We left late in the evening by three separate trains and, at the station at Liphook, were served out with tea and refreshments by the ladies of the town.

Monday 4 October 1915: Southampton

We arrived in the first hours of the morning in Southampton, at the military station where I and several others were detailed off to help unload the train and fill up the transport. All that day we remained, confined to the station, getting very little to amuse us and still less to eat. The great vessel, the *Aquitania*, was lying at the quay, fitted out as a Red Cross ship.[7] We helped to load our transport and tied up our mules and horses. There was one military toil on which I never happened to be engaged – sanitary fatigue. Wherever we were camped, a frequent sight was that of two soldiers walking all over the ground, carrying a bag between them. The men had sticks with a nail at the end of them and were engaged on picking up pieces of paper, empty cigarette packets etc. When their job was completed they carried their load to the incinerator, a simple cylindrical structure which was made of brick, if procurable. At about 4 o'clock the transport ships, carrying the Battalion, left and about twenty minutes afterwards our own ship sailed, bearing all the horses and mules of the Brigade. We had quite a pleasant time, for the weather was mild, but the journey was slow in the extreme. We continually exchanged signals with warships and in addition we had, as escort, a destroyer on each side.[8]

---

7   The *Aquitania* served as a troopship in both the Great War and the Second World War, before an honourable retirement in 1950.
8   The Battalion sailed on the *Empire Queen*, an ex-Isle of Man paddle steamer.

France and Belgium, the trenches

Tuesday 5 October 1915: Le Havre

The morning broke fine and clear as we crowded on the deck to have a look at the new land. We were at the mouth of the Seine, floating and waiting on the tide to allow us to go further. Many more ships, both Red Cross and neutral were standing close by: our escort had disappeared. Soon we were moving on and at about midday we came to a halt in one of the innumerable quays of Le Havre. Signs of the war met the eye on every hand. Trainloads of English wounded were continually arriving. Some bore injured men who were quite helpless and these were carried on the platform on stretchers, others had only minor wounds and travelled like ordinary passengers. The wounded were arriving from the battle of Loos which was fought against the advice of Sir Douglas Haig. The British troops failed to exploit an opening success and their losses exceeded those of the defence. Disappointed and dissatisfied, the British government replaced Sir John French by Haig. We helped to unload our horses and wagons and cleaned up the stables. Meanwhile the Battalion, which had disembarked about the same time, left the dock to proceed to a rest camp, about three miles away. On this journey I saw numbers of middle-aged women with orange-coloured hands and some even had yellow faces. I was told they were munitions workers and that the colour was caused by the poisonous explosive they handled and from which they occasionally died.[1] In the evening we followed the Battalion, and after a weary march reached the so-called rest camp, a canvas abode situated in a veritable quagmire. We had seen no French soldiers except sentries in an assortment of uniforms and all along the route there were notices written in English posted up: 'Keep to the Right'. We were packed, about a dozen in each bell-tent where we had a meal of tea and iron rations. There were many other Battalions around us. We got to bed as early as possible and made ourselves as comfortable as we could.

Wednesday 6 October 1915: Le Havre to Poulainville

At daybreak we had tea with more iron rations, formed up and marched away. We proceeded through a part of Le Havre to a railway station. We placed the wagons and horses on a train and about 10 o'clock we got on the train ourselves, thirty-five men to a bullock-wagon. All the wagons were actually painted with the words: Hommes 40: Chevaux 8.[2] The train stopped about ten minutes in the country to allow us to relieve ourselves. I was told afterwards that French soldiers travelling in a train urinated when it was halted at a station, in the sight of females who vocally expressed their admiration of this exhibition at level crossings. There were hordes of French children to whom we pitched hard tack and tins of bully beef. There was a mad scramble to get these presents and I was relieved that no child was hit by the flying gifts – at least in my presence. The

---

1   The yellowing of their skin was attributed to picric acid, a constituent of the explosive.
2   'Forty men or eight horses', a phrase that would become all too familiar to those men taken prisoner in Europe during the Second World War.

Café society, typical of how many men spent their off duty time
when out of the lines. (Somme Museum, Newtownards)

train set off and travelled slowly all day, through Rouen, and on and on, until it got dark. It was more comfortable than we expected, although we had no cushioned seats to rest on, but the slow motion was not fatiguing in the least, and did not make one weary the same way as an ordinary rapid train.

Le Havre had a good appearance from the sea but on entrance gave the impression of being a dirty, manufacturing town. The docks were very extensive and were piled up with mountains of barbed wire and ammunition. French sentries in their blue and red uniforms were everywhere and English soldiers were very common. The railway we travelled on was double and the trains seemed to carry nothing but material connected with the war. There were sentries at every bridge all along the line. Except for the imposing town of Rouen, we passed through nothing larger than a village. Normandy was a quiet, beautiful countryside. At about ten o'clock we arrived in Amiens; the town to our surprise was very well lighted. We unloaded our transport and set out on a long, weary march. We trudged with our heavy packs right through the town and then along a great road that ran directly north, as I could tell by the shining Pole star. Expressed in the cry "Will they never stop?" It was a dreadful effort and several dropped out, but at last we halted and I was called forth as an interpreter to help to open our billets. They seemed to think my French better than those of higher rank. I approached the first house which was scheduled to hold ten. I knocked at the door, a window opened and I shouted, *"Ouvrez, au militaire."* We were shown a cart-house and helped to push out the cart, then two women brought us straw and left us a loaf, and a lighted lamp.

Captain Samuel Willis in Army uniform. He served in D Company and did not collect cigarette cards! He was killed on 1 July 1916. (Mark Ramsey)

Thursday 7 October 1915: Poulainville

We rose at about 7.30 in the morning and opened the door to have a look at our surroundings. There was a café on the opposite side, 'Au Rendezvous des Chasseurs' and I went inside and had '*Un verre de café*', for which I paid '*trois sous*'. I discovered that we were stationed at the entrance to the village of Poulainville, in which the whole Battalion was billeted. I made the acquaintance of several of the inhabitants and found I could carry on a conversation quite easily.

As we were almost the first British troops stationed in this locality, I said to the French, 'Do you not find it very odd having Englishmen around you to whom you cannot speak one word.' 'Not in the least,' was the reply 'The Frenchmen we had here last came from the South of the Country and we could not understand a word they said'. Indeed in this part of Somme there was a lot of patois Picard spoken which was difficult enough to understand by those who knew French. Cider was the universal, cold beverage and I looked at children drinking it in amazement, some before they had learned to walk. I was much surprised to learn that the Chasseurs hunted the wild boar and that the sport occurred frequently in the neighbouring woods.

I learned that this country had surrendered to the Germans on their victorious advance on Paris and that the Boche had marched down this road on their way to Amiens. The owner of the estaminet was called M. Sire, a farmer and potato merchant. He had a son Joseph, a lad of twelve, who quickly made friends with me. At first M. Sire continually besieged us for souvenirs. His sister, Madame Carpentier, owned the café on the opposite side of the road and had a lovely, little daughter, Madeline, also aged twelve. M. Carpentier was serving in a French Cyclist Corps at the Front. There was also a Madame Sire, a friendly lady and a Mlle. Sire, of over twenty, who assisted her sister in the café business. They were all extremely kind to us and seemed only too delighted to have us with them.

The long, straight road past our door ran from Amiens to Arras and an immense amount of motor traffic used it to and from the battlefield. Much of it was English for

Second Lieutenant Brian Boyd MM, killed in action on
7 June 1917, at Messines. (Alan Curragh)

Arras was a centre of British activity. It was almost impossible to get cigarettes in a shop. The French made their own from a pouch full of tobacco and a book of wrapping paper. At Poulainville we got our first issue of free tobacco and continued to receive it as long as were in France and Belgium. The amount of the ration for each man was based on the requirements of the Regular Army so that in our Battalion we always received too much pipe tobacco and too few cigarettes. These were never the popular brands such as Player's Navy Cut or even Wild Woodbine, but consisted of an inferior quality of tobacco and were called All Flags, Ruby Queens, Ore, Scissors, Trumpeter, Red Huzzar etc. The number we received was about thirty a week. But there was generally in our Battalion a surplus of pipe tobacco which we traded with the French. An exception to this was an occasional issue of BDV tobacco, which I started to smoke because it was plentiful and I found it good.[3] Many a time it served me instead of a meal, so that I always carried a tin of it with me. I continued to use pipe tobacco for the remainder of the time I was in the Army and for several years afterwards. I learned to smoke in 1913 and continued for over forty years. But when I retired, over two years ago, I gave up the habit chiefly because my sons do not smoke.

From Poulainville we sent to all our friends, silk-faced postcards which none of us had seen before. They were embroidered with the brightly coloured flags of the Allies and were embellished with tender inscriptions in French. As a billeting allowance the French peasant received so much per day for every officer and man. The payments must have been generous and promptly made for I hardly ever heard a complaint about them.

Friday 8 October 1915: Bertangles
We had a small route march through the country to the neighbouring village of Bertangles where the 9th Inniskillings were stationed. The land looked quiet and beautiful, rich and full of small villages surrounded by apple gardens. Between one village and the next, perhaps three miles away, there were no hedges. It was a patchwork of fields and woods, the woods occupying the higher ground where the top soil was too thin to plough. The crops consisted chiefly of wheat interspersed with betteraves, mangelwurzel, oats and lucerne,[4] but there were no fields of grass.

---

3   BDV tobacco was imported into Britain in the early 1900s by Geoffrey Phillips Ltd, the letters supposedly standing for Boyd & Dibrell of Virginia. However according to a spokesman from Phillips they were an abbreviation in Latin, *Benedictus dominus vobiscum*, the 'pipe of peace'.
4   Betteraves – beetroot, Manglewurzel – beet, Lucerne – alfalfa

The cattle were kept indoors the greater part of the year and if they were let out, they were attached with halters and fastened to pegs driven into the ground. There were rarely hedges alongside the road but very often a row of apple trees. The farmer when ploughing turned his horses on the highway. From a distance all looked very picturesque. There was a mass of green orchards and peeping through, the while walls of the houses. Above rose the long line of red roofs with the invariable church spire in the middle, but inside the village it was often mean and dirty. Along the roads were innumerable crucifixes and each village had its church spire. The work in the fields was done principally by the women; they were seen everywhere doing all the manual labour, which usually, in our country, falls to men. The few men we saw were elderly and nearly all in charge of horses, they were mostly dressed in some kind of light blue material. Presumably the able-bodied men were at the Front.

Saturday 9 October 1915: Bertangles
After dinner the Brigade assembled in a field adjoining Bertangles and was inspected by a General Monroe, I was told. He was accompanied by numerous red-caps (staff officers).[5]

Sunday 10 October 1915: Poulainville
There was a church parade in the morning, the Service being conducted in the open air. In the evening, M. Sire or 'M. le patron' as he was designated, told me about how the inhabitants of the village left on the approach of the Germans, how he had been relieved of a bicycle, a pair of spy-glasses and shirts, also how they had stabled their horses in the billet we now occupied and he showed us the large holes that these animals had kicked in the plaster walls.

Monday to Saturday: 11-16 October 1915: Poulainville
This was a week of fairly stiff work, consisting of field days and route marches. My pleasant relations with the Sires continued. One afternoon an accident, which might have been much more serious, happened to Madeleine. She was knocked over by a motor and carried into the house in an unconscious condition.

Our Doctor Gavin was sent for and arrived immediately but said that there were no bones broken and she had only a slight bruise on the elbow. The following morning I saw her lying in bed, flushed and smiling, beautiful and looking like an angel. In a few days she got up but her face was pale and her appearance as if she had only recovered from a severe and prolonged illness. Dr M.J.H. Gavin, Royal Army Medical Corps was a New Zealander and a most popular officer. He gained the Military Cross with Bar and distinguished himself particularly at Ypres in 1917, but was killed a few months later by a fall from his horse.[6]

On a visit which my wife and I made to France in 1928, we called at the café Au Rendezvous des Chasseurs. We were hospitably received, Mlle. Sire remembered me

---

5   General Sir Charles Carmichael Monroe, GOC of the Third Army. He was the son of a Scottish father and Irish mother and is remembered as an outstanding regimental officer. He was superb as C-in-C India, his thorough reorganisation of the Indian Army made possible the 'Indianisation' of the Palestine and Mesopotamia campaigns.

6   Captain N.J.H. Gavin, MC & Bar, Royal Army Medical Corps, died on 2 November 1917 and buried in Rocquigny-Equancourt Road British Cemetery, Manancourt.

quite distinctly and the accident to Madeline was recalled, but Madeleine whom I saw and who was now married, had quite forgotten me. We did not go to Belgium on that visit; in fact I have never been there since 1916.

Sunday 17 October 1915: Poulainville

There was a service in the morning in the open air. Afterwards we paraded and each received a new smoke helmet which was worn in a little, waterproof satchel, slung from the shoulder. We then had a lecture from an officer on their use and each man in the Battalion put on his new one and marched through a trench, in which asphyxiating gas was being evolved from a cylinder. This was to test the helmets and make sure that each man could put his on properly while it acquainted him with the smell of the gas. This gas helmet consisted of chemically treated flannel which covered the whole head and was tucked in at the collar of the tunic; it had an eye piece of celluloid. It was replaced by the more modern, but more bulky, box respirator.

Monday to Wednesday 18-20 October 1915: Amiens

We had a route march, in full marching order, to Amiens where we piled rifles in the square, in front of the Cathedral and entered the building in single file. It had a noble, magnificent and rich appearance which made everyone talk of it with wonder and delight. On the outside the doors and several of the windows were protected by sandbag structures which were piled up to an amazing height. Afterwards we formed up, marched out of the town and made our dinners by the roadside, then continued on to the billets. The dinner turned out to be very good, it was made of meat and potatoes to which we added turnips and carrots gathered in the adjoining fields. We expected to see some fine specimens of French maidenhood in Amiens but had to return much disappointed. We found many fellows who readily gave us full instruction as to the location of and rates charged by 'their sisters' for sexual entertainment. "She is *tres bonne ici et ici*" (very good here and here) said one, pointing to his breasts and crotch. I think I saw sheep only once in France at Poulainville. Then a small flock followed an old man, who kept tooting a horn. He was not accompanied by a dog.

Thursday and Friday 21-22 October 1915: Beauval

Acting on instructions received the previous night we packed up about 8 o'clock and the Battalion marched away from Poulainville. I was left behind in a rear party to clean up and at 12 o'clock this number, about fifty men with a baggage cart, all under our Quartermaster Lieutenant J. Long, departed from Poulainville. In most villages, at the crossroads under a grove of trees, there was a dew-pond from which the livestock of the community drank. It was a receptacle of the foulest water and the stench from it was nauseating, especially when a team of horses waded into it to slacken their thirst. A common sight was to see Mademoiselle walk sedately towards it, accompanied by six or seven cows each attached to her by a rope. These animals had never been without a halter and were subdued to an extent unknown to Irish cattle.

Before we left Poulainville, I was shown by the Sires', an account of the local newspaper of our visit to the Cathedral at Amiens. For an entirely different impression of the town of Beauval, see my description of our arrival there on the 2 January 1916. We marched slowly and before dark reached the town of Beauval which was long and

Corporal William Frederick Forbes, who served as a Scout in the
Permanent patrol. He was killed on 1 November 1916. His brother Alec
served in the Divisional Transport and survived the War.

dirty with about three thousand inhabitants. The whole Brigade was stationed around.
Forty of us found ourselves in a barn, among a lot of un-thrashed wheat. There was an
English aerodrome outside the town and aeroplanes were often seen. On Friday we were
on fatigues and in the evening I climbed to the top of the church spire from which I had
a good view of the country around. I also inscribed my name on the lead roof.[7]

Saturday 23 October and Sunday 24 October 1915: Beauval
We had drill and a scheme in the fields adjoining the village. On Sunday 24 October
there was a Church parade.

Sunday 24 October 1915 – Beauval
There was a church parade.

Monday 25 October 1915: Beauval
After dinner we were mustered and marched from the town, along the road to Amiens.
The King was paying a visit to the troops in France and was passing that way, so we
were turned out to do him honour. We stood two deep along one side of the road and
waited there in the mist and damp. During the long wait here we pelted each other
with frozen apples and Norman Paisley was heard to mutter, 'Now I realise why we are
called the standing army!' Paisley was taken prisoner on the 1 July 1916 but he appeared
to have had a fairly agreeable time working with a German farmer. (After the war he
was employed as an officer in HM Prison, Belfast). After two and a half hours, the
first car with King George V and General Joffre passed, and then came Poincaré and
other cars followed. Poincaré was the President of the French Republic from 1913 to
1920. Our band played the royal salute and we, standing more or less in line, presented
arms, afterwards hurrying back to our billets. (General J.J.C. Joffre was in command

---

7   Battalion War Diary: "Left Poulainville for point NW of Lavicogne, where 107th and 109th Brigades
    formed up for attack on above position, advanced in artillery formation for some distance and then
    extended. Stand-fast sounded. Battalion formed up, had dinners and marched to billets in Beauvals
    where men were billeted down after much confusion, owing to proper arrangements not having been
    made for billeting."

Dranoutre, 'Isn't Larne'. James made his point by writing
on the photograph! (McRoberts family)

of the French Forces from the beginning of the war until December 1916, when he was
succeeded by General Nivelle. RNL)[8]

Tuesday 26 October 1915: Couin

We left Beauval about 8 o'clock in full marching order. We went along a series of inferior
roads and after a quick advance reached the village of Couin. There we entered a large
park with a canvas camp hidden under the trees, where we quartered ourselves. It was
very clean, pleasantly situated and with the best of tents. In the evening I went down
through the village but found it exceedingly uninteresting. It formed a rest camp for
English troops.

Wednesday 27 October 1915: Gommecourt Wood

We left on our march to the trenches at about 3pm and advanced along the road in
shallow columns of platoons at one hundred and fifty yards interval. We formed up
together in a field and had tea, then went on our way again, in the same formation.
The night was dry and mild with a waning, ruddy moon on our left. We saw we were
approaching houses and passed by numerous dugouts. Then we entered a tumble-down
village called Fonquervillers, passed round the barricades in the street and next marched
up the long communication trench that led to the front.

In our advance along the communication trench there was a succession of warning
called out by each man as he encountered an obstacle, 'Loose duckboard', 'hole on the
right', 'wire overhead', or there might be a general injunction 'Halt in front, the rear has
lost connection'. Anyhow, progress was always slow, or very slow. My first sensations

---

8   Battalion War Diary: "Received orders to march into trenches for instructional purposes under the
    143rd Infantry Brigade."

were those of wonderment – why were we not fired at, considering the noise we made? And then I saw with a different wonder the tidy, clean, dry conditions of the trenches. The sides were lined with plaited canes which were held firmly in position by strands of wire. The pathway was made of wood and raised several inches from the ground to allow draining. I saw the reeking mouth of numerous large dugouts, always covered by a blanket and heard sounds of revelry. At last we were led to a dugout which was to be my abode for a few days. It was fairly large and capable of holding twenty-four men. The roof was of fir-logs and bunks had been made along the walls from netting wire. A wood fire was burning in an old can, the smoke curling out at any chance opening.

Stationed in the dugout were about six of the existing Battalion, the 5th Warwickshire Territorials, who turned out to be very agreeable, intelligent, young fellows who seemed to know their business well. With further acquaintance our respect increased. This Battalion had been on active service for eight months. At first they had stayed at Messines, in Belgium, where the Battalion had sustained three hundred casualties, there they had only one line of trenches and no dugouts properly so called. They had taken over the present trenches from the French, about four months previously and since then they had suffered only occasional casualties, wounded or killed.

Thursday 28 October 1915: Gommecourt Wood
I got into the working of the trenches. My experience of stand-to or the dawn mists the first morning in the trenches was somewhat of a shock. Very early, before daybreak, I had to tumble out of my bed just after I had apparently settled in. The fact that I was tired after yesterday's march did not matter in the least; this was a solemn rite in which everyone had to willingly participate. It was a wet day and they were very muddy in some parts. There were ration parties, water parties and dinner parties. The Company cook house was in a ruined dwelling down in the village which called Fonquevillers where our reserves were also stationed as well as those belonging to the Warwicks.

Why the village was allowed by the Germans to exist and give shelter to our troops was a question discussed among us. It was often fired into by snipers and occasionally a shell would find its way there, but few casualties ever occurred. The Warwicks had a very neat cook house, on the right flank of our firing line, in a bomb proof dugout, with a wide passage sloping out to the daylight. The rations came at night, right up to this entrance. Our own transport brought the stores to about one kilometre from the village, to which they were then conveyed by a fatigue party, who took the place of the mules and pulled the limbers to the Quartermaster's stores, which were situated amid the reserves in the village.

Guards were mounted along the fire trenches and these were doubled at night, two hours on and four hours off was the rule. In the day time the sentry had a periscope and at night he stood with his head above the parapet. At first we were nervous about looking over it but when we saw the Warwicks gazing around them with indifference we began to do the same.

The Germans were entrenched in Gommecourt Wood about three or four hundred yards away, but little sign of their earthworks was visible. Their front was strongly protected by barbed wire entanglements, fixed to the fir-trees. These defences were practically impregnable, so we were coming round on their left and had enfiladed their first and second lines, with the result that they were believed to have practically all retired to the third.

Friday 29 October 1915: Gommecourt Wood

We still remained as support to the firing line and were covered with trench clay. Our feet were damp and there was no water in which to wash or shave, although we got our water bottles sent down to the water cart, once every day. We never laid off our clothes or boots and were not supposed to take off our equipment, except when on fatigue work. A fatigue party always carried its gas helmets and no equipment, but was accompanied by an NCO with rifle and ammunition. We have been very meagrely fed since we came here but I believe there has been a 'rumpus' and the Quartermaster has been called to account. We expect an improvement in the future.

While in the trenches here I had my first experience of being in the line of fire from heavy artillery. Suddenly there was the sound of several express trains rushing towards me. I was certain I was going to be hit but, to my immense relief, the shells passed over my head. I soon learned to judge from the sound approximately where they were going to burst, but afterwards I had experience of whizz-bangs which travelled quicker than sound and gave no warning of their approach.

Saturday 30 October 1915: Gommecourt Wood

The weather improved and there was no rain but it became colder and there was also a little frost. Occasionally there were artillery and machine gun duels and two YCV casualties were reported from the village. An English aeroplane which was circling around was repeatedly fired at by the German artillery, the shrapnel could be seen bursting around the machine, forming dark clouds, but it was apparently never hit.

At 10pm I went out with a scouting patrol. We proceeded in single file, led by a Warwick officer who was famous for his cool, off-hand doings against the Germans. After warning the different guards we emerged from the sap. A wiring-party was working with a screen out in front to protect it against surprise from a bomb attack. After notifying these parties we advanced over 'no man's land', crawling on our knees and stopping often to listen. The moon, which was half-full, was rising so that each moment the sky was getting clearer and the light brighter. The Germans sent up many more Véry lights or star-shells than we did, why I have no explanation. But from these lights alone it was possible to tell which line was theirs and which was ours. We had Véry lights too and officers carried special pistols to fire them but seldom used them as there was no need. The Germans were better I imagine and lighted No man's land sufficiently for both parties. We now moved on our bellies and were working towards one of the advance listening posts, but the moonlight was so strong that we thought it better to return. Our own working party was making a great din the whole time and the thudding of the mallet could be heard for many hundreds of yards, the coughing of the men and the cringing of the wire were all very audible. A German wiring-party was working on our left and I believe a patrol of some kind passed near us to the right but not a shot was fired, from either side, while we were out.

Sunday 31 October 1915: Gommecourt Wood
It was Halloween today and a parcel came from my Aunt Lennon in Belfast containing many nice things to eat and drink. This was an easy day with little work to do.

Monday 1 November 1915: Gommecourt Wood (Fonquevillers)
It became rather wet and we were still in the support trenches with nothing to do except remain in the dugout. I heard a rather moving story of a young Warwick chap. He was standing quietly with a thoughtful and far-off look on his face. One of our felloes asked him about what he was thinking. At first he evaded a reply but at last answered. "There were only two boys of us in the family, my brother and me. My brother and I are both here, my father is in the Dardanelles and I was just wondering about what the old woman was thinking." A song that the Warwicks used pleased us very much and caught on like an epidemic:

I want to go home,
I want to go home,
Cannons are roaring.
Machine guns are pouring,
I don't want to go to the trenches no more,
Take me over the sea
Where the Allemand[9] can't get at me,
Oh my, I don't want to die,
I want to go home.

I also remember well a conversation between a Warwick and a friend of his who had returned from leave. This letter was recounting his experience while at the Headquarters of Sir John French. He had a bit of amusement in a registered French brothel and he described with gusto the charms of the maidens in the different numbered rooms and told with heartiness of the excitement of a certain ardent loving Scotsman. This was probably the famous No 4 at St Omer, which was both a café and a *maison tol*. A good description of it is found in the *War of the Guns* by Aubrey Wade.

Tuesday 2 November 1915: Couin
At about 4am we were awakened and after donning our 'fall-in' equipment, the company started to leave the trenches in shallow columns of platoons. But so much time was wasted that it was getting clear when we entered the village and it was declared unsafe to go back by the high road. Consequently we had to take a course, more to the right, over the fields in a part of the country where we could not be seen. We must have passed very near where some of our artillery was stationed but all we saw of it were the dugouts and also certain monstrous, wooden guns.

Coming out on to the high road again, the Battalion formed up and, after a heavy march, we reached our rest camp in Couin at about 8am. We were unshaved and dirty and our clothes were heavy with trench mud not to mention that we had scarcely got under canvas when it began to rain heavily. We remained in the tents and the rain

---

9   French word for German.

Madeleine, who eventually married Andre Hotte. (Ulysse Perodeau/Annick Baron)

continued to pour while no one ventured out except the orderlies to get the meals. We lay down at about 6 o'clock and slept luxuriously until about 7 the next morning.

A small stream flowed through the village of Couin and, in it a Sanitary Station had been erected. Here each man of a Battalion, coming from the trenches, could have a hot shower- bath, and there was also an abundant supply of good water for the water carts.

At about 9 o'clock our Battalion went down to the baths, a platoon at a time. There was a room made of wood and canvas where the men undressed. They then passed into the bathroom, where five men at a time stood under a rather miserly trickle of hot water for a few seconds. One had neither enough water nor time but nevertheless the bath was very serviceable and acceptable at the time. We were one of the first platoons to have our wash. We put on our weatherproof sheets, took in whatever clean changes we had, marched to the baths, had our dip and returned. It was still raining.

Wednesday 3 and Thursday 4 November 1915: Beauval
We left Couin at about 8.30am and after four hours marching, on a dull day; we reached Beauval and were installed in our old billets. We had a kit inspection and a pay parade, after which we spent several hours in removing the mud from our clothes. That night I walked around the town and did my best to meet a presentable girl but was unsuccessful. By now I had obtained a parcel from home and a letter from Joseph Sire. This was my first epistle in French and I was as proud of it as a lad with the first letter from his best girl.

Friday 5 November 1915: Pernois
We got into marching order and paraded before the church where we were addressed with a few words from Brigadier T.E. Hickman, CB, DSO. He said that the Battalion

Marius Carpentier, Madeleine's father, who served in a Cyclist Company of the
French Army during the Great War. (Ulysse Perodeau/Annick Baron)

was leaving the 109th Brigade to be attached for a short time to a Brigade of the Line.
It had made a name in Ireland on account of its smartness on parade, its discipline on
the march and the individual, soldierly appearance of the men. He had noticed since we
came to France, a certain falling away in some of those qualities which ought not to be.
He desired this to be remedied and furthermore we were to gather up everything useful
and praiseworthy from the Regulars and to keep clear of anything unworthy we might
see among them. We left with the good wishes of the rest of the Brigade but he wanted
us to come back with laurels of praise from our new Brigadier.

We took the place of the 4th Essex in the 107th Brigade but the change only lasted
one month. We then left and after a march of seventeen kilometres reached the village
of Penrose where my platoon was billeted in a good, brick-built, weatherproof barn. We
were on an outskirt of the village of Pernois where a good road, a railway and a small
river all ran close past the door. Beyond the river lay the main part of the village, a long,
straggling street with dirty houses and innumerable cafés. The countryside around was
hilly and rather picturesque, the formation being limestone. Water could be fairly easily
obtained and there were even a few surface wells. A railway station and level crossing
with a guard of French soldiers were in sight of our billet.

The water supply was often a difficult one in these villages and led to rows between the farms and soldiers. Generally the only fresh water in the village came from a well, which was often hundreds of feet deep, and was obtained only by the tiresome turning of a windlass. It would take five minutes to haul up a barrel of water and for the last few minutes it could be heard bumping against the sides of the well.

One would listen to the water splashing over the edge of the barrel, so that when it came to the surface it was only half-full. It was a common sight to see Monsieur, followed by his sturdy daughter coming from the well, bearing between them a yoke from which hung the barrel half-full of the precious water. But every farmhouse had a cistern below the surface of the yard and often quite close to the midden. Into this tank the water from all the roofs was drained and it was often fitted with a chain pump. This liquid frequently smelled and contained lizards and was used for washing and feeding the livestock. The trouble was when thirty or forty soldiers, fresh from the trenches, started to wash themselves. They were not used to economizing water so it was apparent that the cistern would be quickly emptied. The farmer would suggest that five or six soldiers should use the same water and one half of the quantity only should be employed. He was only laughed at, so he put a padlock on the pump and then the row started. This was often used for making tea when it was chlorinated and boiled and strained accordingly.

Saturday and Sunday 6-7 November 1915: Pernois
The weather was good but becoming colder and we had no work to do. At night W. Victor Gilligan and I searched the village to find an amiable merchant but discovered none. W. Victor Gilligan was well and in 1957, living in the USA.

Sunday 7 November 1915: Pernois
After attending church parade, letter-writing occupied most of the day.

Monday to Saturday: 8-13 November 1915: Pernois
We had two Brigade field days also a good deal of Battalion company and platoon drill. Once again we were under the control of our officers, who were nearly all ignorant, conservative and bullying, to an intolerable degree. In the trenches we rarely saw even one of them. Not one was ever seen in our dugout, not one was ever observed giving a direction of any kind, and their voices were never heard.

Captain S- was intoxicated for most of the time we were in the trenches. I believe he once visited our guard at night. He asked the sentry his name and then what were his duties. The sentry replied. "Is that right?" asked S. of the sergeant of the guard, who was a Warwick. "Yes Sir," replied the Sergeant. "And what would you do in the case of an alarm?" was the next question of the reeking Captain. The sentry gave an answer. 'Is that correct?' queried the Captain a second time. "Not exactly, Sir" was the answer. "You are absolutely wrong," said the Captain turning upon the unfortunate Sergeant, "You are a sentry and you do not know your duty, you should be court-martialled."[10] Such arrogance from an ignorant, drunken officer was unbearable to flesh blood.

Our Lieutenant was scarcely more visible during our stay in the trenches. He never came round to see how we fared for food, he never visited our dugouts and our rifles

---

10 Possibly Captain Slack.

Madeleine at twelve years old.
(Ulysse Perodeau/Annick Baron)

Madeleine, the 12 year old who grew
up to be a very attractive woman.
(Ulysse Perodeau/Annick Baron)

weren't even inspected once. But when in quarters where we had every opportunity of taking care of our equipment, then we were plagued with rifle, kit and billet inspections. Our Quartermaster managed things no better. While staying in billets we were often short of bread and had to purchase French loaves to appease our hunger. We bought soap and went without meat and jam rations, but a few hours before our departure to new quarters, behold hundreds of pounds worth of supplies magically appeared on the scene, dozens of bars of soap, tins of biscuits, pots of meat and jam which we could not possibly carry with us and which were piled up on a corner being covered with straw.

Our letters were certainly much delayed in the process of censoring. In this important duty the officers seemed to behave in a truly careless and disgraceful manner. They held over correspondence for weeks until it suited their convenience to censor it. And they left the letters lying about opened so the contents were perused by prowling batmen.

A number of green envelopes in which we could enclose our letters, was issued occasionally, these could only be opened by the Press Bureau. The writer signed the envelope and undertook to say nothing about the location of his unit. None of my companions ever received Field Punishment No.1 but I had only to go along to the guard-room to see a soldier spread-eagled on the wheel of a limber. At the same time I could read in the newspaper where it had been stated in the House of Commons that tying to the wheel had been abolished.

Sunday to Saturday 14 – 20 November 1915: Pernois
We experienced a week of some of the hardest work in which I have had the pleasure to participate. We had long route marching almost every day, besides we did wood-

Battalion Permanent Patrol Roll of Honour. In the centre is Lieutenant Lack, the Battalion Intelligence Officer; wounded on 2 July, he died seventeen days later. The men are, 1, Lance Corporal J. Dunn, 2 Lance Corporal A.N. Brown, 3 Private J. McDowell, 4 Private C. Trotter, 5, Private T.H.D. Cullen, 6, Lance Corporal W. Cameron, 7, Lance Corporal W.F. Forbes, killed 1 November 1916, 8 Lance Corporal S.J. Johnston, 9 Private A. Marshall, 10 Corporal Brian Boyd MM, killed 7 June 1917, 11 Sergeant J.L. Armstrong MM killed 16 August 1917, 12 Private V.N. Donaldson, 13 Lance Corporal P.G. Pollock, missing believed killed 1 July 1916, 14 Private S. McCall, 15 Private R. Sturgeon, 16 Lance Corporal T. Crothers, 17 Private H. Ferguson, 18 Lance Corporal W. Oliver, 19 Corporal R. Jervis, 20 Private J. McRoberts. (Royal Ulster Rifles Museum)

Café 'Au Rendezvous des Chasseurs' is a private dwelling today.

cutting in the hills near Bonneville, trench-digging in the highlands to the south of Berteaucourt and took part in big Brigade manoeuvres around Vignacourt. We generally were out of bed at 5.30am or 6.30am and were not back in the village again until night had fallen. There were numerous woods and the growth of timber in them was carefully controlled. Wide, straight thoroughfares ran through them with smaller avenues at right angles, so that every part was accessible without difficulty.

For our jam we did not get any of the famous 'Plum and Apple' but for several months our only preserve was marmalade. It came in tins which had a smell of paraffin oil. We only rarely had 'butter'. It arrived in tins also and resembled grease both in its taste and smell. This would not have been too bad if only we had been sufficiently fed. A third or quarter of a loaf was our allowance for the day, with sometimes no jam and very often no butter. But the dinner especially made us feel sick. It consisted of a dixie full of hot water, floating oil and lumps of fat, no potatoes, nor vegetables nor meat nor even salt.

One morning however, our billets were inspected by the new Brigadier of the 107th Brigade and some surprising revelations were made. The Battalion had under drawn bread to the amount of £600. Men were found living in billets with great openings in the flimsy walls, through which the wind blew wet and cold and where painful attempts had been made to remedy matters with straw and mud which was scraped from the street. The Battalion accounts and officers' mess books also made interesting reading to the Brigadier. The Quartermaster was informed that the men must be fed and the billets of the whole company changed. And about our boots, our wonderful trench boots. They had also been found deficient. My own were both cracked across the soles and I have

The actual Café has moved one building to the right.

not known dry feet this whole week, and there was no remedy, no new boots nor boot makers to cope with the repairs required.

Sunday 21 November 1915: Pernois
I was in charge of a bit of sanitary work, making a shelter for latrines.

Monday to Thursday 22 – 25 November 1915: Pernois
I underwent a course of instruction on bombs and hand grenades also how to use them. There were eight of us from each company and Messrs. Corscadden and Mayes were the instructors. We had lectures on the different types of bombs and their construction. We also made a trench for ourselves and practised bowling with dummies and jam-tins which were filled with clay. Then we went to the Brigade trenches at Berteaucourt and practised the formation of bombing parties, to clear the trenches from the supposed enemy. The work was all very interesting and the weather, though frosty and cold, was for the most part dry. Unfortunately I suffered from a sore right foot all the time.

Friday 26 November 1915: Pernois-Franqueville
The Battalion left Pernois at about 1 o'clock and marched westward, through Berteaucourt, until we arrived at the village of Franqueville. The weather was ideal and the distance comparatively short. I, however, had a new pair of boots and a sore, swollen, right foot. The tender foot was the result of bad boots and cold, wet feet for a week. The top of the foot got swollen and it was with pain I put any weight on the toes. The billet in which we were placed was somewhat after the nature of a barn, but we had access to plenty of wood, and soon had a splendid fire going. The owners, an old man and wife, were clean, tidy intelligent people who proved very congenial and we had a pleasant evening sitting around the fire, after the day's march. We also had a wonderful high tea, plenty of bread, sardines, salmon and jam. Verily we are learning how to take care of

FRENCH LESSONS FOR SOLDIERS:
"The Adventures of Corporal Atkins"
with Vocabulary.

PUBLISHED AT THE OFFICES OF "COUNTRY LIFE,"
20, TAVISTOCK STREET, LONDON, W.C.

Price 3d.

French lessons! A booklet that would not have been required by James McRoberts, but would possibly be helpful to Second Lieutenant Corscadden. (Somme Museum, Newtownards)

ourselves and developing into proper old soldiers as well as experienced campaigners. In the yard of these farmhouses there are usually several boxes with wire netting fronts each of which contained three or four tame rabbits which were kept for the stew saucepan. I was told that in normal seasons pigeons were also held but in wartime it was illegal to keep them enclosed.[11]

Saturday 27 November 1915: Ailly-le-Haut-Clocher
We left Franqueville about 8.30 with the weather still keeping cold and dry. After walking for about half a mile, during which I suffered agony from my bad foot, had to report myself as being unable to continue the journey. I am absolutely crippled. Captain CO Slacke, however, allowed me to throw my rifle and pack over his horse's back and thus unburdened I was easily able to foot it to the end. Luckily the march was a very short one.

After passing Gorenflos we entered Ailly-le-Haut-Clocher which was our destination. At first the whole platoon was shoved into an old tumble-down barn, full of chaff and wet bedding. We cleared out this muck, lit a fire inside an old bucket and sat despondently around it. The day was bitterly cold. Soon the proprietress, a stingy, sour-faced old lady was on the scene and she scarcely left us for a moment. She made a race towards the bucket to try and seize our little fire but could not reach it for there were too many round it and they refused to move. She shouted and screamed that we would set the barn in flames, we could have a fire in the yard but not there, she would protest to the officer. But the officer was not about so she shook us by the shoulders and tried to push us aside but we refused to move. Soon half the village seemed to have gathered round us and there were angry looks so that it appeared as if there could easily be a row. But our fellows sat quietly round the fire, nonchalantly smoking and looking into the tiny flames. At an

---

11   Pigeons were used by all armies at this time to carry messages.

An illustration from the *Incinerator* magazine, published by the
Battalion while in France. (Somme Museum, Newtownards)

unusual burst of protestation against the interlopers, a lad would look up with straight, fearless, innocent eyes and with an emphatic sad shake of the head utter the words, "*Non compris*", and all the while each one was enjoying the irony of the scene. It was a huge joke and personally I could hardly restrain myself from laughing. Meanwhile a search was going on for better billets and this proved successful. We gathered up our belongings and moved away about one hundred and fifty yards and took up our quarters in a good, brick, empty dwelling house with glass windows and a fireplace in the kitchen.

At this time we had a Sergeant Major H.J. Lyons, nicknamed 'Dirty Dick' because he was possessed of a most unusual, satanic expression. He had served so long in India that his complexion had become unusually swarthy and in addition he had grey, thick hair and very piercing black eyes. One day I encountered him at the cook house in argument with a sprightly French lady. They were both slanging each other, although neither understood what the other was saying.[12] He was accusing her of stealing from the cook house and she was making fun of him. He asked me what she was saying and having no love for him I was foolish enough to tell him the truth. "She says, Sir, that you only need a pair of horns to become Old Nick himself." To make sure he understood her, she adopted a butting attitude and placed her fists to her forehead, with her forefingers fully extended to the front.

Monday to Thursday 28 November to 9 December 1915: Alley-le-Haut-Clocher
During this period we remained at Ailly-le-Haut-Clocher, the town quite a decent one in French terms. It had two butchers, a hardware shop and several grocery shops all in its favour. High times we had at Ailly-le-Haut-Clocher. We bought a pan, also a saucepan

---

12 Slanging, i.e. teasing.

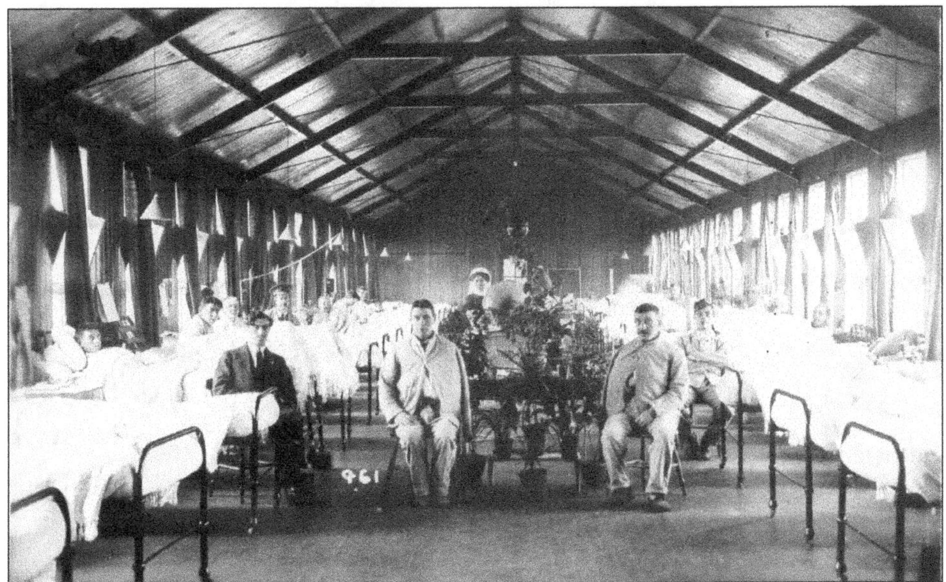

James in hospital, he is supposedly the figure on the right at the rear. (McRoberts family)

and on that old hearth were cooked many a tasty bit of liver, many a pound of beef-steak and many a dish of tapioca or rice. We were as thick as brothers and every parcel received from home was laid on the table or on a groundsheet spread on the floor and became the common lot of all.

I was troubled with my sore foot most of this time but by fifteen minutes of hard rubbing, night and morning, I at last got rid of the pain absolutely. Fortunately I only assembled with the bombers and had little walking to do. We had more throwing of grenades and more lectures, but many of the parades were cancelled owing to the very wet weather. '*Troujours il pleut*' (when it rains, it rains) was the dismal complaint.

It seemed to me that the French people had settled into a state of hopeless despondency. In a café there would be a dance hall with an automatic piano of some kind, but no music or dancing was tolerated for we must remember the War. Ask an old lady in a jovial, bantering manner if she would go for a promenade and although she saw the humour of the suggestion she closed her eyes to it and cried out, "If you want a promenade, go to England, we have not the time – we must work all the time our men are all away fighting."

There must also have been some nervousness about the country's credit. We always got paid in five franc notes but in many places the people absolutely refused to touch this paper money, "*Non bon*" was the reply. Of France itself and its villages and inhabitants, it was hardly worth while writing. The people lived in a state of filth and misery witnessed only in the worst parts of Ireland.

It was the custom of the men to urinate outside their houses against the wall, in sight of the whole village. When the children were let out from school, the boys would immediately line the end wall of the building and start to piddle against it. A part of some school yards was concreted and there were a number of holes in the floor with a drainage system for the use of the girls. Later on I noticed in the larger towns, in the

Joseph Sire at age 12 years.

centre of the square, cast iron-urinals for men. They were roofless structures and only about three feet high and raised about twelve inches from the ground.

Houses were small, badly lit and ventilated and they sometimes flooded. Often the farm midden (lavatory) was in front of the principal door with outbuildings all around it, shutting the dwelling house from the public street. The residence was thus reached by passing through an alley, under a barn perhaps and wading around the edges of the midden. The outhouses were built of wood with a coating of clay plaster. The dwelling houses invariably had shutters on the windows instead of blinds. The roof was carried almost two feet over the walls and, as the majority of the buildings were single storied, the large, airy space behind the eaves was used for drying and storing vegetables, especially kidney beans or '*les haricots*' as they were called. The women in these villages usually wore sabots, which were wooden shoes made in one piece. These appeared very awkward to us but the peasants seemed to manage quite well in them. Contrary to the image of Paris, we found the women unkempt and the children regular ragamuffins, while the sight of a family at a meal could be revolting, even sickening in all its primitive rudeness. In the shops we could really buy little that we liked, unless it had been imported from England.

French bread was very spongy and unsatisfying, also it would not keep. No chocolates were up to British standards, nor were the matches, tobacco, biscuits or cheese. When a French match was struck there was a horrible smell of burning brimstone. If a cigarette was lighted from it, immediately the tobacco was impregnated with sulphur and completely ruined. The only way to ignite it satisfactorily was to wait half a minute, after it had been struck until the head of the match was all consumed and the wood alone was burning. This was slow enough inside a house where there was shelter, but outside, too often, the wind blew out the flame during the period of waiting. I was told the explanation was that the French Government had a monopoly in the manufacture of matches. The French now knew it themselves and were ever on the watch for anything we might leave behind

Andre Jean Charles Hotte, his wife Madeline, Marius Carpentier, his wife Marguerite,
the owners of the cafe, Marie Sire, Eugenie Blanchard, Joseph Sire, Joseph Sire
and Jean Hotte, son of Madeline. The name of the dog is not recorded.

us. "The Germans had little taste, eternally wanting such a country as this," was the comment of one of our chaps. But then they might have done better with the resources.

In the evenings I used to go to a house on the opposite side of the road where a kindly lady and her two daughters lived, the elder of the girls was aged sixteen but had the appearance of one several years older. She was small, well-formed and quite pretty. But I liked to be with her for she could make me understand anything she wanted to say, and she proclaimed herself my '*professeur*' and always corrected the faults I made in talking her own language. She was also much interested in English and had learned a little of it herself. She took me into her confidence and showed me letters she had received from different soldiers and particularly a letter from Edward, an English officer who, falling in love with her winsome smile, wanted a few minutes with her at 8.30 one night, after the men were inside their billets. She had not replied and there had followed a few reproachful lines; '*Je suis desolé*' (I am sorry) was the cry of his wounded heart.

An Indian who could talk French visited her frequently and had wanted to marry her, enticing her with the promise of a dowry of five thousand francs. We were good friends, this little Gilberte and I, but she was young, guileless and sensitive and I indulged in no risky familiarities, although I was confident they would not have been refused. Her full name was Mademoiselle Gilberte Moni, Ailly-le-Haut-Clocher, Somme, but I do not think I ever wrote to her.

Next door to us was a little Belgian lady, a refugee from near Charleroi. 'Madame' I always called her. She had a daughter and a niece with her. She gave lessons on the piano and a somewhat superior style with her. On Sunday evening a party of us took possession of her house and we carried on a rather lively conversation, I acting as interpreter. Paterson, I think, was showing the contents of one of his pockets, explaining that this object was a French souvenir and this other a German souvenir. He then produced a lady's suspender 'and this is an Irish souvenir' he exclaimed. Madame immediately seized

More of the villagers.

it, sniffed it and laughed merrily, declaring it was genuine indeed. *"Après la guerre fini"* (when the war is over) was a common expression among the French. Our soldiers had this rhyme with which they used to tease the girls.

Après la guerre fini
Anglais soldat partit
Mademoiselle she go to well
Après la guerre fini.

She (Madame) said many things and behaved in such way that would make a British lady blush with shame but on leaving, we all declared that she was a fine, honourable little woman whose faults were few.

Friday 10 December 1915: Gorenflos

Leaving Ailly-le-Haut-Clocher we marched over to the neighbouring village of Gorenflos where the Royal Irish Fusiliers were also stationed. I suffered practically no pain from my foot: how satisfied I was, can easily be imagined. I was put in charge of seven others and we had an old kitchen with the best of all blessings, an open hearth. There was also a room behind full of apples. It was locked but we quickly gained an entrance and started pilfering. We made ourselves very comfortable but I had not the same companions as at Ailly-le-Haut-Clocher and the cheer was not up to the high water mark established there. We remained in Gorenflos, which was a rather miserable sort of place and I

The Sire family.

made no particular friends. Mostly I stayed in my billet at night and cleared up a lot of correspondence that was hanging in my hands.

When I was in Ireland I had learned to cut a person's hair and this proved a useful accomplishment in France when I acted as barber to my friends in the Company. We practised the method to be adopted in charging the German trenches in the next great attack. The advance was to be made, after the wire-entanglements had been cut or destroyed in certain places, and the different parties had to pass through these openings in single file, to scatter out immediately afterwards.

The first bombing parties advanced along the enemy's trenches to the right and left and the reserve bombers blocked the communication trenches leading to the enemy support. The assaulting party generally walked over the first line because it was often feebly held and went on to meet the greater resistance in the second and third lines. We practised this assault over and over again. The weather was very wet most of the time. We heard that on the Eastern Front it was finally agreed the Gallipoli campaign had been a failure and all troops were withdrawn without loss, first from Suvla and Anzac on the 20 December 1915, (and from Cape Helles on 8 January 1916).

Saturday 25 December 1915: Gorenflos
This was Christmas Day in France and of course we had no parades. A prize was offered to the billet which was most tastefully decorated for the festive season and we made a noble attempt to win it in our room. With holly and evergreens, postcards and Christmas cards, our rifles and bayonets, we produced a brave and gallant show which just missed the prize by a narrow margin. For dinner we had a multitude of good things, roast fowl and meat, vegetables and potatoes with some excellent Army duff to finish off. After dinner we were engaged in an inter-platoon soccer match in which, somehow, I managed to score a goal. The evening I spent in the billet of Number 4 Section, where there were two pretty children, young girls of about eleven and twelve. At this age the girls seemed to look their best for here they were, sturdy and round of limb with pleasant faces and charming, easy manners and deportment. And they were such hard, willing little workers they touched one's heart.

Sunday 26 December 1915: Gorenflos
After the Church Parade at which our bands under Regimental Sergeant Major Elphick gave a display to the delight of the villagers, we had the *Daily Mail* Christmas pudding

The Sire-Carpentier and Sire-Blanchard families.

for dinner. Then there was a football match followed by letter-writing in the evening. I received many Christmas presents, including a nice, private card from Elsie Graham. I also had an amusing letter from my little brother Sam aged about eleven years, the first he ever wrote I was sure. Sam would later have his own farm called Crookedstone at Muckamore. The letter is as follows, (including some Antrim dialect):

Dear Brother
I am going to try to write you my first letter. What do you think of the old French women? Have you ever seen any Germans yet? I always get mother to read your letters. I would like have been in the room full of apples. We got a barrel of apples but they are all done now. Matthew (another brother presently living at Greystone Road Antrim and with three of a family) is going to Larne every Monday and Tuesday to classes and there is an old lady and she tells them all about hens and how to feed them and to set the clocking (broody) hens and how the kill the lice on them. He says her tongue is a yard long, and he calls her 'Old Fizzenwig', if there are any bugs on you, all you have to do is to write to Matthew. Do you ever try to shoot any of the rats? What do you think of the firing line?

Matthew and Sarah (the maid) are at each other, the same as ever. Matthew calls Sarah 'Old Pintail' and 'Griddle-feet'. Matthew (now a grandfather and living in Detroit, USA) and John (another brother) are at it the same about Tilly (a cousin, now Mrs Matilda Dundee, Lisnalinchy) and Eliza Jane (whom he married?) Matthew would be very angry if he knew I was saying all these things about him. With very good wishes for Christmas and the coming year.
From Brother Sam

Monday 27 December 1915: Gorenflos
This was another holiday and there was more football.

Tuesday and Wednesday 28 and 29 December 1915: Gorenflos
We were back at the old work.

Marguerite Carpentier, the owner of the Café 'Au Rendezvous des Chasseurs', her daughter Madeleine (Hood), with her son John.

Thursday 30 December 1915: Abbeville

I went to Abbeville on an errand for Captain C.O. Slacke. I got a bicycle from the signallers and had a pleasant and quick journey, arriving about 10.30. This was a fine town, population about 20,000, with a fine Cathedral and other churches, a museum and lots of good shops. I saw many Indian troops, who were leaving the country and noted local, fine-looking girls with coal, black air and wonderful, dark, donkey fringes on their foreheads. I understand there were three medical boards in the town and, although I kept a look out for the notoriously famed red lights, I did not notice any and I made no enquiries concerning them. I successfully executed all my purchases and reached Gorenflos after a heavy ride.

Saturday 1 January 1916: Gorenflos

This was New Year's Day. There was a continuous hilarious repetition of good wishes for '*Une bonne année!*' New Year's Day in France had a real holiday atmosphere, entirely absent from Christmas which was only another Saint's day. The very wet weather still continued. In the morning my Battalion paraded and met its own Colonel Chichester for the first time since its arrival in France. I was to have played, in the afternoon, in a rugby match against the 11th Royal Irish Fusiliers but the match was cancelled; instead I did half an hour's pack-drill with the rest of the billet for not having our blankets folded in some certain manner looked for by Captain Slacke.

Members of the village.

In Gorenflos I made friends with lots of pretty little French girls, Marie, Therese, Julie and others, charming little maidens, every one of them was coy, beautiful and impelling. About this time we each got part of a pound box of chocolates as a Christmas present from the British West Indies. It was a long-shaped box of black tin with gold lettering and the Coats of Arms of the different islands, Trinidad, St Lucia, etc, were all engraved in gold on it. I thought the box very pretty and got hold of one and carried it around with me but lost it when I was wounded on 1 July. I saw the chocolates again in July 1916 when I was in hospital, at the Palais de Régates in Harfleur; I was served out with a portion of the same chocolate on several occasions without the tin.

Sunday 2 January 1916: Beauval
We cleaned up our billets and our company set off about 10 o'clock, to march to Beauval. It rained persistently most of the day and we had to wear our waterproofs all the way. At mid-day we halted at Berneuil and had dinner in some empty houses. We started again and as we passed by Candas the light was failing.

It was quite dark when we reached when we reached Beauval and the first electric light pole in the Rue de Recque. We marched through the town in great style, singing loudly. It seemed like coming home, returning to the well lighted streets of this shapely town. We marched up the Rue de Gasse and were put in good billets, well up on the hill. We had accomplished a long march and I felt very fit, much to my own satisfaction.

Monday to Sunday 3-9 January 1916: Beauval
We were attached to a company of the Royal Engineers here; this town was being fitted out to receive about ten thousand troops in the springtime. All possible billets were to be prepared and made habitable for men. Then two or three stands of bunks, according to the head-space, were arranged round the walls. Some of the beds were single and the

'The Merry Mauve Melodies' who entertained the men of
the 36th Division. (Kate Willis Archive)

others were double. They were made of trimmed saplings, about two and a half inches in diameter, with a bottom of netting-wire and by means of a sheaf of straw over the wire, a comparatively comfortable bed was ensured. My duty was to go along, as interpreter, with one of our officers who lacked competence in French, making an inventory of all possible billets, state their size, the need of repairs and the proprietor's name and address. I found the job engaging and discovered I could talk about anything that was required of me. Many towns or villages seemed to possess a most important man, called the *Maire* (Mayor), to whom disputes about billeting and ownership of land were referred. Marriages also were celebrated in his office, although often followed by a Church service.

At first I accompanied Mr F. Corscadden in this work but I found him more of a bother than otherwise. He knew just enough French to worry me and make my position most uncomfortable. He was often told by the old French ladies that he was 'young-looking' and 'ladylike'. When he tried to say something in French, invariably he would be told to tell me so that I could relay the content and they would listen to it.

He was continually looking for rooms suitable for officers. One Madam showed him a room where four Irishmen had stayed and she said she would willingly have four of the same class again. "But this would make a most suitable officer's room", argued Mr Corscadden. "I don't want any officer here, officer much too big", she said, raising her hand towards the ceiling, "officer too much swank", she added, using that English word swank, although she had not shown any evidence of knowing another word of English.

The last day I was out with Lieutenant R.V. Robb. He knew only a few phrases so he wisely kept silent and let me do all the talking with the result that I think I surpassed myself in 'swinging the lead' in a foreign language! I had only a few hours work each day and consequently had lots of time to myself which I employed by advancing an

Joseph Sire at his confirmation.

acquaintance with the three young ladies who were members of the farm where we were billeted. Two belonged to the family, the third and youngest was an adopted child but all three were pretty and all worked very hard from morn to night, feeding the pigs and cows, threshing or winnowing the wheat or chopping the mangle-wurzel. The kitchens were very plainly furnished and books or magazines were absolutely unheard of but one universal adornment was a Singer sewing machine. There was never a fireplace and coal was unknown. Instead there was a stove in the middle of the room with a long, horizontal flue pipe. It burned wood cut into six inch lengths and on the top of it were cooked the meals, consisting chiefly of a saucepan of stew and a pot of coffee. The wood was cut from the branches of trees about the thickness of one's wrist, which were stacked in neat piles in the yard and often thatched.

The bread was always baked at a *boulangerie* and the loaves were all white rolls about two feet long, but only four inches in diameter. The different varieties of bread made in the homes of rural Ireland and raised with sour milk and baking-soda such as potato bread, oat cake, soda cake and potato-oaten bread were absolutely unknown here. These very understanding young ladies told me that they believed that many women in England did little work, that they considered manual work a disgrace and kept many servants to do it. I answered that such was often the case. They seemed amused at this and told me that it was the custom for everyone to work in France, man and woman, rich and poor, that although a mistress might have a maid, she considered her as much a lady as herself and both did their share of the household work.

Certainly these girls seemed comfortably well off yet they were working hard every day, doing all kinds of dirty, manual farm work such as cleaning out the byres etc. In the evening they would dress and behold an astonishing change. A little paint was added and there they were three elegant, healthy, fine girls. With you youngest, Lea, I

Sergeant William Kelly, 15 Platoon, severely wounded on 1 July 1916. (McRoberts Family)

was on very friendly terms. Together we used to milk the little Bretonne cows and slice the mangel-wurzels down in the shadowy cellar. But we had to make a noise working most of the time otherwise there would be a shout from the eldest girl wanting to know what we were doing. The middle girl, Clara, was the most beautiful but small, motherly and subdued. She had been engaged for seven years, her fiancé being an officer with the French Army. She showed me several of his letters written from the trenches, letters of a deep, adoring love. One day she received a letter, in English, from a Sergeant of the 2nd Essex. I translated it and put into English the reply she made in French. Gabrielle was the name of the eldest girl and she was red-haired. Many more people I got to know – Lodi, Simone and others.

Monday to Saturday 10-22 January 1916: Beauval

My interpreting being over, I returned to my work with the company. One day I was on guard, it was a pleasant twenty-four hours. Corporal Scott was in charge and entertained us during the night with a recital of the story of his life in the world of cross-country running. At night it was remarkable how clearly the star-shells shone; even at this distance from the front, their light gleamed on the pools of water on the road. In the early morning, about 5.30, we had a bit of fun with the girls going to Saint Frères jute factory, bold and unrestrained they were in language and deportment.

I was also at the jute factory and noticed that the machinery had been made in Belfast by Combe Barbour Ltd.[13] Another day I visited the Machine Shop and French Sawmill, taken over by the Royal Engineers. The next day I was with the billeting party under Sergeant Calvert. Sergeant William H. Calvert was a good-looking capable and

---

13   A linen making and engineering firm.

Ground over which the Division fought over in August 1917. (Royal Ulster Rifles Museum)

most decent NCO Shortly after this he was sent to Harfleur on a bombing course and accidentally killed.[14] He had a brother, Norman, in our Transport who survived the war and afterwards went to Australia.

The billeting party, if it were necessary, removed the straw to another quarter of the barn and after this, the bed frames were put up and the netting wire fastened to them. A detachment of Scottish soldiers in kilts who, when mounting ladders to the loft, were a source of some hilarity among the French girls present. In general Scotsmen were popular with the French. I frequently had lots of interpreting to do which took me away from the main work. Once I was called to the orderly room where I found Sergeant Major Mackay bewildered by a small elderly Frenchwoman shouting in patois for all she was worth. On my appearance her eloquence was directed at me but for quite some time I couldn't really discern what she was trying to say although I kept reiterating, '*Oui, oui, je comprends bien.*' Finally I noticed a certain word '*fumier*' kept repeating itself, so eventually I said, '*Oui, oui, je vous comprends bien, madame, mais qu'est que c'est que le fumier.*' Then she conducted us all out into her yard where she triumphantly pointed out '*le fumier*' or midden. I understand then all she wanted. She had no one to help her, her men were all at War, the midden had not been emptied for three years, the English soldiers were young and strong, they did not appear to be too busy and all she wanted was to have the midden removed to her land outside the town. Next morning the Army obliged with a working party and transport and I walked at least one mile outside the town to where she pointed out her particular patch of land.

Sunday 23 January 1916: Doullens

There were church parades in the morning. I went to the Church of Ireland and the service was conducted in a schoolroom. Sir D. Haig was in town that day and was

---

14   Sergeant William Henry Calvert, No 14264, killed on 7 February 1916, the son of W.H. and Margaret Calvert, of Cliftonville, Belfast. He is buried in Grave Div.Q.19.5, Ste Marie Cemetery, Le Havre.

present at the meeting in the Soldiers' Home with the Presbyterians. After dinner, Moore Parkhill and I, having obtained passes, walked to the town of Doullens. This was a rather fine specimen of a town with several good streets of imposing appearance. There was one YMCA building at which we had tea and buns. When the cafés opened at 6 o'clock we entered one, attracted by the sounds of revelry within. It was a small place with two rows of tables at each side and a tiny open space in the middle.

There was dancing going on and anyone could join in when he liked. If there was room for him he could have a partner from either sex; a girl of twenty or the barmaid herself or, now and then, even a French soldier with a frightful beard or a young English driver with his brown bandolier. The music never ceased. It came from a mechanical piano keeping up quite a pace. Moore and I sat at a corner of one of the little tables drinking beer and coffee. We did not dance for I did not know the steps but we sat enjoying the gay scene. To us, rather dour no doubt Ulster-Scots, the Frenchmen seemed obtrusively extrovert and rather loud in attracting attention to themselves in an immature way.

Moore Parkhill could speak French and was slightly older than the majority of us. Shortly after our visit to Doullens he was sent home and commissioned. He survived the war.

But about the dance. One could see that it was a social institution and what a beautiful healthy one. A lad would bring in a girl with him and they would dance quietly, as if they did it for the physical pleasure and then it was the girl who spoke, '*Merci bien, Monsieur*,' perhaps adding '*Au revoir*' as she rejoined her family group. So we sat and drank more beer until at last it was nearing 8 o'clock and it was time to leave. We walked quickly to Beauval discussing these people, our allies.

Tuesday 25 January 1916: Berneuil

'A' Company, 14th Royal Irish Rifles, left Beauval and marched to Berneuil. I went with the advance party which left at 12 o'clock, under Sergeant Andrew Yates. We passed through Bonneville and Montrelet on the way. The Battalion left about two hours later and went by Candas and Frienvillers. The weather was mild and the march reasonably pleasant. That night we slept in an old barn which was wet on the floor and without any straw. It was really cold. Sergeant Andrew Yates was killed on 1 July 1916.[15]

Wednesday to Friday 26-28 January 1916: Berneuil

We moved into better billets, where we were quite comfortable and occupying the attic of the third floor of a big, old building which accommodated the whole company. Friday was a big Divisional day with aimless marching and retreating all morning.

Saturday to Monday: 29 January to 7 February 1916: Domart

We remained at Berneuil and the weather was for the most part unsettled. In the morning we had company drill and in the evening we did pioneer work. I walked twice to Domart on business and, favoured with good weather on both occasions, I had quite a pleasant time. Domart was a pretty, well-built, little town with good shops. The Army Ordnance

---

15   In this entry James is incorrect, Sergeant Andrew Breakey Yeates, No 16112, age 31 years, was the son of the late Henry and Mary Jane Yeates of Agincourt Avenue, Belfast. He was killed on 16 August 1917 and is buried in New Irish Farm Cemetery, grave V.F.3. This was the first day of the Battle of Langemarck.

The 14th Rifles football team. Back row left to right, Sergeant Powell, who commanded the firing party at Private Cobain's funeral and who later fought on the Somme, Company Sergeant Major Griffiths, Private Kirkwood, killed on 6 May 1916, Sergeant Clarke, Private Craig, goalkeeper, Private Kyle, Private J. Martin, referee, Quartermaster Sergeant J. Holmes. Second row, Captain McKee, Lieutenant Wedgwood, killed on 1 July 1916, Sergeant Harper, Lieutenant Mayes who tutored the men in hand grenade throwing, Lieutenant Hooton, from Nottingham, who was killed on 5 August 1916. Front row, Private Brian Boyd, killed on 7 June 1917, Private Beattie, Private N. Donaldson and Private J. Donaldson. (Nigel Henderson)

Corps had a station there, to which the big guns were sent down to get a run through after having been in action for some time. A sight which I saw on several occasions was a dog turning the churn to make butter. There would be on the outside of the wall of a farmhouse a vertical wheel, about five feet in diameter which was turned by the weight of a large dog in a cage. If the dog did not lift his feet quickly enough his weight carried him down to the rear of his cage where the points of several nails made him quicken his pace. The same of motive power was used in the employment of a horse to drive a thresher, as recounted by me on the 19 March 1916.

The road to Berneuil was a pleasant one and as I swung along between the lines of tall ash trees on either side, with the winter sun shining on the damp fields around, my thoughts took an agreeable turn. I seemed to be walking along by myself with no pack or equipment, apart from my belt, so that I felt free and forgetful of the War, for a moment at peace with the world. Dreamily I pictured a time when the days of concord would dawn and how I would spend my holidays when the War was over. One day the orderly sergeant took the names of all those men with any knowledge of Chemistry, it seemed that persons with such learning were required for the manufacturer and employment of asphyxiating gases. I gave my name with the academic Honours I had received in Chemistry. But to no avail, the unchangeable ways of the British Army, the chap from our company who was selected had no certificates, he had worked in a druggist's shop in a street off the Falls Road and was preferred to a man who had passed his Intermediate

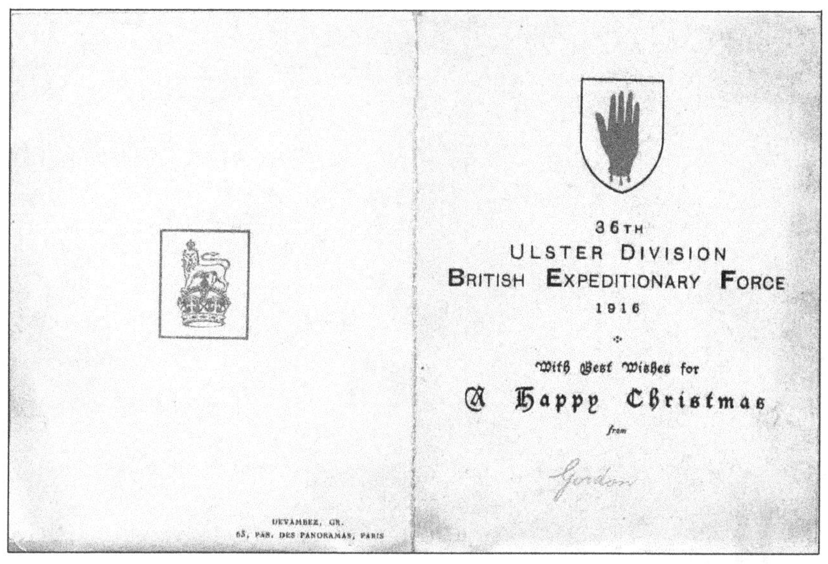

36th Divisional Christmas card of 1916. (McRoberts Family)
and (below) the inside of the card, really quite accurate. (McRoberts Family)

Science from Queen's University, Belfast. But of course I had been spared participating in this heinous form of warfare.

Exasperated, I wrote to Mr J.W. Finnegan secretary of Queen's University asking him my chances of a commission. After a week when at Varennes, I had a reply that the only way to get a commission would be to wait until I got leave and then obtain an introduction to Colonel Wallace at Newcastle, County Down, further to the consent of my own Colonel. While at Berneuil I was given various jobs of interpreting with satisfactory results which increased my confidence in myself. My name had been put

Private William McFadzean VC, his award earned on the morning of 1 July 1916. (Nigel Henderson)

Second Lieutenant Corscadden. (Nigel Henderson)

forward for a stripe since before Christmas but it was found there was no need for promotions, all the vacancies being filled by the NCOs' who came in drafts from the reserve Battalion.

Some of these boys had only been in the Army for eight months, while some were frankly undesirables of whom we were relieved when the Battalion was over strength but, who in the meantime, had obtained stripes and were now in command of fellows who once looked down on them as objects of ridicule. For example, there was a smart, good-looking chap who proved a source of particular annoyance for he was a living example of the fact that the wages of sin were sometimes promotion. He had been a Private but a few days after our arrival in France he returned to Le Havre with venereal disease. The hospital in which he was treated was supposed to be full of all ranks, including the chaplaincy. Anyhow, he got well, escaped the rigors of a winter in the country, was sent to the base and a made a Lance Corporal and as such returned to us. Bien beau, as they said in French.

To rise, at least by straightforward methods, seemed impossible, to escape to another job, under another unit, was barred and to gain a commission was exceedingly difficult; besides I did not really wish to go back home for further training again. I was on guard for twenty-four hours and while on sentry duty, exhibited my command of French by challenging "*Halte, qui vive?*" instead of demanding 'Halt, who goes there?' The Corps Commander, the Earl of Cavan, passed twice in his motor and the guard was called out and smartly presented arms, while the General Salute was given by the bugler both times. He was immensely pleased and on the second occasion stopped his car to congratulate the Sergeant on the smartness the guard and said he would report the matter to Headquarters. The Earl of Cavan was the Lieutenant General commanding the XIV Army Corps in 1916 and 1917. In 1918 and 1919 he was the General Commander

Sergeant W.H. Calvert, ex-YCV and
North Belfast Regiment UVF, killed on
7 February 1916, age 24 years, buried
in Ste Marie Cemetery, Le Havre, the
son of William and Margaret Calvert of
Cliftonville, Belfast. (Nigel Henderson)

Private Alex Campbell, mortally
wounded on 6 April 1916, he died the
following day. (Nigel Henderson)

in Chief of the British Expeditionary Forces in Italy. His titles and decorations are too
numerous to list.[16]

Tuesday 8 February 1916: Pouchervillers
The Battalion left Berneuil at about 9am and marched to Pouchervillers, a distance of
about twenty kilometres. The roads were heavy and the march tiresome. We passed
through Bonneville, crossed the Doullens–Amiens Road a little to the south of Beauval
and reached our destination about 4pm. The town was of the better type and seemed to
be a centre of engineering activity. A certain street was guarded and out of bounds to
everyone, the story told, in confidence, was that long-range guns were placed there on
beds of concrete. We were put in a barn, a rather comfortable spot for the night.

Wednesday 9 February 1916: Varennes
We left Poucherville at about 9am and marched through Toutencourt on to Varennes.
The route was about eight miles but bad weather and heavy roads made the march
anything but pleasant. Varennes was reached at about mid-day where we were placed in
middling billets, cold and anything but waterproof. About this time I first discovered

---

16 Field Marshal Frederick Rudolph Lambart, 10th Earl of Cavan, KP, GCB, GCMG, GCVO, GBE.

vermin on my clothes and I never got rid of them the remainder of the time I was in France and Belgium. The fumigation my clothes got after I was wounded the first time only quietened the pests for a few days. About once a week we removed our clothes – in the summer we would strip completely – and ran along the seams of our underclothing, trousers and tunic, with the lighted end of a cigarette. Then we could the joyful sound of the crackling of the lice from the heat.

Thursday 10 to Monday 14 February 1916: Acheux
Varennes was a village but it was only two kilometres from the important centre of Acheux. This town was the terminus of the new broad-gauge railway that now ran from Candas and was in its final stages of completion. The position for the shunting rails was now being cut out and the tracks laid. At the railway station at Acheux the French train driver, instead of making his engine whistle every time he wished to start, raised a horn to his lips and gave a short toot. There was a considerable amount of this tooting, which highly amused our fellows and made them toot also.

A party of engineers and a company of the 16th Royal Irish Rifles were supervising the work.[17] The workmen were supplied by the Battalions in reserve. This was believed to be a vital point at present and the whole Ulster Division was there, holding a part of the line itself. It occupied the road to Amiens and was supported by exceptionally strong artillery, whose men with their long troops of horses were observed everywhere. The bombardment of our own aeroplanes was seen every day while occasionally a Taube ventured over and was subjected to a treat from our lads.[18]

Our Battalion marched out to the railway every day. Reveille went at 5.30am, breakfast was at 6am and the parade was at 6.50am. We travelled to our work, piled arms and were told off to our different duties, many to navvy work and some to carrying rails or pushing buggies. The weather was often very wet and cold, we even had some snow. When it was good, we found the job quite pleasant, but generally it was a most muddy, unpleasant one and we often returned to our billets very wet and dirty.

While at Varennes, we were all issued with the new waterproof coats provided by the Army. We found them very useful so that we came to the conclusion that a fur coat and waterproof were far more serviceable and adaptable than a greatcoat to withstand all kinds of inclement weather. Our fur jackets were made of goatskins the hair of which was coloured black and white, they were quite warm. When we marched through a French village the ladies would greet us with a bleating noise. The next winter, however, we were issued with leather jerkins because the goatskins became very heavy when wet.

Mid-day dinner was brought out by the cooks in their field-kitchens at 12 o'clock, when we had an hour off work. We ceased our labours at 4pm. In Acheux there were two fine shops where all kinds of luxuries could be purchased also an Expeditionary Force Canteen and a YMCA hut, where Canon King often served at the counter. Canon R.G.S. King afterwards became Dean of St Columba's Derry, which position he held until about 1948, when he retired to the South of England, where he was still living in 1957.

During the day we were allowed to go shopping for fifteen minutes, in small parties under an NCO, and never did tea and pat-a-cake make such a tasty and welcome meal.

---

17   The 16th Rifles were the Pioneers of the 36th (Ulster) Division.
18   A German single-engined monoplane observation aircraft.

Captain John Griffiths, a former pupil
of Larne Grammar School, killed on
1 July 1916, buried in Ancre British
Military Cemetery, Beaumont Hamel,
the son of John and Jane Griffiths
of Chester. (Nigel Henderson)

George Kirkwood, who was mortally
wounded on 6 May 1916, dying
three days later. He came from
Alexandra Park Avenue, Belfast and
pre-war had played for Brantwood
Football Club. (Nigel Henderson)

A noticeable sight at Acheux was a big observation balloon which ascended in good weather, often to a great height. It was attached to a motor-car, was shaped like a sausage and seemed to be made of khaki-coloured material.

Tuesday 15 February to Saturday 19 November 1916: Varennes

Fifty men of 'A' Company went up for a course of instruction to the trenches, with the 8th Royal Irish Rifles. The pick of the Company were chosen but I was retained to save the remainder from troubles with vicious Froggies.

Saturday 19 February 1915 – Varennes

In the evening, just at sunset, a violent artillery action started up at the Front. At the continuous, thundering noise the lads went out into the street and the whole sky flashed red and fierce as if with the streamers of a northern sky. After an hour and a half the tremendous tumult ceased and all was calm again. We thought of the fifty chosen lads up there and wondered how they had come through this angry strafing.

Sunday 20 February 1916: Auchonvillers

It was a very wet morning and the Church Parade was cancelled. In the evening a working-party was told off for a machine-gun emplacement that was being made. We were under Lieutenant H. Hooten[19] and marched through the important town of Forceville but, beyond it, we halted for ten minutes at a reserve line of the allies, comprising very strong

---

19   Wounded on 1 July 1916.

Private Albert Laughlin, No 15139,
who was killed on 1 July 1916;
he came from Battenberg Street,
Belfast. (Nigel Henderson)

Second Lieutenant E.R. Ledlie, who was
wounded in a trench raid; he was the son
of Dr. Ledlie of Strangemore Terrace,
Crumlin Road, Belfast. (Nigel Henderson)

wire-defences, fine trenches and dugouts. We then approached Mailly-Maillet and along the road we came upon that regular succession of peculiar, concrete skeleton towers which I had noticed first on approaching the trenches at Fonquevillers and saw again at Doullens. They looked like concrete pylons of a simple form but they were on the roadside and followed its curves. Edmund Blunden in his *Undertones of War* refers to them as "the curious concrete obelisks which here are used for telegraph poles."

We passed a wood, in which several big guns were concealed under screens of tree branches. One was being pulled through as we passed and immediately afterwards the shell swung round on a derrick into the chamber. The road to the big guns was a corduroy pathway that is, one made with logs about six inches in diameter, laid touching each other. Mailly-Maillet had a fine appearance, perched on the top of a hill with a big wood at its side. The town was practically deserted by its civilian population and was now left in the hands of English troops who had canteens, messes, a cinematograph, baths etc. We marched through the town and as darkness fell we entered Auchonvillers. It was dangerous to pass along the Main Street, which commanded by German fire, so we went along a path at the back of the houses through orchards and gardens that led to our communication trench which was called First Avenue. We entered it and advanced to within two hundred yards of our first line.

The trench was in a bad condition and ran perfectly straight along the side of a road. We started to make a bend it in and deepen it, while some helped the machine-gunners to finish their dugout. The night was very clear, cold and dry with a full moon riding queen of a glorious sky. We worked hard but otherwise were left undisturbed at our task.

There were, however, signs that the war was close at hand for six German shells fired at the village, exploded with a tremendous noise. A long spell of rapid fire, English by its sound, occurred on our right; some working party had apparently been caught. We stopped labouring at 11 o'clock and marched back, through the town. The place was horribly ruined, only one wall of the Church remained and scarcely a house was standing whole, some being level with the ground. At Mailly-Maillet we had tea and early in the morning we reached our billets.

Monday 21 February 1916: Varennes

The fifty lads were back from the trenches with no casualties. They had been in the middle of the bombardment on Saturday and had hair-raising yarns to tell. They were standing-to when the German cannonade started with shrapnel and high-explosive. For twenty minutes the shells fell on either side of the trench, everywhere but in it, and still our artillery was silent. The men and officers got anxious; they expected an attack and everyone had his ammunition out at his elbow. The officers walked up and down behind them. "Keep cool men," they said, "not a shot until the Germans reach the wire, then give them hell." Soon after that our artillery started pouring high-explosives into the German first-line and tearing up perches[20] of it at a time. Several of their batteries became silent and after some time our guns ceased too. Such was the story they told and many more tales besides; the latest novelties of Fritz, silent guns, whizz-bangs and aerial torpedoes; stories of the White City, the Redan, the Sunken Road and famous *Sucrerie* which was captured by the French with such awful loss of life. Stories of trenches which were up to the thighs in water and a loaf of bread that had to satisfy nine men for a day. The battle of Verdun opened on the 21 February 1916, and the fierce fighting continued intermittently until September 1916.

Thursday 24 February 1916: Beaussart

We were working at the railways in the morning and in the evening packed up and marched to Beaussart, arriving there after sunset. A fair covering of snow was on the ground but were placed in good billets with wire-beds and were served out with straw mattresses.

Friday 25 February 1916: Beaussart

The weather was showery and we remained in billets all day. Some of the lads had to go to the railway at Acheux but our Platoon had been on fire-pickets the night before and we were not asked to go on any work. This village might be shelled any moment and, in the event of a fire breaking out, a number of men had to be ready to go and extinguish it. There were many artillery men in these billets and we had guns placed in every covert in this district. In the village, at the side of the graveyard, just behind the church, there was a howitzer known as the 'Big Gun at Beaussart'. When it spoke the whole ground trembled. It sat there, below a thin pleating of osiers, between two immense wheels, with its short, wide muzzle gaping into the sky. The village was small with one street. It had no shops and very few cafés but there was an excellent Expeditionary Force Canteen.

---

20 A perch is 5½ yards or 5 metres.

Saturday 26 February 1916: Auchonvillers

All were directed to different working parties attached to the Royal Engineers. We all walked to Mailly-Maillet and there each party was formed up and marched off. Ronnie Campbell and I were joined with two sappers. We carried several heavy planks with us, up to the entrance of First Avenue. There we commenced work, finishing a dugout for the members of an observation post of the artillery. Ronnie Campbell was a quiet fellow, from a good home I should say, with whom I became friendly at this time. His death is related about six weeks later. It was said that his commission in the Army Service Corps was sanctioned the day he was killed. Every 1 July for years afterwards a wreath to him was laid on the Cenotaph in Belfast. I thought of calling on his parents, for I was the last person probably to speak to him alive, but I shrank from this ordeal.

The ground was covered with snow and slight snow showers continued all day. Strafing was heavy and many shells could be heard bursting close to us. The dugout would be very secure and comfortable when finished. The walls and roof were composed of circular, steel plates named 'elements' but more often called 'elephants'. The dugout had thus the shape of a Roman arch and the floor was a raised, wooden one. The whole structure was deep in the ground which would be levelled in with a packing of sandbags, full of flints and perhaps a seam of concrete. The two sappers were nervous and shouted when a shell burst near them. After the work was finished they would not leave the dugout because a few explosives were falling. At last, when it was getting late, they had to move out but we had not gone far when a shell burst close to us and they lost their nerve. A few perches further on, a house was blown into atoms, and a cloud of dust and smoke, just at our side, not more than fifteen yards away, and the sappers took to their heels. Sensible guys, some might say!

Ronnie Campbell and I walked on quietly, watching the display of two soldiers who had lost their self-command and were doubling away from us. Anyway we overtook them on the road to Mailly-Maillet. Someone must have been wounded in Auchonvillers that day and had been carried down to Mailly-Maillet, for drops of blood, distinct on the white snow, marked the whole way. Eventually we reached our billets all right, some of the other parties had a little difficulty in getting safely away but no one had been hurt.

Sunday 27 February 1916: Auchonvillers

More snow had fallen during the night and a party of us spent the whole morning clearing the streets of Beaussart. In the evening I was on a large working party that went to the trenches at Auchonvillers and spent a few hours in cleaning out a communication trench leading off Second Avenue. We were not disturbed, but immediately on returning to our trench the ground was swept by a powerful searchlight. Many of us had been working above the parapet and undoubtedly would have been spotted. Edmund Blunden in his *Undertones of War* says that this searchlight was ours and that it was originally erected by the French.

Monday 28 February 1916: Auchonvillers

We squared up our billets in the morning and, in the evening, left Beaussart for the trenches. We carried our greatcoats, fur jackets, waterproof coats and rubber sheets with the small haversack, on our backs. Darkness had just fallen as we entered Auchonvillers, in shallow columns of Platoons, with an interval of three minutes marching. Our

Platoon loaded their rifles, marched down the main street and entered Second Avenue. The trench was deep, also wide and in a tumble down condition, its floor was not paved and its sides were not boarded or wired. A thaw was on and we splashed on, in single-file, through the darkness. We were up to the thighs in water sometimes and of course our socks and trousers were wringing wet. We did a left-wheel and went forward along the Sunken Road for several hundred yards, then into a trench again. A high hill was on our right, with dugouts and wooden huts built into its side.

Then a sharp turn to the right and we began to mount the hill, by a series of steps, known as 'Jacob's Ladder'. Next we went along a trench, deep I mud with sharp, narrow turnings, named 'King's Street'. The march seemed interminable but at last we reached the firing line where the 9th Inniskillings were standing-to. We fixed our bayonets, stood-to also, and the Inniskillings withdrew. We had two saps on our part and parties were led down to their posts. I was told to stand down and try to locate a dugout for myself. I managed to find one which in this part was known as the 'big dugout'. It had been about ten feet by six feet but the back end had all fallen in, leaving a big hole looking out to the sky. The doorway was facing the Germans, as these trenches were supposed to have been occupied at one time by the Hun, and so everything was the wrong way about. The sides and floor were of dirty limestone. It was about 9pm and I was wet up to the thighs also I was in a bad temper. The Inniskillings had sent down their waders for us, so they said, but we had not received them. Searching among a pile of dirty sandbags, lying on the floor, I came upon a couple of waders and changed immediately, putting on a pair of dry socks. The waders were good ones and felt comfortable, although they were an odd pair, both being made for the left foot. I pitied the lads told off for guard, who had to do duty all night with boots, socks and putties oozing with dirty water.

At midnight three of us were sent down to No 7 sap to relieve the fellows who had been there since 9pm. The way was long and torturous and the sap-head was just in front of our own wire. We continued here until stand-to in the morning. We had a cartridge in the breach of our rifles and a box of Mills grenades at our side. Our instructions were not to fire until necessity warranted it and we were not to challenge anyone approaching the wire but to treat them with a bomb immediately. This general order did not apply when patrols of our own were out. We wore a pair of gloves and a pair of mitts while on sentry in the winter. The gloves were of the ordinary pattern with separate divisions for each finger and thumb. They were of knitted, khaki wool and were worn in the usual fashion on the hands. The mitts were larger and made of cloth. Each had only two divisions, one for the thumb and the other for the fingers. The right and left hands were joined by a length of tape which was worn round the sentry's neck. Thus the second pair was always available as pouches into which the hands, clothed with the first pair, could be pushed. Also about this time we were issued with steel helmets or 'tin hats' as they were called, up to this we had worn the soft cap only. The night was cold and dark and we could not see beyond our own wire, which did not inspire us with any great confidence. It was composed of wired trestles, piled one on top of the other and tied together. It did not look a formidable obstruction to remove and the wood appeared old and rotten. The night passed quietly, however we were relieved before dawn and got back to the dugout.

Tuesday 29 February 1916: Auchonvillers

Breakfast was brought up from the village by a party from 'B' Company. In the morning I went down to the support trenches, at the foot of 'Jacob's Ladder' to draw waders. Passing along muddy King's Street I had a view of the position. I saw our trenches on two hills with the Sunken Road between. On the other hill was Donegall Pass, the new trench made by two of our Battalions in a single night, one hundred and fifty yards out in No man's land and named Donegall Pass by our Irish Primate, John Baptist Crozier. Looking to the other end of our line I saw the famous *Sucrerie*, marked by several isolated buildings. We carried back the gum-boots, but a pair could not be found for everyone and some had to pass their whole spell of duty in this awful quagmire with ordinary boots and putties.

At 6pm two of us went on sap duty and remained there until midnight; six hours in a viscous mud-hole. Tapping, such as might come from mining, had been reported from No 8 sap the previous night and we listened carefully for the noise again. Sure enough we heard the tapping, at regular intervals, during the whole evening. We listened to the transport to Beaumont-Hamel, coming in just after sunset, and the voices of the drivers could be heard, not to mention the noise of the carts and horses. Why we did not shell them I did not know. A dog, over on the other side, kept up a continuous barking for a long while and a cat also lent her musical notes.

When I visited Auchonvillers in 1928 I could not, in the time available, definitely identify any of the old landmarks. The houses had all been rebuilt in red bricks so that they presented a totally different appearance to the whitewashed walls with which we were so familiar. The trenches had completely disappeared except for a small section at Beaumont-Hamel which had been preserved intact as a memorial to the Newfoundland troops.

Wednesday 1 March 1916: Auchonvillers

I had a bit of a doze sitting in the dugout, during the remainder of the night, but from stand-to in the morning until it occurred again in the evening, I was on guard in one of the bays. With the periscope and the aid of field-glasses I had a good view of the village of Beaumont-Hamel and the trenches held by the Germans. When I was getting ready to go on the sap at midnight, a terrible explosion took place close at hand, the ground moved physically beneath our feet. On going to our tryst the lads there told us the sap held by the Inniskillings, on our left, had been mined and blown up, that the whole earth had moved and heaved and that the place had burned like a bonfire for some minutes. We heard in the morning that eight Royal Engineers, who were counter-mining, had been buried and that five had been rescued unconscious, but three were killed.

Thursday 2 March 1916: Auchonvillers

I remained, most of the day, in the dugout where we had a fire and I enjoyed a bit of a sleep. I went on sap duty at 6 for a spell of our hours only. A German, with a clarinet over in Beaumont-Hamel, entertained us for a considerable time, playing a solemn, slow tune in loud, clear notes.

Company Sergeant Major John
J. Mackey, who was wounded
while on a fatigue party close to
RE Farm in September 1916. He
had formerly worked for Messrs
W McCalla and Co, and was
awarded the Distinguished Conduct
Medal. (Nigel Henderson)

Sergeant J. Makemson, who served
in A Company. He was severely
wounded on 1 July 1916 and sent
home to recuperate. On returning
to France he was posted to the 12th
Royal Irish Rifles and was taken
prisoner during the German attack
of March 1918. (Nigel Henderson)

Friday 3 March 1916: Auchonvillers

This was our last day in the trenches and in the evening we carried our waders down to the village. We suffered the cruelty of carrying heavy officers' kits right down Third Avenue and through the village to the dump on the other side. At 5.45pm everyone stood-to in marching order, expecting to be relieved abut 8, but we remained there, with our terrible packs on our backs, and our greatcoats, fur coats and waterproofs, trebled in weight with mud and water, hanging on to our shoulders. So we endured in the dark and cold and the minutes passed so slowly.

At about 11 o'clock the relieving Battalion arrived and we waded down to Third Avenue. Here we had huge trouble in progressing, as we carried our wide, bulging kits and it was with infinite trouble that we got past long files of men laden with planks going up to their work in the mines. My shoulders were painful with the continual wearing of the equipment for four days, now with the pack in addition, they seemed to be breaking. Everything has an end, however, and at last we were struggling through the village of Auchonvillers. At the dump, we were allowed to leave behind our greatcoats in the medical station. I took advantage of this and we were enabled to finish our journey to Forceville. The whole platoon was packed in a small barn where we got into our blankets and lay as still and close as sardines in a tin. It was about 5am.

Saturday 4 March 1916: Forceville

We rose from our slumbers and had breakfast at about 10am. It was a cold, bleak day and snowing softly. Dinner and tea came in quick succession while between times we did our best to clean ourselves, but the clay was still damp on our clothes and equipment, so it was hard to remove. It was also difficult to get water in this part of the town with the result that when I had my rifle cleaned and face satisfactorily washed, it was time to go to bed.

The scarcity of clean water in the villages of the Somme was unbelievable. To shave I have sometimes used an egg-cupful of our tea, on other occasions I have gone out and searched for a puddle of rainwater in the street. In shaving, some of the chaps used a piece of sheet metal the size of our breast-pocket and made for the purpose. It was highly polished and had the advantage of being unbreakable but never gave so clear a reflection as a glass mirror.

During the night I had a disconcerting experience. The barn we occupied was the usual sort in the country, a construction of wood and mud plaster with a roof of heavy, red tiles. Outside, as it happened, four horses belonging to the Army Service Corps had been chained to a rope attached to the two wooden posts, forming half the corners of the barn. Inside, against the wall, along which the horses were tied, Lance Corporal A. Nelson and I made our bed. Carefully and with thought it had been laid down and we were soon in a deep, luxurious sleep, undisturbed by the tinkling and clanking made by the horses on their chains, as they restlessly moved about that cold, snowy night. From my sleep I was awakened by a terrific noise. Around me I felt falling, a mass of wood, earth and stone so that I believed I was buried. With vexation I thought that the worst had happened at last, and that I was entombed in my sap-head by the explosion of a mine. I realised the calamity that had happened but I was quite cool and hope came immediately.

I found I was not hurt for I felt no pain, I was not completely buried for I sniffed the air and found it fresh; there was not even the smell of gas. I felt someone moving beside me and knew that he lived too. Such was the delusion under which I laboured. Then I heard a voice say, "Anyone hurt? Strike a light." 'Was it safe to strike a light – was it wise?' I thought. But the light was struck and then the spell fell away. I was still lying in the barn with Nelson but around me was a whole mass of roof-tiles, rafters and caked mud while my blankets were wet with snow. Outside the horses were plunging about madly for it was them who had caused the trouble. With their tugging, they had shaken down a part of the wall and roof of the barn upon the sleepers below. On the face of it, it was miraculous that none of us had been hurt, considering how close we were lying. But our bed was destroyed for the reminder of the night and it still was 10 minutes to 12 o'clock. The blankets were wet with the snow which had fallen along with the tiles, and through the great opening more snow kept falling, slowly in soft, wet flakes. There was no room to shift our bed, nothing we could do but lie and stick it till the morning. Lance Corporal Albert Nelson was afterwards killed on the 1 July 1916.[21]

Sunday 5 March 1916: Forceville

The Battalion went by platoons to the baths at Acheux where every man had a few seconds under a spray of water and, leaving behind his old underclothing, was given a clean change in return. Forceville was a fairly large town and it seemed to be an important

---

21   Lance Corporal Albert Earnest Nelson, MM, No 6322, killed on 1 July 1916, the son of Albert Edward and Mary A. Nelson of Bryson Street, Belfast. He is buried in Connaught Cemetery, Thiepval, grave III.A.7. 0.

centre at that time. All day its streets were crowded with men and horses like some huge fair. But the men were all clothed in one colour, khaki, the lines of horses drew big guns and military wagons, the mules had limbers to pull along while the motors were huge so that they moved slowly and heavily. The motor despatch-riders dashed quickly through it all, and at the crossroads there was a military policeman directing the traffic. Then a Battalion of men from the trenches entered the town, they moved slowly and unsteadily while there were many stragglers. The majority of the men still wore their blue, steel helmets also their feet and legs were wet and brown with mud while their tunics and faces were white with chalk. Their fur coats, waterproofs and rifles were attached to then in every conceivable manner; often they would be chanting an obscene song. Another song to a well-known hymn tune was:

The Bells of Hell go ting-a-ling-a-ling
For you but not for me:
For me the angels sing-a-ling-a-ling,
They've got the goods for me.
Oh! Death, where is thy sting-a-ling-a-ling?
Oh! Grave, thy victory?
The Bells of Hell go ting-a-ling-a-ling
For you but not for me.[22]

At Forceville there was also a fine canteen. In the evening, several shrapnel shells burst over the town but no one was hurt it seemed. As our billet had been made uninhabitable by the tricks of the horses during the night, we had to move to fresh lodgings. We got into good quarters and in the afternoon there were a lot of inspections and a list of deficiencies were taken. I could not lay my hands on my greatcoat which I had left behind me in Auchonvilliers but I did not mind if I never saw it again for it was not serviceable, being too heavy when wet and the tail gathered too much mud.

Monday 6 March 1916: Mesnil
In the morning we cleaned up our billets and prepared for a move. A Taube came over during the day and dropped several bombs. One of our fellows was hit in the chin and nose while standing near me outside the billet. Some more damage was done and there were several narrow escapes. Two artillery horses were killed and one of our own shells which had not exploded fell into a stable and buried itself deep in the floor, narrowly missing a soldier and two mules. The anti-aircraft guns were familiarly known as 'Archies' and were often seen behind our lines. They were mounted on lorries which were drawn in to the side of the road and were accompanied by other vehicles which contained the crew and ammunition. At first we collected the nose-caps of German shells that had exploded and marvelled at the amount of solid brass or aluminium in one and the precision of the scales that were engraved on them. We left Forceville in the evening and marching through Martinsart, arrived near dusk at the ruined and deserted town of Mesnil. Twenty of us were put in the priest's house, a fine, large, brick residence.

---

22 A British airmen's song from the Great War, it was a parody on the song 'She Only Answered Ting-a-ling-a-ling'. Lines five and six of the song quote St Paul's words on the resurrection in 1 Corinthians 15: 55, used in the burial service: "O death, where is thy sting? O grave, where is thy victory?"

We had the whole building to ourselves, for in case of a bombardment the cellar could only accommodate twenty.

There were many books lying about the rooms, some of them very old and bound in costly leather. They were chiefly of a religious or ecclesiastical nature: *Histoire de l'Eglise*, *Les Oeuvres de Cardinal*, *Les Meditations de Saints* etc. There were also books on Horticulture, Health and Cooking. Close to the house was the Church which had suffered rather badly. There were many shell holes in the roof and walls. Inside all was debris, and the harmonium was a wreck, while the statuary had been removed. The village had been pretty and well-built at one time but now it was the abode of only rats and soldiers.

Tuesday 7 March 1916: Martinsart

The spick-and-span craze had seized the Company again, fostered by the arrival of a new Major, H.C.J. Bliss and the departure of Colonel Chichester to hospital. We had an inspection of rifles and equipment at 9am. Notwithstanding the fact that water was tremendously hard to obtain we were expected to turn out with perfectly clean clothing and equipment besides being properly shaved and washed. We were subjected to a lecture for not being up to the mark by the Sergeant-Major J.J. Mackey and that bright Lieutenant R.V. Robb.[23] So the Platoon stood up on the road, in the place where we might be shelled at any moment, and were harangued about a spot of candle grease found on a cap. In the afternoon the rest of the lads went away on a working party and I went to Martinsart with Quartermaster Sergeant Moore to buy some extra provisions. We found only several small grocery bars in the place, but after a bit of exhilarating bargaining with the sprightly French ladies we gathered up some beer, wine, tinned fruits and biscuits. On the road back the guns were in action close by our sides.

Wednesday 8 March 1916: Mesnil

In the morning at 2am were awakened according to orders and dressed to go on a working party. We were dismissed however as it had frozen so persistently that the ground was too hard to dig. During the day we had another inspection. I was much annoyed by an attack of diarrhoea that took me continually to the latrines which were placed in a rather cold and breezy orchard. The latrines consisted of a long pole supported about eighteen inches above the ground and a trench at the back, the whole being surrounded by a canvas screen. Often there was no screen or stick, there might only be the trench. There was also some snow on the ground. It was a most miserable and exhausting time for me, for as soon as I had cleaned my boots and entered the billet to warm myself, I found it necessary to go out and thereby dirty them again.

Thursday 9 March 1916: Mesnil

The fellows left early on a working party and I went on sick parade. I was given the diarrhoea mixture, a slimy, repugnant draught, hard to swallow. My internal organs began to take a more normal condition of working and on returning to the inspection room at 5pm, I had a normal temperature and was told to carry on.

---

23 Lieutenant Harold Victor Robb, died of wounds on 3 July 1916, buried in Belfast City Cemetery, grave I 39.

Friday 10 March 1916: Mesnil
There were more inspections, except for which, we remained in the priest's house where we maintained a good wood fire all day. Timber could be had quite easily from the many ruined houses about. I got a few letters written also.

Saturday 11 March 1916: Hamel
There were still more inspections, the spick-and-span idea had gone mad. As it was falling dark we left, by platoons, for our positions in the trenches. No 1 Platoon was to be the ration party and was to be placed in cellars in the ruined village of Hamel. This village was 16 kilometres from Mesnil and was reached by descending a hill which ran at right angles to a part of the German trenches and was enfiladed by their machine gunners and snipers. Going down this road we walked in single file, five paces apart. The next platoon was at a five-minute interval behind us. We marched silently along and arrived amid the ruins of Hamel without mishap. The night was misty. We were placed in a good cellar below a lot of ruins and the 11th Inniskillings, whose place we took, filed out silently, laid hold of their packs and went away in the gloom. We had just got our respective places booked when the section had to go on a ration party to draw the next day's rations from Quartermaster Sergeant Moore's store at Mesnil.

We carried our rifles with bandoliers and at the store we got the rations of coke and bread, all put up in sandbags and labelled for their respective destinations such as 'platoon', 'police', 'signals', 'cookhouse', 'officers' etc. Each man carried two bags, tied together and the weight was not too great. Then we travelled down the exposed road to Hamel to be told off to receive ammunition for the Lewis gunners. So we had another journey to Mesnil and a heavier load to bring back. Meanwhile tea had been drawn from the cookhouse and we all had a strengthening drink before lying down for a rest.

Sunday 12 March 1916: Hamel
Today we were on a ration party at Hamel. We rose at 5.45am, stood-to in the cellar and at 6.15 went to draw breakfast from the cook house. The four cookers were placed about a kilometre out of the town, on the road to Albert, under the railway embankment. The view was pretty in the morning sun and mist, a broad, well-kept road, with a high wooded hill on one side and on the other the double railway track, high above the road and sheltering the cookers. After dark the road to the cook house can be used but in the daytime one must go along the deep trench made at its side. After having delivered the breakfast to several points widely apart we had our own. Then the dixies had to be washed, filled at the well and carried to the cookhouse, again along the same hard-bottomed communication trench. Carrying the dixie in the trench was usually done by a pair of men with a yoke between them from which the vessel was hung. Later on the dixies were replaced by large thermos flasks.

Similar work had to be done for dinner, tea and supper, potatoes and vegetables had to be cleaned or peeled and extra water drawn. Fortunately the wells were quite easy to manage here, being only about ten feet deep. We finished roughly about 10.30pm, truly a day of work, but the weather was fine and warm with lots of sunshine. In the morning there was a mist but in the evening the declining sun shone fully in the enemy trenches. Three great lines of German trenches could be seen plainly running along a bare hill, east and west on a slope to the right of us and across the valley. Our trenches opposite them were in Thiepval Wood, but they changed direction to north and south as they ran along the summit of an elevation towards Albert.

The German lines which were situated in front of us were lost to view behind a hill. Down in the valley was the railway where the cookers were hidden and along it ran a large stream, the River Ancre, with areas of marshy ground. These went through 'no man's land' and abounded in waterfowl which had become quite habituated to the shelling that went on continually. With the shrapnel bursting over them or the hot particles of iron falling, steaming and sizzling in the water, they remain un-alarmed. From the ruins over our cellar, with our field-glasses, we had a good look at the three German lines and the sights were especially interesting when they were being bombarded by our artillery. Of course our billets – in fact the whole village – were very open to the Germans and there was a lot of sniping. As one walked about, it was 'phiss' and a German bullet six inches from one's head was a common affair.

Monday 13 March 1916: Hamel

It was a beautiful spring morning with primroses and daffodils growing up amid the ruins. During the day I was on different fatigue jobs among which I had to take a box of ammunition over to the Castra Nova post where Jack Armstrong was. He was in charge of a guard, on a small bridge over the River Ancre, and the men were having a classy time, sitting in the sun, on the meadow land reading and writing. I think Jack Armstrong was the soldier I admired most. He was handsome and spoke French and some German. None of our concerts were complete until he had recited 'Gunga Din' and 'The Green Eye of the Little Yellow God'. He was a Lance-Corporal and in the Permanent Patrol. I was out with him in 'no man's land' dozens of times and I always admired him for his coolness and resource. I was with him on the 1 July 1916, when I was wounded; he was decorated with the Military Medal for his services that day. After I left France and Belgium he was promoted until he became Sergeant Major but he was missing after the Battle of Ypres in 1917.[24] Over the river where our support line was, the shrapnel was bursting in great, black clouds but that did not matter. After stand-down in the evening I went with the ration party to Mesnil and coming along the road we were treated to a few snipers' bullets.

Tuesday 14 March 1916: Hamel

This was a repetition of Sunday's work but I had an extra bit to do and how it was done was illuminating. Six of us, who had been trotting after rations all day, were sent into the firing line to repair a bit of a trench that had fallen in. After a long walk we arrived at the spot to be sent back for shovels to go up again to do thirty men's work before coming back to draw the supper.

---

24 Company Sergeant Major John Leslie (Jack) Armstrong, No 16175, died on 16 August 1917, the son of William and Emily Armstrong of Clifton Park Avenue, Belfast, commemorated on the Tyne Cot Memorial.

Private Thomas Martin, who was known as 'Tom' in A Company, killed on 6 May 1916. He came from the Springfield Road in Belfast. (Nigel Henderson)

Private J.H. McBratney of Comber County Down; he was one of those of A Company who was killed on 6 May 1916. (Nigel Henderson)

Wednesday 15 March 1916: Mound Keep

We had more good weather and I had not much work to do all morning. I evaded it and spent my time reading the *Adventures of Gerard* by Conan Doyle. After dinner our billets were subjected to a heavy bombardment from shrapnel. I was in the cellar when it started, but some of the lads outside had narrow escapes. More walls were levelled above us and blasts of hot, dusty air swept through the cellar at each explosion. The trenches were also bombarded and Sergeant C Penman was killed and buried in the chalk.[25] Several other lads, mostly officers' servants, who were engaged on cooking the dinner were buried in their dugout but although severely hurt they were all able to walk down to the village.

We left the village at dusk, the 11th Inniskillings taking our place, and marched along the road past the cookhouse to the last barrier beyond which the transport was not allowed to come. The road on our side of the last barrier was hidden in places from German observation by high, vertical nets camouflaged with branches of trees. Also, to prevent the enemy from looking into our trenches, it was necessary to roof certain parts with sandbags; this made progress through them more troublesome than usual.

There, two platoons took over an outpost called Mound Keep, guarding the railway, the double broad-gauge line that ran to Albert. On arriving there I was put on guard, at a gas alarm post, out on the edge of a wood, behind our supports. We were on this post for twenty-four hours. The gas alarm was a copper shell-case about fifteen inches long, suspended and intended to be used like a dinner gong. It was found at intervals all over the trenches but was never used while I was there. It was a beautiful, moonlight night and looking over the parapet I had a fine view of the trees with the wire entanglements fixed to them, while beyond that were the marshes, with the slow river winding in the

---

25   Lance Sergeant Charles Penman, No 16936, killed on 15 March 1916, age 19 years. The son of Mrs A. Penman of Lyle Street, Belfast. Hamel Military Cemetery, Beaumont Hamel, grave I.E.15.

middle. The German line was just on the horizon, behind Albert, and shelling took place at occasional intervals during the night. The bursting shrapnel was a beautiful and fierce sight, the shell at the moment of exploding glowed like a huge, red ball, high up in the sky. The waterfowl made a continual, gabbling din as they fluttered about the marshes with its long grass and the bullfrogs croaked all night long.

Thursday 16 March 1916: Mound Keep
We stayed on the gas alarm post at Mound Keep until we were relieved at 6pm. The guardroom was a shed built up against the railway cutting and its sides and roof were of sandbags. It was a roomy and comfortable place for six men and one NCO. That night I slept in a dugout with wire beds, our blankets had arrived and I had my clothes off for the first time in six days.

Friday 17 March 1916: Mesnil
This was St Patrick's Day and it was beautiful and spring like. The previous night I had received a box of shamrock from Meg and I wore it today in honour of her and the fair country in which she lived with its noble Patron Saint.[26] At 8 o'clock our section fell in and we marched through the small wood to Martinsart where each had a bath in a tub and were allowed to take as much time over it as we liked. In the evening we prepared to move, two platoons of 'D' Company coming to take our place.

I and several others had a bit of excitement from a German machine gun. We were wheeling some officers' kit in a dog cart, with muffled wheels, along the road to a dump in the small wood. 'Tat-tat-phizz-phizz', up went the cart and we fell flat on our faces, rolling over to the side of the road where there was some cover from a thorn hedge. 'Tat-tat-phizz-phizz' continued the bullets, passing through the thorn hedge a few inches above our bodies and some striking the middle of the road and glinting off with a flash of fire. Then all was silence and we rose, gripped the dog cart and began to move stealthily on. We had not gone many yards when the ominous rattle started again, and again we hugged the mother earth. During the journey to the dump, and back with the empty cart, this performance occurred several times and we gave a sigh of relief when we reached the railway cutting again. At 6.30 our section marched away from Mount Keep and we found our billet in Mesnil, in a comfortable little cellar which contained five of us.

Saturday 18 March 1916: Mesnil
In the forenoon it was a clean up all around and after dinner the whole Company was inoculated against typhoid by the Medical Officer, Captain M.J.H. Garvin. The injection was put in the left arm, near the shoulder and the operation was practically without pain but we all went to bed early.

Sunday 19 March 1916: Mesnil
I awakened with a stiff, painful arm and a thick taste in my mouth but did not find myself otherwise out of normal. Many of the fellows complained of being sick and having headaches, anyhow we were all allowed to pass the day as we liked. I remained in bed until mid-day, then arose and did a little bit of writing in this little book. I have been

---

26   According to the *Ballymena Observer* half a ton of shamrock was shipped out to the Ulster Division for
distribution among the troops.

scribbling now for over an hour and have brought the journal up to this day. So here I sat, amid the ruined houses of Mesnil, in this deserted farmyard. The day was sunny and warm while the blue sky was curtained with hazy, white clouds. The birds were chirping as they fluttered amongst the rafters or sought nourishment from the cold, empty hearth.

This had been a pretty village in a great, agricultural district and the binder, emblem of prosperity, was found in every ruin. In this yard there were two of them drawn into a corner, an Osborne and a McCormick machine.

I also inspected a travelling threshing machine which had been made in Germany. It not only separated the straw and chaff but it also cleaned and bagged the wheat. It was worked by a horse in a box treading on a moveable staircase. His weight caused the staircase to move down and he had to climb quickly upwards, otherwise his hindquarters came against the points of some nails at the lower end of the box. Aeroplanes, friendly and hostile, were up in the air all morning and received each his peppering from the guns. 'Oh, that this war were over, the world was weary of it!' An American lady had written that Europe was sick of the war. Someone had found in this statement another proof that a woman could not be entrusted with a secret. Would that I were free of this tyranny which every good soldier of the King must bear without a murmur. Oh, to be at liberty again, to be back at one's profession, for the Army was no profession for one with intuition or imagination. I was classified as an intelligent and capable Private, a very useful man but one to be kept in his place.

Monday 20 March 1916: Mesnil
We had an examination of arms by the doctor, N.J.H. Garvin in the morning and during the evening we had no parades. These have been two of the best days' holiday since we came to France.

Tuesday 21 March 1916: Hamel
Tonight the Battalion left Mesnil for the trenches and Sergeant James E. Makemson and I went early to find out the position for the platoon. In July 1956 I heard Sergeant James E. Makemson speaking on the BBC of his experiences on 1 July 1916. He was shot through the arm that day. After a spell at home he was sent to France, to the 12th Royal Irish Rifles, but was taken prisoner during the retreat in 1918. He now has a good position as Deputy Gas Inspector for the Belfast Corporation and is looking forward to retiring at the end of 1957.

Sergeant Makemson and I proceeded to Hamel by the long way, through the wood and along the trench beside the Grand Ligne. Our platoon was to hold a portion to the north of the town. The trenches were good being exceptionally dry and tidy after the long spell of good weather. The German positions, exactly opposite, were not visible from our parapet and, being on the other side of the hill we had no view beyond our own wire. But the German trenches, to the right of the hill on the other side of the river, were very plain.

In the hollow there were the river and marshes and also a long space with no trenches, the forward positions being held by outposts, the most important of these was the Greystone Bridge, opposite the Mill which was situated between the two lines. This description of our trenches and the German fortification, as seen from Hamel, is partly repeated under the dates 12 March 1916 and 3 April 1916. From Hamel we had a good

Second Lieutenant A.J. McClellan of Ballyboley, Larne, a good friend of James McRoberts, killed on 1 July 1916. (Nigel Henderson)

Lieutenant William McCluggage, killed 1 July 1916. (Nigel Henderson)

view across the valley, of the shelling of the German trenches in front of Thiepval Wood. It was noticeable at this time that many of our shells fell short and burst in 'no man's land'. We were told that this was the fault of American ammunition.

Tuesday 21 March to Monday 27 March 1916: Hamel

We had a spell of six days in the trenches and I was on sap duty each night, on some occasions for four hours but on others for two hours. The first day was dry but inclined to be cold. On the second morning we had a good fall of snow and the weather continued bad until we left, a slight improvement being observed the last day. The trenches got dirty and matters a little uncomfortable but still far from intolerable. During the day we had a lot of sandbagging to do, the old sandbags having rotted away in many places. One morning a signpost was observed outside our wires and on looking at it, through the telescope, we could read the inscription in English, 'God punish England'. That evening Mr F. Corscadden and two men immediately after dusk, left our sap, advanced about fifty yards toward the post, fixed a wire to it and returning, hauled in the suspicious object, nothing alarming occurring at all. The words were crudely made by a pencil on what seemed to be the rough side of a wooden box.

One night a large patrol entered the Mill but found nothing, although we expected the capture of machine guns or prisoners. The last night I was on a patrol of ten men under Mr R.V. Gracey. We remained out from 10pm to about 2am and entered a great valley between the two lines. On the side of the hollow, nearer to us, we found a great number of curious excavations which aroused our suspicion and astonishment. We thought at first they were shell holes, but as we met more of them we noticed they were all in a rough line and of a certain, similar construction, as if a few hundred men in extended order, had worked for abut thirty minutes and then suddenly ceased. 'Strange,' we said and went to examine the other side of the valley but met nothing unusual. The depression gradually widened out at the left and here we approached the German wires and lay still. We could distinctly hear the talking and shouting while there was a big amount of laughing. Several star shells fell right on top of us but we were left undisturbed and returned to the safety of our own lines. We each carried forty rounds in our pockets and ten in the rifles, besides having four Mills bombs. Our bayonets were dulled, our faces blackened and we carried no equipment, we made certain of our direction by the wind and stars for the lines run due east and west at this point.

Monday 27 March 1916: Mesnil
We had thus a fairly good time in the trenches also enjoyed a liberal supply of food and coke. I left early with a party to prepare the billets in Mesnil. Our Platoon was going back to the priest's house. I had had the blankets drawn for the boys and a fine fire lighted, only to find on their arrival all of us were for guard, so another night without sleep. Six of us, under Moore Parkhill, were on the duty, at the end of the village on the road to Martinsart. We had a pretty good guardroom, lighted a fire, gathered up some rations and had a fairly decent time altogether.

Tuesday 28 March 1916: Mesnil
The guard was relieved for a few hours while we had a cold and unsatisfactory bath in the village, after which we returned to duty and remained there until relieved at 6pm. The weather was quite fine now although it was cold, especially in the morning.

Wednesday 29 March 1916: Mount Keep
We went on a working party, the weather keeping fine and buried a cable near Mount Keep.

Thursday 30 March 1916: Authuille
We worked at the making of new dugouts in the trenches at Authuille.

Friday 31 March 1916: Martinsart
We filled sandbags for the Royal Engineers at Martinsart.

Saturday 1 April 1916: (All Fools' Day) Martinsart
We made no jokes – it was more than a joke to be here. We filled sandbags in the square at Martinsart for the Royal Engineers, to protect a bomb store. The day was glorious, but we had a lot of work to do, about seventy-five bags from each man were expected.

Sunday 2 April 1916: Hamel
The weather was lovely and we had no work to do as we were going to the trenches that night. In the morning I was lying outside in the garden, reading an old *Strand Magazine* of the year 1909. I was interested in an article which was about universities and a commercial life so I did not trouble to look up at the Taube above me, although the shells were busting quickly and I had noticed the signal, by whistle from the sentry, warning men to take cover from hostile aircraft. Suddenly there was a loud rushing noise

and realizing what was going to happen, I dashed into the priest's hall and took cover behind its walls. Immediately the bomb burst, filling the air with dust and made a large hole in the garden next door, about fifteen yards from where I had been lying. I was told that the aeroplane was a Fokker which was a mystery and menace to the RFC.

After dinner we tried to organise a football match in a field near us but it was hot, besides there were ditches, shell holes and wire so that the project was not a great success. We left the village after sunset at about 7 o'clock and arrived safely in the trenches at Hamel.

We were posted to a part of the line to the right of where we had been stationed formerly. Numbers 1 and 2 sections were put in a classy dugout in which there was space for the number of men and standing room as well. It was down, deep in the ground and reached by descending a shaft of over a dozen steps. The evening was beautiful and it was a wonderful sensation arriving dry and clean in the trenches also going into a spacious dugout. I was not on sentry-go that night.

Monday 3 April 1916: Hamel

I was on day duty, two hours on and four off, thus I had the short night free, except for perhaps an hour or two on a working party. During the winter months at stand-to in the morning a ration of rum was issued to the troops in the front line. It consisted of a small glass of the spirit which was poured from an earthenware jar by an officer and I took it along with the others. In the summer we had a small glass of lime juice several times. French soldiers, it was said, had a daily ration of wine. This night I helped to deepen a sap-head. From our sentry post one had a fine view of our wire, silhouetted against the skyline. The German trenches which were exactly opposite were not visible at all. I was out on a small working party that night.

Tuesday 4 April 1916: Hamel

The weather continued to be good and I remained on day sentry. The two hour spell passed very quickly, basking in the sun, and in my leisure moments I read *The Master of Ballintrae* but found it much less interesting than *Kidnapped* or *Treasure Island*. There was a lot of shelling.

Wednesday 5 April 1916: Hamel

In the evening, while I was on sentry, the Germans threw over ten trench mortars. These could be seen coming through the air; in appearance they were like footballs. They generally arrived in pairs, the one a few yards behind the other and they exploded with a tremendous uproar, sending up a huge amount of earth and darkening the sky with dust. I was peppered with dirt several times. That night I was on patrol, under Mr R.V. Gracey, examining the damage done to our wire by the trench mortars. We were out for about three hours, cold business I found it.[27]

---

27   The Battalion War Diary states that this patrol was carried out on the night of 4 April and was commanded by Second Lieutenant Gracey. The enemy trench mortars were silenced for a while when the supporting howitzers delivered counter-battery fire. The weather was described as fine and the trenches dry.

Memorial plaque to McFadzean
VC. (Nigel Henderson)

Private David McKeown, killed
on 6 May 1916. He came
from Tudyniskey, Dromara,
County Down and was 24
years old. (Nigel Henderson)

Thursday 6 April 1916: Hamel

This evening while I was on sentry, our wire and front trenches were weakened by a number of high explosives, these shells I am willing to admit annoyed me at the time. They came ringing through the air then as they approached the ground they seemed to rush forward, towards the listener with a terrible vicious hiss. It was impossible to believe that they were not going to explode at one's feet. I stood in a trance, for about an hour listening to this music and I confess that as I ducked double in the trench, I felt my eyes rolling in my head.

As a result our wires were messed up a bit and two repairing parties went out after dusk. I was on the smaller one. There were three only of us without a covering party, Lance Corporal Jack Mahood, R. Campbell and myself. We had a number of fresh corkscrew iron pickets to be inserted in the ground and several coils of barbed wire entwined around them. We had finished and just returned to the dugout when a bombardment of our lines suddenly started. The hour was about 9pm. The dugout was a large one with an entrance at each end and Ronnie and I had a corner of it to ourselves. We thus had two walls on which to hang our belongings and to perch our candles.

I remember Ronnie anticipating a quiet time until stand-to because we had been on sentry all day and a working party in the beginning of the night. Besides he had received a parcel that day and was looking forward to a peaceful glance at the magazines it contained before we went to sleep. Then an alarm went and Ronnie left by one doorway and I by the other. Usually he and I, at stand-to, occupied the same bay but this night he held it alone. I was in a bay along with a fellow called George Knott and I started shouting in order to encourage him and myself. After the war I heard of Knott as a railway employee somewhere about Clones.

The bombardment was increasing in intensity and everybody was ordered by Sergeant Major J.J. Mackay to stand-to. Coming out of the dugout into the open, the sight was terrible and the din astounding. We took up our places in the front line, fixed bayonets and loaded up ten rounds. I was a little frightened at first for the high explosive was tearing up our trenches. As I glanced along the line, great clouds of smoke could be seen rolling up to the sky where the explosions had lighted. Whizz-bangs came bursting over our heads, spreading their deadly shrapnel and trench mortars were crossing over thick, their course traced through the air by a trail of sparks. Machine guns were pumping and pumping. At last, Mr R. Renwick came round, and we received the joyful instruction to blaze away. We got up on the fire step and starting off, each and all of us obtained his nerve. Our artillery had got going and the shells were roaring overhead like so many rushing, express trains. Our rifle fire was sweeping the ground and glancing off our wires.

We could not see the enemy trenches but with the sight at normal and firing low, we could depend on finding their lines. The whole air was full of a roaring, shrieking music, like what one could imagine when a huge forest was on fire, urged on by a mighty wind. I kept firing away. I looked to the right and saw that the Inniskillings did not appear to be engaged. I looked behind and saw the village beneath the flares of bursting shrapnel. The Germans sent off many star shells which added to the scene, and their occasional red and green flare signals added to the colour.

Our ammunition was running short now but more was coming, brought by the officers' servants and bandsmen. David Paterson was among them, giving a cheerful word to everyone. 'Want any ammunition Mac?' 'Yes, throw me a couple of bandoliers.' 'Right O,' and hauling up his bandoliers he went on his way shouting, 'Here comes Gunga Din – any more ammunition for the Home Defenders?' Kipling's 'Gunga Din' was a familiar recitation by Jack Armstrong of our Company. I was up the trench several times on messages, 'Pass up word to 'D' Company to stop that machine gun,' Ammunition at the double for 'B' Company,' 'Shovels for 'B' Company, the ammunition is buried.' I saw that the parapet had been blown in at several places and I realised that some poor fellows must have lost their lives.

J.G. Henderson, usually a dull, uninteresting fellow rose to the occasion and found himself evidently in his element. "Well done lad," he said, addressing himself, "you get a cigarette case" and, putting his hand in his pocket, he pulled out his cigarette case and laid it on the parapet. "Well done, again, lad," he continued, "a notebook this time," and on he went with his performance.

The question was now raised what had happened to the big covering and wiring parties under Sergeant J. Makesom outside the sap? Then came word that Bertie Laughlin was wounded.

Meanwhile Doctor M.J.H. Garvin had arrived and I was sent down to the village to bring up the stretcher-bearers. I got off the fire-step again, my rifle was scorching hot, its action was still and the oil was boiling out of it. Down the communication trench I met the stretcher-bearers coming up. In the firing line once more, I found we had a lot of casualties; the firing had ceased now, the bombardment having lasted two hours. Until almost daybreak, I helped to remove the wounded, first Alec Campbell, then S. McAdam and then H. Coates. Alec Campbell was usually known as 'Fatty' to distinguish him from Ronnie Campbell as they both belonged to the same Section. It was strange that they both should be our only fatal casualties in that section that night, for 'Fatty' died in the ambulance before reaching hospital.[28]

This was severe work; the patients had received bad wounds which had been dressed in the nearest shelters. The stretcher-bearers stripped to the shirt, smeared up the elbows in hot blood, were pulling off tunics and trousers, cutting away shirts and applying first-aid dressings. When ready to be shifted, the patients had to be hauled along the narrow fire trenches to the communication trench, where they were put on stretchers. At every sharp turn they had to be hauled off the stretcher, pulled round the corner and placed on the stretcher again. All this had to be done in a narrow passage where there was no room to stand sideways and support the body of the poor, wounded fellow. Simpler turns could be mastered by raising up the stretcher, outside the trench.

Down in the Medical Officer's place the wounded had accumulated and a dead Sergeant, W. Stephenson from 'D' Company, was laying there, his face covered with a ground sheet.[29] Returning to the dugout I found the lads had stood down, extra sentries being posted. I was astounded to learn that Ronnie Campbell was missing, believed to be buried in the trench. Immediately afterwards a party that had been working on the place, returned to give us the news that it was indeed Ronnie – they produced his pay-book. His rifle and steel helmet had been blown to pieces: his head could not be found.[30]

We then had a drink of hot cocoa that had been kept for us and lay down for about an hour's rest until stand-to called us out. During the day we cleaned out the trenches and disinfected the places still stained with blood and particles of flesh. Report had it that the Germans had entered the trenches on our left occupied by the South Wales Borderers and leaving some of their own dead had got back with a number of prisoners.

I then heard the story about the big wiring and covering squads under Sergeant J.E. Makesom, outside the sap. When the bombardment started, the wiring party got back to the trenches carrying back several wounded, but the covering squad was isolated out in 'no man's land', about twenty yards in front of our wire, and one of the party, Bertie Laughlin, was wounded by one of the first shells. They could not return on account of our rifle fire, so they took cover in a shell hole, where they lay together with the wounded chap, all clinging to the earth. A trench mortar alighted about two yards from them, they heard it striking the ground and allowed it four seconds to explode and blow them all sky high, but it was a dud. Then J. Brown volunteered to creep back, under the wires of the sap and ask for the rifle fire to be stopped for a little time to give them an opportunity of returning. He accomplished this, returning with Lance Corporal Nelson to the party and carried back Bertie Laughlin.

---

28 Private Alex Campbell, No 14173, died on 7 April 1916, the son of Mrs Campbell of Nore Street, Belfast.

29 Sergeant William Stephenson, No 19849, died on 7 April 1916, age 25 years, the son of William R. and Fanny Stephenson of Fitzwilliam Street, Belfast, buried in Hamel Military Cemetery, I.E.18, Beaumont Hamel.

30 Rifleman Randolph Churchill Bestall Campbell, No 14168, killed on 6 April 1916, age 21 years. The son of Mr H.A. and Mrs C.E. Campbell of Cyprus Avenue, Belfast and a native of Ballynahinch, County Down, buried in Hamel military Cemetery, Beaumont Hamel, grave 1.E.20.
Rifleman Alec Campbell, No 14173, died 7 April 1916, age 19 years, the son of Agnes and the late Louis Campbell of Nore Street, Belfast. Buried in Forceville Communal Cemetery.

Lance Corporal A.E. Nelson, who
served in A Company and was killed
on 1 July 1916. (Nigel Henderson)

Private Norman Paisley, taken prisoner
on 1 July 1916. (Nigel Henderson)

Jackie Brown received the Military Medal for bringing in Bertie Laughlin.[31] Bertie Laughlin survived and almost any day, is to be found in the office of R.G. Laughlin & Sons Ltd., Hardware and Cutlery Merchants, 19 Queen's Square, Belfast. In 1957 he is absolutely fit but still bears on his face the mark of the wound received that night. Both Brown and Lance Corporal A. Nelson were recommended for the Distinguished Conduct Medal and D. Paterson was mentioned for courageous conduct.[32] He was sent with water to a machine gunner but could not reach him by the trenches, so he climbed up over the parapet and, guided by the sound, arrived at the spot. The machine gunner, a picture of desperation behind his steaming machine said, "Who the hell are you?" "14th, with water," Paterson replied. "God bless your little soul" was the answer. Another story was told by 'D' Company about Captain S. Willis. The Captain was struggling along with a box of ammunition for the lads when a voice was heard from the fire step, "Sammie, Sammie, come quick'" The Captain hastened to the distressed man, who, bending forward, asked "Any cigarette cards Sammie?"[33] Another story from 'D' Company was how they pissed on their rifles to cool them.

Friday 7 April 1916: Hamel

It was quiet after the storm, dead being reported by the artillery observers along the German wire. News also reached us how the enemy had raided trenches on our left occupied by the South Wales Borders and had returned with a number of prisoners.

---

31 Private Jack Brown came from Avoca Street, Belfast, he would be seriously wounded on 1 July. Two brothers were also on active service.
32 Brown and Nelson both served in 'A' Company.
33 Captain Willis was killed on 1 July 1916. He was the son of the late Jacob and Mrs Willis: husband of Mary Christina Wilis of 'Lynncrest', Coleraine Road, Portrush, County Antrim. He is commemorated on the Thiepval Memorial, Pier and Face 15A and 15B.

These South Wales Borderers belonged to the 29th Division which had recently returned from Gallipoli. Their first impression was that there was no fighting here and their comment invariably was, "You should have been at Suvla Bay." There was an end to such talk after this bombardment and raid.

Saturday 8 April 1916: Mount Keep

It remained fairly quiet and we left the trenches in the evening, being relieved by the Inniskillings. We went to Mount Keep where six of us had a comfortable and secure dugout.

Sunday to Friday 9 – 14 April 1916: Mount Keep

We remained at Mount Keep; the weather was good the first two days but got cold and wet afterwards. We did twenty-four hours' guard on the road at the barrier, carried rations and cleaned up about the railway. On the whole we had an easy time and best of all we had a canteen with us.

Friday to Thursday 14 – 20 April 1916: Hamel

I was on the permanent patrol for the trenches. We entered Hamel in the afternoon and ten of us, all old scouts, took up our residence in a fine cellar where we soon made ourselves very comfortable. We had a good stove, found quantities of wood to chop and did bits of extra cooking for ourselves. There were two iron beds in the place and the rest of us made easy mattresses for ourselves by stealing several hundreds of sandbags. At night, the approach to the cellar was swept by machine gun fire and we had many a joke dodging the energetic and persistent gunner Fritz. The permanent patrol was a happy lot and we had numerous good sing-songs and much clean fun in that old cellar. 'For the moon shines bright tonight' and 'You are going back to Dixie' were favourite tunes but we did not despise 'Just before the battle Mother.' The proper version of this song I think is:

> For the moon shines bright tonight on Pretty Red Wing,
> The birds are sighing, the night wind crying
> But we preferred to sing:
> For the moon shines tonight on Charlie Chaplain
> His boots are cracking for want of blacking
> And his tight, baggy trousers they need mending

Before we send him to the Dardanelles

Near the Mill, we were divided into parties. A companion and I stretched ourselves as sentries on the grass while Mr Lack and two others entered the building.[34] They were a long time away but at last they returned and taking our places, we were given the opportunity of visiting the Mill ourselves.

We were out scouting practically every night but sometimes it was a listening patrol in the dip of 'no man's land'. This was cold, freezing work and although we maintained a post out there, each night from 8pm to 3am, we never noticed any Germans. One night

---

34   Second Lieutenant R.L. Lack was the Battalion Intelligence Officer; he was mortally wounded on 2 July and died on 18 July 1916. Buried in Thames Ditton (St. Nicholas) Churchyard.

we entered the Mill that was supposed to be an enemy outpost and credited with being fortified with a machine gun. We explored the numerous rooms, cellars and lofts but found nothing, not even a souvenir to carry back. A horse rotting in the middle of the yard was the only interesting relic in the ruin.

Another night Mr R.L. Lack, our Platoon Commander, was challenged by a German sentry in a sap by a word which sounded like 'Onai', repeated twice. The sentry then fired at a range of six yards and missed. He, or probably another sentry behind him, flung a weak concussion bomb which exploded in his own wire doing us no injury. Our lads then threw in two bombs which exploded successfully, and retired safely. Other interesting souvenirs discovered were a pair of German jack boots, a dead German practically buried, a good specimen of a German rifle and a German hand-grenade.

During the day we were on observation work which was carried on from several posts, the chief one looked across the valley, over the top of the Mills and into the German trenches on the other side. We possessed a fine telescope and had a good view of an open traverse which showed very plainly everyone passing up or down it or into what seemed to be an officers' dugout.

The old waiter of this latter place was a well-known figure to each of us. He was tall and stout with red face and snow-white hair, while he wore corduroy trousers, black cardigan and a small, dark circular cap. He moved very slowly and I could often see his shadow before he appeared. He washed his pots outside the dugout.

In general, the Germans were big and well-built but there was a striking exception in the appearance of several small, slim, youthful figures who were dressed in dark, bluish-grey material, with round caps having a black band. They sometimes had black belts. Also several were seen with spiked helmets but I never observed anyone with equipment or rifle.[35]

Working parties in shirt sleeves, with picks and shovels, I often saw. From another observation post we could examine the country behind the German lines. During the last days of the spell, the weather became wet and the trenches got into a very muddy condition. About this time I visited the Catacombs where our reserves were stationed. These consisted of huge subterranean galleries excavated into the limestone where it rose sharply from the valley of the Ancre. They were perfectly dry and safe but very dark and a bit musty.

Thursday 20 April 1916: Martinsart

We left Hamel in the evening and walked out to the wood at the south of Martinsart, where there were many huts and tents and the Battalion expected to be ten days. The Permanent Patrol went into a hut along with a lot of Lewis Gunners. The huts were singular, having wooden sides about four feet high, roofs of felt and doorways with no doors or windows. The roofs were covered with brushwood and earth to disguise them.

---

35 From various sources it seems that McRoberts may be describing Germans in the pre-field grey blue coats. He may have been seeing reservists who were wearing older pattern blue jackets (they could have been old Bavarian or Württemburg State jackets) than the new M1915 uniforms which tended to differ from the earlier field grey M1908 in pattern and colour. It was not uncommon for this to happen due to a shortage in kit. The hat is the standard *feldmütze* but probably with the new band that covered the normal red band. The Army was changing over to black leather from the earlier brown, even to the extent of re-colouring pre-existing brown equipment.

When we arrived there we got our blankets, made cocoa for ourselves and retired to rest in a very contented frame of mind. The bed was wonderful.

Friday to Thursday 21 – 27 April 1916: Martinsart
We remained in Martinsart; the first few days were wet and cold but suddenly the weather got very hot with stifling, sultry days when one had scarcely the energy to breathe. On the 23rd, Easter Sunday, we had a service in the open air, under Rev. J.J. Wright, the Presbyterian Chaplain but it was seemingly a very dull affair and from where I was standing, I could not hear a word of the address.

Easter Monday 24th April was given as a holiday to all whom it could be allowed. In the morning there was an inspection of billets, but after that the time was spent in sleeping, writing or reading as each one felt inclined, football was my choice. In the evening, because of a clear sky which promised excellent weather and with the numerous aeroplanes overhead, it was a very exhilarating and benefiting game of football in which I took part. The Irish Rebellion started in Dublin on Easter Monday, 24th April 1916, and when over three hundred lives had been lost, the insurgents were forced to surrender on the 29th April. The whole uprising, when we read about it in the papers, was incomprehensible to us. That evening the two Companies, 'A' and 'B', left Martinsart to take up their positions as reserves, 'A' in the cellars of Authuille, and 'B' in the dugouts of Thiepval Wood. The Permanent Patrol had made arrangements to be attached to 'B' Company when, without warning, our chief Lieutenant R.L. Lack, was taken away in the ambulance, suffering from an attack of measles, the preparations were cancelled and we remained where we were. The spell was therefore spent in a fairly agreeable manner. We had little to do by day and only a certain number of us went out on night working parties, to Thiepval Wood, to assist the Royal Engineers.

The way these working parties were managed was very unsatisfactory to my mind and showed lack of organisation. There should have been far more Royal Engineers and Pioneer Battalions to do the engineering work that was required. In each Brigade there should have a pioneering Battalion which should have been stationed as close to their occupation as possible, and should have had nothing to do but their work. They would have understood their duties and knowing the task had to be done by them, they would have taken an interest in doing it well.

Take the case of the infantryman who came out of the trenches seeking a certain amount of relaxation for a few days. He was then a considerable distance behind the firing line, when he was told off for a working party attached to the Royal Engineers. He marched four miles, perhaps through woods and difficult paths, carrying his rifle and ammunition. After a journey of an hour and a half, he and his party were put under the charge of a little shrimp of a sapper and ordered about by him. Their minds were in rebellion, they did their best to avoid the work, their NCOs' made excuses for them so that after muddling about for several hours and doing a minimum of effectual work, they started on their weary journey to the camp, through the slippery paths in the wood till they reached their billets, fed up to the world.

A job that was often given to infantrymen was the carrying of heavy logs or burdens along narrow and troublesome paths. This work could have been done ever so much more quickly and effectively by a mule and one of the numerous affairs that were lying about everywhere here, which the French used for taking harrows, barrels of water and such unwieldy loads a long distance. There was a lack of imagination, lack of ingenuity and lack of straight-forward, organised methods.

Twice we had a splendid swim in a corner of a swamp of the River Ancre, just outside Aveluy, and sitting on the grass, with the shells swirling overhead, we let the hot sun do its natural work on our wet, naked skins. It was glorious, clean and healthy, such a contrast to the cramped and dirty lives we often lived, sometimes in dugouts full of smoke and sometimes in vermin-creeping cellars, with never our clothes off.

Friday and Saturday 28-29 April 1916: Albert

On Friday evening I walked into Albert with Norman Paisley. We ran the risk of being caught out of camp bounds but were unmolested. The town was large and most of the houses were standing. They afforded fine billets to the English troops but there were only a few shops left, most of the civilians having departed. That evening Albert was full of Scottish troops, clean, sturdy fellows who paraded up and down the streets as though in a town at home. At the centre of the square, however, the town had suffered severely and whole houses were level with the street. The Cathedral was damaged a lot on one side – that towards the enemy – but its most striking feature was the golden statue of the Madonna, which now hung horizontally over the edge of its tower looking down on the town below instead of standing up perpendicular and majestic as in the days of yore.

The town of Albert was afterwards completely destroyed by continuous bombardment. The Virgin and Child were struck by a shell in 1915 and bent down to an angle of fifteen degrees, below the horizontal. It remained in this position for a long time and there was a superstition among the soldiers that, when the effigy fell, the war would end. However in March 1918, when the Germans seized Albert, the Virgin was shot down by the British because the tower was being used as an observation post. Albert was the home of Jules Verne (1828-1905), the author of *Around the World in Eighty Days* and other well-known novels.

The guns seemed to be just outside the town and were in action as we left; their shells could be seen describing great, fiery arcs in the darkness and bursting on the top of the ridge to the north-east along which the German trenches lay. The weather was very hot these days and the orchards were all in bloom. Who will gather the apples in the fall? Hordes of English troops as last year, or who will it be? The siege of Kut-El-Amara in Mesopotamia ended on 29 April 1916, with the surrender to the Turks of three thousand British and twelve thousand Indian soldiers through starvation.[36]

Sunday 30 April to Saturday 6 May 1916: Thiepval Wood

The Battalion moved into the trenches in Thiepval Wood, to the east of the River Ancre and the Permanent Patrol took up their residence in two dugouts, where they were fairly well off. The Wood was moderately close, consisting chiefly of tall pines and dense hazel shrubbery; the trees were green and the cuckoo called its wonderful note. The Front Line was a disorderly looking place; it wound out and in among the trees, many of which had fallen, cut down by travelling shells or uprooted by explosions.

---

36 The 6th Indian Division, commanded by General Sir Charles Townshend, whose inept handling of the siege led to the disaster. While Townshend was held prisoner as an 'honoured guest' his troops suffered brutal treatment at the hands of the Turks. He never again held a command.

Private David Paterson, the cheerful and energetic Drummer Boy. (Nigel Henderson)

Sergeant Carl (Charles) Penman, killed on 16 March 1916. (Nigel Henderson)

The trenches to the right, occupied by 'D' Company, were in a particularly bad condition, for here the German line was only a matter of seventy yards away, and this part had suffered severely from continual bombardment by trench mortars. The trench was a long, winding, wide excavation with few traces of a fire step or other evidence of a regular made trench. It was certainly a dangerous, forbidding looking spot and during our stay we had many casualties there. Lance Corporal W. Lauchlan, who was one of my friends, being in our harrier team, was killed instantaneously by a trench mortar. Years afterwards, I met his father, who was farm manager for Messrs. McCrum, Watson and Mercer at Milford, County Armagh.[37]

The artillery on both sides never ceased firing and all day the Wood was subjected to a constant bombardment from shrapnel, high explosives or trench mortars. The trench mortars were especially hated, on account of the furious destruction wrought by their explosion. Every forenoon and afternoon casualties or dead were being carried down Elgin Avenue, the communication trench, to the first-aid post. In anticipation of even greater slaughter, a straight trench was being made for the wounded, with a Dead House to put the bodies into, out of the way, in a general action.

The Permanent Patrol was abroad every night, except the last, but we had orders not to interfere with the Germans and consequently we made ourselves into a listening post, with hours from 8.30pm to 2.30am each night. We generally crept out and took up a position on the near bank of the Sunken Road. This highway lay in a cutting, about midway between the two lines. The Germans were out working at their wire each night

---

37 Lance Corporal William McLauchlan, No 15443, the son of William and Elizabeth Stewart McLauchlan of Milford, County Armagh. Killed on 2 May 1915, age 19 years, buried in Authuile Military Cemetery, Authuile, grave D60.

and noises of their digging, handling wire, talking and coughing were always audible. They seemed to have a covering party out also, for sounds of shuffling could often be heard, close at hand, on the other side of the road in the long, withered grass. The forms of men could even be sometimes distinguished.

One night a little bit of bombing and firing took place on our left and since the artillery was beginning to come in, it looked as if there might be a general strafe. Immediately in front of us a gong sounded and men were seen rising in front of us and retiring back at the double. Soon afterwards everything quieted down but on other nights, various little interesting incidents took place.

In 1928 when my wife and I went to France, we visited Thiepval. The area occupied by the Wood was covered with undergrowth, about seven feet high, and the decaying debris of war was lying amid it, but I did not venture further. The ground around the Wood was completely restored and, except where there were cemeteries; it now bore crops of betteraves and wheat. I was told that after the War, companies of Chinese labour had been employed for months with mechanical ploughs in levelling the ground and almost every day there were explosions and casualties among them.[38] The road in front of the Wood, where we used to patrol, was tarred and I travelled on it in a motor car to the top of the hill where the Memorial to the Ulster Division now stands. It is a replica of Helen's Tower, Clandeboye, County Down, and from the top of it an extensive view of the battlefield can be obtained. The caretaker, who lived in the tower and was married to a French girl, was a County Down ex-service man.

(On 6 May) Last night, a raid was arranged to be made by the two Battalions on our right, belonging to the 32nd Division, namely the Lancashire Fusiliers and the Highland Light Infantry so that evening we did not go over the parapet but remained in our dugout. At about midnight our artillery opened and soon there was a terrible duel in hand. For about an hour and a half the air was filled with huge, flashing, terrifying lights and hummed with the concussion and roared with the noise of exploding shells, while all the time there was the incessant rattle of machine guns. Amid the uproar there could be heard the noise of some huge, tall tree which had been stricken, or the shrieking of roots, hurled out of their old beds. On the left, where 'A' and 'B' Companies were, the German shrapnel was off its range and bursting very high, with the result they had not a single casualty that night. But on the right, 'D' Company came in for a terrible mauling from shrapnel and trench mortars, whole platoons were buried and put out of action.[39]

When matters cooled down, the work of digging out the bodies began, but some had to remain buried up to the neck for several hours before they could be extricated. One poor fellow, if he had been uncovered sooner, would have been saved, but he had to remain buried and bled to death from a wound in the leg. Lieutenant JL Walker and

---

38 Some 100,000 Chinese served in a support role with the British Army on the Western Front, a similar number with the French, fewer with the Australian Expeditionary Force. Ten of these in British service faced a court martial and were executed for the murder of civilians or fellow Chinese. Many more simply faced a summary form of justice and were shot out of hand. In 1918, near Locre in Belgium, a unit of the Royal Welch Fusiliers were ordered to round up 'escaped' Chinese labourers and in so doing shot between three and eight of them. Corns, C. & Hughes-Wilson, J., *Blindfold and Alone: British Military Executions in the Great War* (London: Cassell, 2001)

39 Battalion War Diary: "1.15am, out of touch altogether with 16th Lancashire Fusiliers on our right. 1.25am runner arrived from 'D' Company reporting all well, but ten casualties. His name was Private Milligan and he must have come through heavy fire to reach us."

many others were fatally injured and a still greater number were severely wounded. It was a bad night. With the breaking day the work continued and eight sandbags of flesh remains were gathered up and sent down to the burying ground.

The raiding party succeeded well in catching great numbers of Germans in their dugouts and killing most of them, they brought back five as prisoners. Before daybreak the order came 'Stand-to, Germans over the parapet.' We stood-to and a large party of Germans was seen gathering up their casualties, men who had evidently been caught out on one of their working parties. The order 'No Firing' was passed and they were allowed to finish their work in peace. We left Thiepval Wood the next evening, being relieved by the 9th Inniskillings, and arrived safely back in the huts beside Martinsart.

Sunday 7 May 1916: Thiepval Wood
There was to be a raid by the Inniskillings tonight.[40]

Monday 8 May to Sunday 14 May 1916: Lealvillers
Strange and conflicting reports arrived about the Inniskillings, but what seems to have happened was this. The raiding party did its work well and was returning with prisoners, when the Germans opened a bombardment and commenced raiding the trenches to the right occupied by the Dorsets. The Inniskillings bayoneted their prisoners and on reaching the English trenches, found Germans in the place of the Dorsets. The latter it seemed, mistaking the Huns for the returning Inniskilling party, had allowed them to get right up to the trenches. The 10th Inniskillings, who were in reserve, had to be called up to clear the place and several prisoners were made. The Dorsets lost men and prisoners while the Inniskillings suffered heavily also. This agrees, more or less, with the account of the happenings of that night as related by Mr Charles Douie of the Dorset Regiment and the Royal Munster Fusiliers in *I Was There* (p. 829).

The day was cool and fine for marching, so setting out early [9am as per War Diary] we made an excellent journey, through Hadeauville and Varennes to Lealvillers, where we were quartered in fairly good billets. It was with a feeling of relief and delight that we look upon such a wonderful sight as women, and cheered the first few we saw. It was over two months since most of the Battalion had seen a woman. Varennes was a good deal changed and was the centre of much activity; the streets were full of machine shops, stores, hospitals and transport. The new railway was now in full working order so that the dump with its workshops remained one of the dockyards at home.

Monday to Friday 15-26 May 1916: Lealvillers
We remained at Lealvillers, the weather was glorious and we experienced a pleasant time. The following extracts are a description of life in Lealvillers which I wrote to my mother on 21 May 1916: This is an interesting part of the world, just behind the firing lines, where the rail heads are and where every tiny village has been converted into a hive of industry. At one corner of the village is a hospital with its Red Cross flag floating high. At another is the divisional smithy and further along the street is the mechanical workshop for motors. Then there is the pumping station where a motor pump raises water from an enormous depth, replenishing the wooden trough for the horses and filling the water

---

40   Battalion War Diary 7.5.1916: "A day of rest, church services and plenty of sleep."

Private Thomas George Sloan who came from Elswick Street, Belfast. He was killed on 6 May 1916, aged 26 years old. (Nigel Henderson)

Sergeant William Stephenson from Fitzwilliam Street, Belfast, who pre-war had been a draughtsman working for Messrs. Workman, Clark & Co. He was a well known and popular figure in the local sports scene. He was killed on 6 April 1916, aged 25 yeas old. (Nigel Henderson)

carts for the cookers, also supplying the bath house and laundry where thousands every day get a wash and clean change. Then you should see the steamroller on a road that has just been made with the soldier driving it.

In the mornings we had a lot of work to do. Sometimes we went to the railway dump, outside Varennes, where there were trains to unload and scores of motor lorries or horse transport to fill. The material handled was generally timber and tree logs. The dump was well managed and no one was murdered with heavy labour, and yet a great amount of work was got through. Other days we, or perhaps the whole Brigade, would practise for the big event at the dummy trenches outside the village. These were marked out with a plough and day after day, we went through all the movements that were considered necessary, even marching over the growing wheat fields. In the long summer evenings we had concerts, whist drives and more concerts.

Several times in France the whole Battalion would be paraded and a proclamation would be read by the Commanding Officer. It would be stated quite coldly, without any trimming, that Private so and so of the Umpteenth Regiment has been sentenced to death by field court-martial for sleeping at his post and the sentence of death had been duly carried out.[41]

Saturday 27 May to Monday 12 June 1916: Lealvillers
We had Battalion sports and I tried to run in the mile but after covering half the course at a good pace, I felt as if I would burst, so I dropped out. A few days previously the Brigade was assembled to take farewell of their Brigadier General Hickman who said he had to leave us, at the call of duty, though much against his will. In bringing to our notice the new Brigadier – General Shuter – he stated that he was introducing him to a Brigade second to none in the British Army. About this time the exploits of the YCV were being boomed abroad in Belfast, and down at the base at Le Havre new troops were told to take an example from the coolness and steadiness of the gallant 14th.[42]

There were not many interesting French people to meet in the village but there was a little girl, down in a café, with whom I have had a parley or two. She was called Susanne, was aged about seventeen and had a wonderful, little, developed body worthy of a matron, and a pretty little face to match. A rare lassie was my little Susanne and she lived here with her aunt, while her mother was at Vermelles. In the first days of the War, her brother and sister were killed at her side by a German shell and she was wounded in three places. She was sent to Amiens, was operated on, and now awaited the end of the war, for the big advance that never came.

At night we could hear the noise of the machine guns up at the Front. Only a few days ago, Acheux was shelled all morning with shrapnel and high explosive, with the result that there were numerous casualties. We were working at the dump at Varennes that day, in sight of the exploding shells. During the last week at Lealvillers we had several strenuous Brigade days, in the region of Warloy and Baixieux. We had been relieved of our blankets and had to sleep in our clothes. The Battle of Jutland was fought on 31 May 1916.

On 5 June 1916, Kitchener was drowned within sight of the Orkney Islands when the cruiser in which he was travelling to Russia struck a mine and, in less than fifteen minutes, had disappeared beneath the waves taking with it eight hundred men.

Tuesday 13 June to Thursday 15 June 1916: Aveluy Wood
We packed up our kits and left Lealvillers. We marched through Martinsart, then round to the Albert-Hamel Road and finally found we were to bivouac in Aveluy Wood. The ground was very wet and muddy while the weather promised badly. We were served out with khaki canvas coverings, each one of which was supposed to shelter six of us. The first night we passed rather miserably, but eventually the weather improved, and we made quite a comfortable billet. We constructed a sandbag wall to protect us from Fritz's machine gun bullets and put revetment on the other sides, while a little leaves and small

---

41   Up to this date three members of the Division had been executed by firing squad.

42   According to the War Diary this was 26 May 1916 and while Hickman may well have expressed his regret in leaving, however, he was leaving at his own request to return to the House of Commons and much to the relief of General Nugent. In conversation with Haig, Nugent was told, "If I were you, I should put no obstacle in his way of returning to his parliamentary duties." Quoted in a letter from Nugent to his wife dated 11/12 May 1916.

branches made a comfortable floor. At night there was a lot of machine gun and artillery fire so that several fellows were wounded or killed by stray fragments. Mr F. Corscadden of my Platoon was mortally wounded by a ricochet, which had first hit a tree.

The whole Brigade had come to this Wood and each day great working parties were furnished. These made pits in Thiepval Wood to contain tons of iron rations and they carried up bombs, trench mortars and small ammunition in unprecedented quantities. They helped to make the Headquarters dugout on the Martinsart-Englebelmer Road, and to dig many miles of new trenches for telephone wires. Everything pointed to an advance in preparation but I have the old complaint to make about the organisation of working parties.

This will be better understood by giving a typical day. We rose at 5.30am, had breakfast at 5.45am and fell-in at 6.30am. The party would then be told to go and report at Martinsart, to the Royal Engineers, and we would be carrying our rifles, equipment, and ammunition and probably waterproofs. We reached Martinsart after an hour's walk and found no one expecting us. After about an hour's waiting, we would march back past our billets to do work in Thiepval Wood. The communication trenches would be packed with working parties so that the pushing and congestion was cruel. Arrived at the scene of our work we would probably have to return for picks and shovels because these had been lifted by another party. We often never got started our work until between 11 and 12 o'clock and then we knocked off for half an hour about 3pm to have dinner which consisted of iron rations, or a Maconochie. Maconochie was the name of a tinned stew consisting of potatoes and vegetables with a small piece of tough meat, all cooked together. When a tin was opened it had, for me, a most repulsive appearance, which was only slightly improved when the mess was heated. We resumed work and probably stayed until about 5 o'clock to get it finished, then marched back for tea. The best hours, those in the morning, when we were keen, were spent in wearisome, sickening wanderings and delays. On every working party we wasted hours of valuable time.

Friday 16 June to Friday 23 June 1916: Thiepval Wood

On Friday morning a party went up to Thiepval Wood to carry trench mortars and all morning they were pulled about by three artillery officers who each wanted them for different purposes at the same time. After staying from 8am to 4pm and having done very little real work, our officer marched them off and the artillery put in a complaint.

One day I was in Thiepval Wood and saw one of our aeroplanes flying very low over the German lines. I thought he was going to fall and apparently so did the Germans for, from Thiepval village, a dozen machine-guns suddenly opened fire.

Such a clatter they made, nevertheless the English machine escaped, but the episode made me think that the Germans were stronger than we had ever suspected; there was at least four times the machine-gun fire from the village that had ever been heard before. In my opinion, they had been tempted to show their hand.

Meanwhile the 14th had received their meal of iron rations and at 9pm were marching away, with full kit, to Hedauville. My Platoon had reached Martinsart when we received orders, from General Shuter, to return. We left our packs in Aveluy Wood and marched back to Thiepval Wood, extended and started to pass sixty pounders through the Wood up to the front line.[43]

The night was pretty calm except for a salve of shrapnel from the enemy which, however, did not touch any of us. We were starving with hunger and had been famishing[44] all week, as we were living on iron rations. I was cursing the system, the relentless stupidity which brought all this pain on us, who had committed no demeanour while the real guilty ones lived free from any physical discomfort. To crown matters it began to rain heavily and everyone was soon soaking to the skin. Still we passed up the trench mortars, then the 'pipes' and finally the detonators. It was getting clear, 3am, in spite of the new Daylight Saving Bill, when we crossed the River Ancre and in the early, damp morning and wandered back, in groups, to Hedauville.[45]

Saturday to Tuesday 24-27 June 1916: Hedauville
We remained at Hedauville and the weather was unsettled. I was in a comfortable billet but we had no blankets nor straw, and we lived practically on iron rations along with tinned fruit and biscuits which were bought in the canteen. A lot of French Artillery had its Headquarters here, as they were to take part in the great attack.

The bombardment started on Saturday morning. During the day the sound was not too obvious but in the evening and night the noise was loud and continuous, the flash of the guns and the flares of bursting shrapnel made the whole horizon red. Reports came in that two villages in German hands were burning, that we had sent over gas successfully and that our raiding parties had done well. Small groups of German prisoners came down the line, they were dirty and distressed but all were strong-looking youths with, I must say, the typical Hun expression made familiar by photographs in our papers. We had no work to do, only submit to inspections and lectures but for me there was map drawing. I made copies of the secret maps of the German trenches, on both sides of the River Ancre showing our advance as we hoped it would be.

Tuesday to Thursday 27-29 June 1916: Martinsart
On Tuesday 27th at 9.30pm we left Hedaville in single column of platoons for Martinsart and for equipment we were carrying only our small haversack together with waterproof sheet. The last civilians were being forced out of Martinsart and we met them struggling along the road like refugees in a picture. Each had a cart piled with household effects. The grandmother with the children would probably be on top, in charge of an elderly, senile man. Behind came three or four docile cows followed by the women of the party. It was a sad procession. In addition we bore, however, an extra bandolier of ammunition, two Mills bombs and hard rations for a couple of days, all contained in a sandbag.

We expected to cross the parapet early on Thursday morning, the 29th, and all arrangements had been made for the venture. We came by cross-country to Martinsart and, on the way, had a magnificent spectacle of an intense artillery bombardment. We arrived safely in Martinsart on Wednesday morning the 28th and were placed in good

---

43   Ammunition for the artillery, each shell weighing 60lbs.
44   Starving.
45   Battalion War Diary 17.6.16: "All men on work parties. 2nd Lt. Corscadden wounded in Aveluy Wood whilst sitting writing in front of his bivouac. He was sent to hospital, but died next morning."

Lieutenant J.L. Walker, who was among those killed on 6 May 1916. (Nigel Henderson)

billets with wire beds. During the night I slept well, although the din was great, and German shells often threatened to burst in the roof of the old barn. During the day we survived, leisurely making tea and munching biscuits. My thoughts were all about the advantages of living a farmer's life in Ontario in the company of a wonderful, female companion.

The German bombardment had nearly ceased but our heavy guns continued. Down in the wood and among the huts where we used to be billeted, there was a number of very heavy artillery, including a huge, twelve-inch naval gun known as 'Lucky Jim'.

We all expected to be over, in Germany, within the next twelve hours. In the afternoon, the order was changed and we were told that we were marching back to Forceville that night. Rumour had it that the British had broken through in several places to the North, while the German reserves were concentrated here to meet our attack. The weather was wet and I pitied the fighters who had to make the advance.

During the morning, while the shells were occasionally bursting into the town and orders were still unchanged, three lads paraded through the streets in fancy costumes and caused much amusement by their droll antics. One was dressed as a lady, having a huge blue hat with feathers and an old skirt. He showed the additional charms of a beautiful, long, low, brown neck and suggested a full and bounteous bosom. The others were equally good in their make-up and action, being fine examples of the thin, weedy-looking, typical French village lad. I might say that the civilians had all been evacuated from Martinsart and these articles of clothing had been abandoned by them. We left Martinsart and after a walk, retarded by endless miles of ammunition trains, we found comfortable wooden huts in an orchard in Forceville. On the 29th we remained in Forceville, doing nothing in particular.

Friday 30 June 1916: Thiepval Wood
We left Forceville in the evening and marched across the fields, platoon by platoon, to Englebelmer into Martinsart. Tomorrow many of us would over the parapet. I had not time to moralise, so I did everything in a matter-of-course way. We scouts under Mr R.L. Lack led the way. 'Follow green' was the order, for there were green lamps along the roads, to show us our direction. The green lights led us through Aveluy Wood, down to the railway line, along it for a short distance, then we passed over the march and the River Ancre by the North Causeway, recently made by the Royal Engineers. Next, we went up Elgin Avenue to our assembly trenches in Thiepval Wood.

The night was good and the bombardment was going on briskly with Fritz replying occasionally. Other Battalions were streaming up in the dusk and trying to get into their respective assembly trenches. There was a bit of confusion and I, a scout, had a lot of running to do. The night passed uneasily for the most part, there was the bombardment all the time, the crash of falling trees and the hiss of flying shrapnel. My health at this time was, as ordinarily, good, but the hardships and the insufficient food were telling on my body. My teeth, which I had tended so carefully, ever since I understood their immense value, had suffered under the diet of hard biscuits, especially such teeth as had been stopped. There were also two swollen lumps on one side of my jaw. These subsequently disappeared altogether, just after I was wounded and down in Le Havre, enjoying a rest and a bit of eatable food.

During this night, Private W.F. McFadzean of our Battalion gained the first Victoria Cross in the 36th (Ulster) Division although he lost his life. In a crowded trench, a box of bombs skipped and two of the safety pins fell out. He immediately threw himself on top of the bombs which exploded, and he was blown to pieces, although only one other man was injured.[46]

∽

We wait in our dugouts,
The vile-smelling water
Leaking into our boots.
All is quiet
All is silent.
Not a bird in the sky
Nor an insect in the ground.[47]

∽

---

46 Private William Frederick McFadzean, No18278, C Company. The son of William and Annie McFadzean of 'Rubicon' Creagh, Belfast. He has no known grave and commemorated on the Thiepval Memorial Pier and Face 15A and 15B.

47 Hannah Carson.

Saturday 1 July 1916: Thiepval Wood[48]

The 108th Brigade came under heavy and accurate machine-gun fire at Beaucourt Station and from St. Pierre-Division. Beaten back, they regrouped, but each time they advanced machine-gun fire cut them down. Like the 109th Brigade they were forced back to the German 'A' line trenches, where they remained until the following day. 107th Brigade was to pass through the two leading brigades and attack 'C' and 'D' lines and finally the village of Grandcourt. Despite heavy casualties the 'C' line was captured and here they awaited orders. General Nugent, realised the situation was untenable ordered the attack stopped. However the order did not reach 107th Brigade and they made a last minute dash across open ground and despite horrendous casualties reached the trenches in front of Grandcourt. Here hand-to-hand fighting took place, but they eventually forced the enemy out of the trenches. German reinforcements were rushed up and despite dogged resistance the survivors of 107th Brigade were pushed back to their own lines. Early the following morning, the observation post on Mesnil Ridge reported that there were still some Ulster troops in the German 'A' line trenches.

General Nugent ordered Brigadier General Withycomb to assist and reinforce these men. Withycomb gathered together the remnants of 107th Brigade plus two machine guns, placing this makeshift unit under the command of Major Woods of the 9th Rifles. A third of the men were casualties before they reached the enemy trenches, where they stayed for the remainder the day. The 49th Division relieved the Ulster Division on the night of 2 July; 107th Brigade were relieved the following morning by the 48th Brigade. In two days of fighting, the Ulster Division lost 5,500 officers and men, killed, wounded or missing.

The Ulster Division was then only Division of X Corps to have achieved its objectives on 1 July 1916 and the men of the Division received many awards for bravery, including four Victoria Crosses.

I spent the early hours of the morning in an old mineshaft, quite convenient to Headquarters, along with the other scouts. While out on a message down Elgin Avenue, I had a very narrow escape from several high explosive shells, which burst on the other side of the trench, the concussion sent me dottering and the heat scorched my face, but the huge shrapnel pieces missed me. The moment I heard the first one come, I got down in the trench and gripping my rifle with both hands resigned myself to what seemed the inevitable.

The attack was not to open until 7.15am when the Inniskillings were to cross the top. At 6.30am, our guns, which had been sullenly shelling all night, opened a hurricane blast on the German lines, our trench mortar batteries were in action too. It was a glorious, summer morning with a blue sky and dazzling sunshine. The din was magnificent and so we sat in the old mineshaft, laughed and sang. A rum ration had been issued in the early morning and some of us had more than our share. The Germans began to retaliate and their high explosives came diving into our front line.

---

48 On the night of 30 June, the Division moved to the trenches in Thiepval Wood in preparation for the battle the following day. At zero hour, 7.30am on 1 July, the 108th and 109th Brigades spearheaded the attack, with the 107th, held in reserve. The 108th Brigade attacked with two battalions on either side of the River Ancre plus the 15th Battalion Royal Irish Rifles of 107th Brigade. Their objectives were the railway station at Beaucourt and the machine-gun posts located in and around St Pierre Division.

Then as our troops mounted the parapet, the enemy machine guns and shrapnel opened furiously. I was in a dugout but I could understand only too well what was happening. For over an hour, the machine guns hummed and sang while the high explosive burst with deafening roar among the trees.

German prisoners were coming back in large numbers; they were fine specimens of men. The Germans had not been issued with steel helmets on the 1 July 1916: the men I saw were wearing what I have heard described as 'pork pie' cloth caps. These had two ornamental buttons, about the size of a halfpenny, one above the other. One button always had three concentric circles in the German colours of red, white and black, the other had different colours representing the state from which the owner came. But they were in a sad, humbled condition and if you looked at them angrily, their hands were up in expostulation with the cry, 'Pardon, Pardon Kamarad.' They brought out treasures of beautiful cigarettes and cigars, which they offered eagerly, also watches, compasses and penknives. One German offered me a box of cigarettes, which had blue lettering on them with golden mouth pieces. They looked very nice but I declined them chiefly because I was too thirsty to smoke. Behind him was another man holding up two cigars and pushing them forward under my nose, but I rejected them also.

Reports came back with a runner: we had got to the German trenches all right, but our losses were very heavy, and all communication with our old trenches practically impossible as the enemy was maintaining a terrific sweeping fire on No man's land. Our Adjutant, Captain A. Mulholland, was getting anxious and Mr R.L. Lack with his scouts was asked to go out and find exactly how matters stood. We made our way slowly up to the front line, meeting streams of wounded and tramping over many dead bodies both of our own men and the enemy. After a mad race across the open, I dropped into a shell hole to get my wind and see where I was. Lifting my head over the edge, I could discern no one alive. There were lots of dead about while the shrapnel was sweeping the ground and bursting into a thousand, angry, hissing, flying pieces. The machine guns were ever tinkling.

The day was glorious and I could see Grandcourt, a picture of red roofs still, amid a wood of green foliage. The whole landscape was speckled with the clouds of bursting shrapnel, and miles away beyond Grandcourt, our shells were bursting on the German roads. Another rush and another friendly shell hole, again a rush and I was through the German wire, there was little but the posts left, and into the German first line. I found I had arrived, not among my own fellows, but among a mixed lot of the 108th Brigade. The Germans were being bombed out of their dugouts and certain trenches where they had taken refuge. They were wonderfully game, considering what they must have come through, and caused a lot of casualties among our men. The German trenches, in any part where they were, a little less shattered, showed that they were deeper and much broader than ours with a higher firing step. The revetment, which was very neat, was invariably used, instead of sandbags, wire and iron stakes, as with us. Consequently, I would say that our trenches were better, but the Germans far excelled us in the construction of their dugouts. These were sunk deep in the ground and reached by a long, wide flight of steps. The staircase and its sides were sheeted with timber while the dugouts, which were large and spacious, had floors, sides and roof of wood also. There were spring beds, tables and chairs, and beautiful valises made out of cattle-hide with several clean changes of clothing. It was known to be cattle-hide because the hair was still remaining on it. There were also pictures of girls and of the Kaiser, bottles of beer, plenty of chocolate, black bread, biscuits and some kind of sausage.

I now made my way to the right, getting nearer the road to Thiepval and came into contact with my own Battalion. They were in 'B' line where they were getting it very hot from the German shrapnel and had lost nearly all their officers. There seemed to be nobody who had any authority and groups of men were sitting in clusters everywhere, doing nothing at about 12 noon. I now met Jack Armstrong who had found a German officer's valise, full of maps and the both of us determined to go back with it and report ourselves to Headquarters. The way we went was quite short this time and I reached our trenches safely. I was going down Elgin Avenue when a whizz-bang burst over my head. I felt a burning sensation on the left side of my neck and saw the red blood pouring down my tunic in a gushing flow. I took out my first-aid bandage from a special pocket in my tunic, and Jack Armstrong tied it round my neck.

Our Adjutant, Captain Mulholland, who was outside Battalion Headquarters, stopped me in my race down Elgin Avenue and asked me where I was going. I said I had been wounded and pointed to the blood stained bandage around my neck, so I was allowed to proceed. I threw my rifle and all my equipment up on the side of the trench and in my hurry and delight, I forgot all about the few souvenirs I had in my pouches. One of the souvenirs was a cigarette case embossed with a picture of the Kaiser and the words *'Gott mit uns.'*[49] I saw no German helmets. I was very much afraid of blood poisoning and made my way quickly to the first aid where I had a fresh bandage from John Doran, a stretcher-bearer of ours. Then I went away down the communication trench, where I met endless fresh troops of the 49th Division, rushing up. Next, I walked past Authville and over the River Ancre. Then I passed through Aveluy Wood and into Martinsart where I received a bowl of tea and my medical tag. After that, I walked to the collecting post at Englebelmer where I got into a transport wagon and after a long journey, through Acheux, came to Clairfaye. Here the wounded were arriving in hundreds from three Divisions which all seemed to have been practically held up. On enquiring I found most of my own officers were casualties and that my old friends McCluggage, Dunwoodie, Griffiths and McClellan had come to a bloody end. I was bandaged and inoculated and that night went to bed between two blankets in a marquee. William McCluggage was an old Grammar School boy and an engineering student at Queen's University, Belfast.[50] In 1914 he got his final, but on the outbreak of War, as he had been a member of the Officers Training Corps, he decided to join the Army and was commissioned to the 12th Royal Irish Rifles. John Griffiths was a Welshman and had been mathematical and chemical master at Larne Grammar School since 1909. He had a commission in the 12th Royal Irish Rifles and was a particularly nice chap. I first met HH Dunwoodie when he came for a year as a junior master, to Larne Grammar School. I was therefore very surprised, on entering Queen's University, to find him there as a student in Civil Engineering. It

---

49 'God with us'.

50 Lieutenant William McCluggage, A Company 12th Royal Irish Rifles, killed 1 July 1916, age 23. The son of Thomas and Annie McCluggage of Ballyboley, Larne, County Antrim. Second Lieutenant Hugh Henderson Dunwoodie (Dunwoody on the Commonwealth War Graves Commission), 9th Battalion Royal Irish Fusiliers, died 31 July 1916, age 26 years, the youngest son of Robert and Eliza Dunwoodie of Holywood Road, Belfast. Captain John Griffiths, killed 1 July 1916, age 34 years, awarded MID for this action, the son of John and Jane Griffiths of Chester.

must have been embarrassing to him, while being an immense joke to the other students, when I told how he had taught English and Latin and how I had never dreamed of calling him anything but 'sir'. He had a commission in the Royal Irish Rifles. I have made reference to Allan John McClellan in my entry dated 6 February 1915.[51]

Sunday 2 July 1916: Lealvillers

I slept until about 11am. In the morning I found several pals from the Company but they knew very little about anyone except themselves. More wounded kept arriving. After endless lining up, I at last found myself marching away, with several hundred others, to the railway station. It was dark and the field was full of stretcher cases, lying silently, wrapped in their blankets. I slept that night amidst a lot of freshly made hay.

Monday 3 July 1916: Gezaincourt

In the light of early morning, a train arrived and took us along to Gezaincourt where I had tea, bread and another rest in a marquee. Then I fell into the end of a line of several thousands of wounded men to wait my turn for a hospital train. For hours I kept moving nearer the front and it was getting dark when I found myself at last in a train bound for Rouen, I supposed. All night we travelled slowly but were well attended to by the RAMC orderlies in the train.

Tuesday 4 July 1916: Harfleur

About mid-day we arrived in Le Havre and were divided into different lots, according to the severity of our wounds. I was sent with a party which was put into motor ambulances and had quite a journey to the Palais de Régates, a fine, palatial building in Harfleur, sited on the shore, a matter of ten yards from the sea.

A letter I wrote to my mother, with an account of the fighting on the 1 July, was published in the Larne Times and was described by my old schoolmaster, Mr William Kennedy, BA, of Larne and Inver National School as the only account of the fighting he had read in which he understood what had happened.

I had a bath, then a blue uniform and pair of slippers was issued to me, also I had my wound examined and dressed.[52] The Sister remarked it had been a near escape for me, as the injury had just missed some big arteries, and she said she could see the blood throbbing in the open wound. There was a chap beside me who had a big, dark swelling

---

51 At 7.30am the Battalion followed the 10th Inniskilling Fusiliers forward and into the German front line trench. During the advance Frank McIllroy's brother was killed, but Sergeant Powell told him to keep moving, which he did. It has not been possible to tell if this was the McIllroy brother who managed to have the free weekend off while at Randalstown. The Commonwealth War Graves Commission (CWGC) website quotes two men named McIlroy of the 14th Battalion dying that day. Rifleman Robert Henry McIlroy, No 18299, age 25 years, the son of the late Mrs Agnes Henkins, no known grave and commemorated on the Thiepval Memorial, pier and face 15A and 15B. Also Rifleman Samuel McIlroy, No 1903, attached to the 109th Light Trench Mortar Battery, age 26 years, the son of David McIlroy and Catherine McIlroy of Blackstock, RFD, No 2, South Carolina, USA, a native of Belfast. Buried in Connaught Cemetery, Thiepval, grave III.A.5. There is no spelling of McIllroy on the web site.

52 This uniform was known as 'Hospital Blues' and was worn with a shirt and red tie. It was issued to men were sufficiently recovered to go outside the hospital for walks etc. While wearing the uniform soldiers were not permitted to enter public houses or to drink alcohol in public. It was also an offence for members of the public to supply alcohol to such men.

on the back of his hand. The doctor looked at it; then squeezed the lump and, to our astonishment, a black shrapnel bullet instantly slipped out. I slept soundly in a beautiful, clean bed that night in a room with hundreds of others. The Sisters were smart, hard-working girls, all of good build and appearance so that I got to admire them more and more each day. One was a Belfast girl from Dundonald.

Wednesday to Wednesday 5-12 July 1916: Harfleur

I remained in hospital; the life was monotonous but what could I not endure with a patient mind now! The routine was as follows: rise at 5.30am, wash the floors, make the beds and clean up until 7.30am when we had breakfast, inspection by the Medical Officer at about 11am. Then there was dinner at 12.30, tea at 5.30 and supper, which I rarely attended, at 7pm, while we must all be in bed by 9pm. The weather was generally fine and it was charming in the evenings in front of the Palais, the sea and sky were a picture while many ships, aeroplanes and dirigibles were always in evidence.

We were not allowed beyond the precincts of the Hospital but we could talk over the railings to the people on the beach. Sometimes it was French girls, wading and bathing. At other times it was English children who had lived all their time in France and talked both languages equally well, but by their gesticulation, they were French. Beautiful, clever and healthy they were. Their sympathies and nature were English; for they did not like their schoolmates who, they said were always hurting each other and were noisy and spiteful.

The patients in the wards were of all the nationalities of the Empire and some of them had seen service in Gallipoli, Egypt, South Africa or India. Several were skilful on the piano and others sang; so that in the evenings we never lacked entertainment. I also found a number of novels, *Brothers, Mightier than the Sword* and *The Locum Tenens* gave me thoughts on which to go to bed. There was a lot of work to be done in the morning, floors, chairs, lockers, tables and forms had to be scrubbed or washed, and windows had to be cleaned. The wound got on well, being carefully dressed every day. The sister, when she first saw it said that I had experienced a very narrow escape from death and that there was something in the world for me to do yet. The doctor said I would never die in my bed.

Thursday 13 July 1916: Le Havre

In the evening, I received my old uniform, which had been through the fumigator also, a certain of amount of kit and went by motor bus, along with a number of others, to No 4 Convalescent Camp. These quarters were situated on the outskirts of the city, upon a high hill, which could also be ascended by flights of steps and were beautifully arranged.

There were huts of the usual build and a great number of Indian marquees, also a YMCA building and a canteen. There were picturesque gardens and lots of quaint, rustic work in evidence, among the well-kept lawns, all of which gave the Camp a quite festive appearance.

Friday to Friday 14-21 July 1916: Le Havre

I remained at the Convalescent Camp and had a pleasant time. Duties were few and leisure plentiful but money was limited to the amount of five francs received the second day on arrival. In my spare time I read Robert Elsmere and *Letters of a Subaltern to his*

Wife. These letters gave some interesting comments on the Army Acts and soldiering, which I found agreed very much with those found by myself from experience. These may be summarised as follows: The training and drill received by regular soldiers were of practically no value to them on active service and did not help them the least in the day of battle. Drill, over which we spent so many months of toil and brain fever, had a dull and weakening effect on a man's initiative. In the hands of hundreds of our officers it was the mask under which was hidden their incapacity, their intellectual barrenness and their gross stupidity.

A civilian army with civilian officers who proved their capacity in ordinary life and who had received practical instruction in their weapons would be a match for any regular army whose whole thoughts were about drill or ancient regimental customs and who could not conceive a good idea without its being tied with yards of red and golden regimental tape.

We had good food in the convalescent camp. There was also a lot of fun with the association of different troops from all parts of the War and I, who had been in the Battle of the Somme, could look in the face of those of those who had been at Ypres, or Suvla Bay and compare notes and impression. I heard many stories of Egypt, the Turks, camels and Cairo. There were also bathing parades in the sea and an excursion to a cinema, which I enjoyed to the full.

I remember before the picture started at the cinema the whole audience had to stand to attention – perhaps for fifteen minutes – while the national anthems of all the allies were played. The main picture was a long, fairy story called '*Le jambe de muton*', which was rather childish and boring to us. An evening down in the city on pass, I spent very pleasantly and thought sorrowfully of the days in store for me.

The French have a far more realistic attitude to the natural functions of their bodies than we have. In a shop window in Le Havre there was on display, among the postcards for sale, a picture of a French soldier, dressed in the old uniform of blue coat and red trousers, he had exceedingly long whiskers and a huge grin on his face for his pants were down and he was defecating into a German spiked helmet.

In any stationer's shop, it was possible to examine hundreds of untouched photographs of perfectly nude ladies, which were on postcards, with dotted lines on the other side for the address and stamp. But on such pictures only ladies were shown and the poses were all decent. In certain shops, however, it was possible to get 'mademoiselle et monsieur' cards, which were not on public display. These had pictures of stark naked men and women and there was no imaginable posture of their bodies that was not depicted. There was a famous 'red light' street in Le Havre called Rue de Galions and I would have liked to see it but my stay was too short.

Every family seemed to come down to the beach with a large, gaily-coloured parasol, or even a tent. Under its shelter, papa read his paper and mama knitted while the children played around. I remember a small girl remarking that I was '*frize*' (curly) and when I smiled at her, she was delighted. "Oh, he understands me," she exclaimed to her mother. "Yes," replied the mother, "they know more than we suspect."

I had my first letter from home this month: my mother seemed to be very thankful for my survival, wished I could get home of course, and spoke of those who had fallen, among which she mentioned Allen John McClellan. I also received this diary and my pocket book from the front. My wound began to close up and finally it no longer required any dressing. The numb sensation about the neck and cheek still remained, so that on leaving the Camp, the Commanding Officer marked me for a month at the Base.

Lieutenant R.L. Lack, the Commanding Officer of the Permanent Patrol, died from wounds on the 18 July, also Lance Corporal Paul G. Pollock, who was missing on the 1 July. A sister of Pollock's wrote to my mother asking for my photo, which was sent to her, and in due course there arrived a picture of Mr Lack surrounded by his twenty scouts. This picture is in my possession. Pollock's father was the Presbyterian minister in charge of St. Enoch's Church in Belfast. The previous summer he had spent a month with his family at Seaford and preached to the troops one Sunday.

Friday 21 July 1916: Harfleur
A party of us left the Convalescent Camp at Le Havre in the afternoon, and went by motor bus to the Base Depot near Harfleur. There were a great number of stations here, and the endless rows of canvas tents together with the large number of huts were imposing. A fine attempt had been made to add a touch of beauty to the place and there were numerous, promising flower gardens.

There was a good number of our Battalion on permanent jobs in that place and lots who had gone down sick had since received promotion and were now settled comfortably, apparently for the remainder of the war. Here I met some of my Battalion who were recovering from their wounds, and it did my soul good to be among them again. The food was plentiful, money was to be had and I was looking forward to a month's holiday. It was reported that the Division had gone away north to the Belgian Frontier and was being filled up with drafts of Englishmen, such as the King's Royal Rifles.

Saturday 22 July 1916: Harfleur
I received the full kit of a soldier, including a rifle and equipment similar to my old one. I was also medically examined and the doctor, although I explained the nature of my wound, calmly gave me a big 'A', remarking that he thought a paralysed cheek would not annoy me much. I was in a boiling temper as I burst into my tent, which was occupied chiefly by men who were going up the line for the first time. They were being addressed by a man of the Salvation Army, or such like, in a khaki uniform. Turning to me, as I entered, he said "Young man, are you ready to go?" "No, I am not, but the flaming doctor says I am," was my indignant reply. He was rather startled and presenting me with a New Testament, which I accepted, he withdrew from the tent.

Sunday 23 July 1916: Harfleur
There was a Church parade in the morning; everything was strictly precise in regimental propriety and in the evening I was warned off for guard.

Monday 24 July 1916: Harfleur
We mounted guard at 8 o'clock in the morning and had the ordinary, agreeable time for the following twenty-four hours.

Tuesday and Wednesday 25-26 July 1916: Harfleur to Étaples
We were warned off to leave for the front in the evening. The party, about fifty men from the Division, paraded at 7.30pm in full marching order, and was inspected by the

Commanding Officer, who was apparently of the old type, his only ribbon being the King's Medal for South Africa.

He had a few words to say to us about smartness. The aim of a soldier was to be smart, smart in camp, in billets and in the trenches. Walk smartly and carry out orders smartly, salute smartly and never slouch. If we did this nothing more could be expected of us. We were then marched away and drafts from other Divisions joined us so that a large party marched the distance of six kilometres to the Railway Station. We had a pleasant journey along a broad boulevard and past the hutments of many thousands of Belgian refugees.

We got into ordinary carriages, not cattle trucks as we had expected and journeyed all night, arriving about 8 o'clock in the morning at Rouen. We stayed until 5 o'clock in the evening, confined to the railway station and made lots of tea for ourselves from a plentiful supply of iron rations. That evening, again in carriages, we had a journey through a very interesting and beautiful country. In each carriage there was a notice posted warning one to keep silent, to be on guard, that hostile hears are listening. It read as follows: '*Tarsez-vous Mefrez-vous. Les ovelles enemies vous ecoutent.*'

The landscape was more English in appearance than I had been accustomed to in France. There were meadows of fresh-mown hay and the old, familiar scent reached me through the carriage windows. There were fine, big farmhouse, also there were hedges dividing the fields and long, winding, shady lanes, so it was the old English style altogether. Then it got dark and I fell asleep but we continued travelling all night.

Thursday 27 July 1916: Étaples to Steenwerck

Shortly after daylight, I awoke as we were approaching the great stretch of camps that formed the English base at Étaples. The ground was sandy, rough and broken while the sea was a short distance away, almost hidden in mist. The cottages were small and of a plain, countrified style. We went on past Boulogne and Calais, the first striking me as a big, flourishing town, the latter as more of the village type. The country had now quiet a changed appearance, with canals and long drains full of slow, running water, reeds, small stunted trees, rowboats, and fishing lines. A great effort had been made to drain the land as much as possible and a large amount of it was under wheat, oats and potatoes.

Then we came to the big, busy-looking town of St. Omer and, about 11am in the morning, we alighted at Hazebrouck, We marched through the town, laid down our rifles and packs in a field and made tea for ourselves, but had no milk – which did not really matter. A walk into town showed me some fine shops, all the good displayed being English. It had quite a British air and there were restaurants with the menu in English, showing it was possible to get ham and eggs, but I had not a sou. At 6 o'clock, we went again to a passenger train and after a short journey reached Steenwerck.

We formed up and set off to look for our Battalion. We marched along a great, wide road with a wonderful row of trees on each side and having also, a broad-gauge railway or tramway line. The surface of the road was formed of stone setts, like the streets of a town at home. The '*pavé*', it was called and, although it made a noisy highway, it wore and looked well. Northern France was a country of good roads but what particularly struck me was its splendid system of direction signs. These were numerous and of a uniform pattern. They were all of cast iron and the blades were about two feet long but their height varied from six to eighteen inches. The lettering was cast iron also, and was painted white on a light-blue background. The blade, on an important road would contain up to eight names arranged in order of their lengths, which would be given in kilometres carried to one decimal place. The first name would be in letters about two inches high and the others would be in reduced sizes. For pedestrians I thought the signs could hardly be improved, but for motorists the lettering was rather small.

The country was more like home and there were many big farmhouses, all built of brick; none of the wood and plaster style here. The fields were about the size of our own and bounded by heavy hedges.

Belgium

Thursday 27 July 1916: Near Red Lodge

We passed a notice board which read *'Limit de État'* and the next second we were treading the soil of Belgium. The ground was of a rich, rough nature and the heavy land would be waterlogged in winter but now carried great crops of potatoes, oats and hay. The few people we saw smiled welcomingly to us and if to greet more new and agreeable acquaintances. At last, after wandering a lot, we met Mr J. Long, our Quartermaster, who took us to where the transport was camped and where we met many old friends. We had tea with bread and slept that night in a bivouac.

Friday 28 July 1916: Messines

We rose early and after a short march, came upon the Battalion who were quartered about a wood, some in farmhouses; others in dugouts. I had much pleasure in seeing many old faces who I had given up as lost forever but very many were absent and in the places were strangers. I stayed that day about a farmhouse with some of the other boys and we had much to talk over. I recounted to them my experiences, while they told me about the awful days they had come through since the 1 July and the hard spells of marching on the long journey which had landed them here. I was told that they stopped for the night at a town larger than usual, where there was a *'masion de tolerance'* and so eager were the chaps to gain admittance that a queue was formed. One fellow whose trousers were held up by means of a nail was so pitied by the mademoiselle that she kindly took the trouble to sew on a button. He was sure proud of that button.

Only for a small fraction of the way had they been helped along by a train and another day by motors. About this time I noticed all our transport appeared with the Divisional sign of the 'Red Hand of Ulster' painted on a white background.[53] That evening an unfortunate affair happened. I was in the barn of the farmhouse and the building was being shaken every few minutes by the explosion from a twelve inch gun of which ours was in action, in the wood, behind me. Suddenly a bigger roar than usual sent the slates reeling off the roof and outside there was a cry for stretcher-bearers.

The gun had burst and a huge fragment of steel, roughly fifteen hundredweights I should reckon, had been hurled up into the air, had passed over the barn where I was and crashed into the side wall of a building beside me, severely injuring two of our lads, one of whom had just arrived along with me that morning. Of the unfortunate artillerymen, six were killed outright while one died in agony from horrible injuries and several were

---

53 The 'Red Hand' symbol used by the Division was the left hand, the UVF used the right.

slightly shaken or wounded. I have been asked if I ever saw men praying in the trenches and I must answer I never did. I found men met death as they had lived, and when I write that a man died in agony I may mean he died cursing and swearing with all his remaining energy. We could do nothing; one always felt such a helpless mite in the presence of these awful explosions of modern warfare.[54]

That evening we marched into the firing lines; the weather was very hot. A tremendous amount of work had been done on these communication trenches to resist the pressure of the heavy soil and water in winter. The sides, right to the very bottom, were lined with sheets of corrugated iron and the floors were wooden and raised about two feet, so as to allow a free channel underneath for the water.

The country was level with many thick hedges and a light railway ran right up almost to the front line and most of it could be worked in the day time. The hand-pushed buggies made the duty of bringing up rations and construction material very easy. The dugouts were only shrapnel proof and had to be very carefully constructed to keep out the water.

The best were those which had been made by the Canadians and which were often very neat and effectively constructed. It was out of the question to think of making dugouts, deep down in the ground, on account of the wetness of the earth. Our front line was in a dilapidated state with the ruins of sandbags but there was a fairly good second line about one hundred yards behind.

The German trench was a matter of three hundred yards away and very difficult to follow in this level country with its many hedges. On the left, on higher ground, stood the village of Messines and the way to it was by the road along which the London Scottish made their charge in the beginning of the war. On the right were Ploegsteert Wood and Armentières with its mill chimneys.

Saturday to Wednesday 29 July to 2 August 1916: Messines

During the time I was in these trenches I had very few duties. I was with the reserve bombers, in the second line, and throughout the night we did guard duty against a surprise attack by gas. In the daytime it was tremendously hot and it was with difficulty I exerted myself. Flies and mosquitoes were troublesome but this part of the line was very quiet and the artillery action was limited each day to a few trench mortars and salvos of shrapnel fire.

We actually got paid in these trenches on one occasion, so free were they from disturbance. In Flanders, in a corner of many of the fields, scattered over a wide area, there would be a dozen graves of soldiers who had been killed in 1914, before this line became stabilised. They were all marked with wooden crosses and half of them were British, belonging chiefly to the cavalry regiments.

In the Somme, when I was there, isolated graves were unknown. In the churchyards of the villages immediately behind the line there would be a dozen graves of French soldiers, each marked with a wooden cross which was surmounted with the cap of the deceased. The cemetery at Beauval had a most imaginative appearance. Generally the civilian graves were adorned with sculptures which were more ponderous and elaborate

---

54 Battalion War Diary: "Our 12" gun near Battalion Headquarters blew up, killing four and wounding several – a piece six feet long and weighing a ton was hurled 150 yards through the roof of a house."

than those in England. Aeroplanes were being used and fired at as usual but we had no casualties during this spell.

Thursday 3 August to Monday 7 August 1916: Piggeries

We came out of the trenches, being relieved by the 10th Inniskillings in the evening; there was no necessity to wait here until nightfall. 'A' and 'B' companies went into billets, in a big farmhouse called the Piggeries, and my quarters were in a wooden hut there. People were still living on the farm and the horses, cows and roving pigs were still there, although the situation of the place was only a matter of half an hour's walk from our firing line.

Fields of wheat were around us and the binders were already started their work. In the same fields, along the thick hedges, were our batteries, gun posts and dugouts for the artillerymen. The German shells came over and I have often seen them exploding among the stooks of wheat. As we lay on our beds at night, with the howitzers in action around us, we wondered what ties held these people, especially the womenfolk, to such a hideous place.

During the six days we were here, I was on several working parties for the Royal Engineers, carrying bags of cement and shingle up to the communication trench to the second line. It was hot weather and, as there was generally a heavy mist or haze, I did not know why the trench railway was not used. The King's Royal Rifles employed this railways right up to within one hundred and fifty yards of the front line in the day-time. The cement, I believe, was for a dugout for Headquarters.

Tuesday 8 August to Saturday 12 August 1916: Messines

We went out of our billets at the Piggeries to the Front Line, 'A' Company taking up a central position and I was with them until Saturday. The place was very quiet, never a shell came near us by day or night, but owing to the nonsensical and malign regulations enforced upon us, the time was a very hard and trying one. These orders were given by the Brigade or Divisional Headquarters, also to add to our humiliation and exasperation they were enforced by those new officers whose experience of warfare had been obtained at Newcastle in Ireland.

Of all the inhuman regulations the worst was that all men must wear their equipment, at all times, in the trenches. There was no necessity for such a command; I never saw a German in the front line with his equipment on and I had seen dozens of them. The outfit was heavy and sore to wear, for the one hundred and twenty pounds of ammunition alone must have weighed over eight lbs. The weather was hot and suffocating, so that crawling in and out of our earthy holes, we had to be always harassed by this dragging, scorching load. How much better to have kept it hanging on pegs, inside the dugout?

Every time we moved a few yards out of a dugout to draw a dinner or empty a dixie, we must have this burning leather pulling at our aching shoulders and lean bones. In fact we were treated in these trenches as if we were unnatural criminals, doing punishment, instead of the only survivors of a great fight. We must even eat with eight pounds of lead pressing on our stomach; we must sleep our occasional sleep with one hundred and twenty pounds as a pad on which to rest our side and we must dig and fill sandbags, our limbs tied in an entanglement of leather straps.

There was much important work to do, for winter was coming on and we were holding a Battalion front with a Battalion of half-strength. That was not the only thing we had to grumble about, for we practised continual gas alarms. When the wind was blowing on our backs toward the German trenches, we used to have to wear our masks on for hours at a stretch. Not one day for practise only did we do this when the wind and conditions were favourable for a German gas attack, but day after day, and sometimes twice in the same day. It was a gallant attempt to break our hearts by some means.[55]

And the new officers used to run boldly up and down the quiet trench – they never wore equipment or donned gas helmets – threatening and bullying the men. At stand-to every morning and evening these same heroes found fresh opportunities to show their extreme powers. At stand-to every man must parade to the fires step and face the German lines with his head over the parapet. He must remain in this position during all the stand-to and woe to the man who tired, or fed up, stepped down for a moment from his cramped position on the narrow fire step.

What was it all for? And what was stand in for? I have asked that question a hundred times and I have received two answers which were always the same. One said it was on old custom of the British Army: then was it not nearly time that the British Army knew it did not come to the trenches only to show its veneration for such silly old habits? The other answer was that sunset or sunrise was a favourite time for an attack to be made: but surely the enemy was not going to attack until he had destroyed our wire, and he could not do that without giving us sufficient warning. Else what was the use of wire?

That reminds me of another incident. One of the chaps at stand-to asked his officer to have a look, over the parapet, at our wire which in his opinion was too scanty. 'Oh no, I don't look over the top. The Captain has told us that we must on no account show our heads above the parapet.'

A redcap (officer of the Brigade) passed along the reserve trench one day and we expected to hear him say, 'These trenches will be terrible in the winter, we must see about doing this and that to improve conditions.' Instead he strode along, proudly followed by his string of orderlies, until he spied someone's equipment. 'What is that doing there?' and he pointed out the obnoxious thing with his cane. 'That's mine Sir,' replied a Tommy in shirt sleeves, sweating and filling sandbags. 'God damn it, man, what do you mean? Get in on, get it on.' An example of how to speak to a degraded criminal, and thus Tommy groused, so that the world said he was lazy while it smiled its patronising smile.

The great, redeeming feature about our stay here was that the grub was good. We received one third of a loaf per man per day, and proper dinners, once we actually had a second course, a nice dish of rice, sultanas and milk. My sand-bagging won the admiration of a Royal Engineer Officer and our own Commanding Officer, Lieutenant Colonel F.O. Bowen.

On the 7th August 1916, I posted home a copy of the Battalion magazine, *The Incinerator*. It was No 2 Vol 1, and was dated June 1916. It was edited by U.S.H. Monard who, in 1957, is still living. On the front was an incinerator and on the back the words of Colonel Chichester: 'I am proud of my young citizens.' There were articles such as 'Fuel and Ashes', List of deaths since arrival in Frances, Sports Corner, several drawings,

---

55 Battalion War Diary 8.8.16: "A quiet day. A large paper balloon coming from a south easterly direction alighted in the field at the back of La Grande Munque Farm. Evidently sent by the enemy to test the wind. All ranks warned to be particularly alert for gas attack"

'Between the Strafes', 'Some French' by Professor Boyd de Brian etc. There was also among the 'Advertisements', one from Sergeant Jones which proclaimed, 'Come to me all you weary ones, and I will tie you to the wheel of rest.'[56]

Saturday 12 August and Sunday 13 August 1916: Hill 63

This day I packed up my kit and left the trenches to join the Permanent Patrol, which was billeted in dugouts in the wood on Hill 63. It was fine getting back among those fellows, to be in the midst of maps and telescopes and away from all the regimental tyranny of the Company. The first night I had a good, long sleep and the next day I was orderly.

Monday 14 August 1916: Anton's Farm

I was on the Battalion observation post in the front line, near Anton's Farm, and from this point a good view was obtained of part of the ruined village of Messines but it was very rarely that any movement was observed. That night I was to go out on patrol but the moonlight was too clear for such work.

Tuesday 15 August 1916: Hill 63

I paid a visit to the Brigade Observation Post, on Hill 63, from which an extensive view could be seen of the German roads and fortifications behind their front line. That evening the Battalion came out of the trenches and the patrol went into tents, amid the trees, near Red Lodge.

Wednesday to Monday 16-21 August 1916: Red Lodge

We had an easy and pleasant time as were close to the Divisional canteen and we had lots of money to spend. We went on no working parties but instead we moved out in pairs, into the country, to look for carrier pigeons and spies. I cannot say we had any very substantial results, but we gained a good knowledge of all the roads, cafés, shops and the girls who served in them.

A number of the women worked for the Royal Army Medical Corps washing clothes. There was a large hygienic station on the Steenwerck Road where a fine shower-bath and a change of so-called 'clean' clothing was given out to over one thousand men every day. It was unfortunate for us that fruit was not so plentiful here as on the Somme, but we helped ourselves to blackberries and beans.

The people here talked a peculiar language, I supposed it was Flemish. It was a written language, for the public notices were printed in it and it looked very like Scotch but everyone knew French and a very good smattering of English for that matter. The public notices were in three languages, French, English and Flemish which could all be seen, side by side, on the Church doors. In every village in Belgium there seemed to be at least one café named 'Lion Belge'.

Some of the farmhouses were very pretty and I especially liked the roofs of red and black tiles, the red in the edge and black in the centre which along with those fancy,

---

56   *The Incinerator* was produced during the months of May and June 1916 only. It is probable that many of the editorial team fell in the opening days of the Somme battle the following month. See Bowman, T., *op. cit.* , (Manchester: University Press, 2003).

black ridge tiles was a fine combination. The weather was unsettled with several thunder showers.

Monday to Monday 21-28 August 1916: Mac's Post
We did a spell of seven days in the trenches at Messines this time; the weather was changeable, sometimes very hot and sunny but occasionally raining heavily. I was on Mac's Post (Brigade Observation Post) all the time. The atmosphere was good for observation and we had an excellent time watching the roads and paths behind the German lines and trying to place them on the map. I found this a difficult job, for the ground in view showed only the tops of hills and the important things, such as rivers, railways and roads were nearly always hidden from sight.

Sometimes in the evenings, when the sun was behind me and lighted up the villages occupied by the enemy, the effect was very beautiful. A perfect Dutch picture of green trees and red houses with windmills was displayed, also Church spires and factory chimneys, rising one behind the other, further and further back. I could see the people in the fields working the hay; a real beautiful landscape it was but I could only admire it.

There was a Church spire and a tower I liked to gaze at very much, although I could see only their tops above the trees, in the distance beyond Warenpon in the valley of the River Lys. But two such graceful architectural objects I had never looked upon before. They were of different styles of building and one was taller than the other, but I could never decide which was the more elegant, chaste or clear in outline when they were gilded with the sinking sun and set in a sky of mellow blue. And yet I was not there to admire such things; I was to look for machine gun emplacements, new trenches and other signs of active warfare lurking in that pleasant land. What a humiliating job!

I was out on two patrons but nothing particular happened in either. The chief danger was from machine-gun fire for the ground was level and the only cover was the old trenches, which were very abundant. The grass was long and dry while there was a great deal of old wire, so that we had to walk warily for the Germans sent up a big number of flare lights.

Returning from a patrol, I had to report at Battalion Headquarters and I was amazed at the fuss there was over the exact number of life-preservers which we had on loan. However the controversy was eventually settled and the adjutant, Captain A Mulholland, gave my companions and me each an oval shaped cigarette from a large box of them on the table.

During the last few days, a great lot of gas was carried up to our front line in heavy, steel cylinders. I suppose an attack by gas was mediated at an early date. The cylinders were stored below the fire step in wooden chambers made for the purpose, but which I had always supposed to be for the purpose of drainage.

Tuesday 29 August 1916: Red Lodge
We practised a raid which our Battalion intended making during darkness, after an attack with gas. That night, however, it was raining heavily and the wind was in the wrong direction, so the raid was postponed. We had a good sleep instead and another twenty-four hours of life fairly well assured.

Wednesday 30 August to Saturday 2 September 1916: Messines

It was wet all day and we again practised our raid. We had the German trenches marked out on the ground with white tape, so that each man would know exactly what to expect. I wondered how it would turn out when it came to the real thing for I had my suspicions. We were told by the Commanding Officer, Lieutenant Colonel F.O. Bowen, that he did not see how there could be any casualties; the Germans would be in a state of coma, a very nice word to use, so that I wondered if our leaders knew the enemy had machine guns, artillery and gas helmets.

After dark, the rain ceased and there was a very slight breeze blowing in the direction of the German trenches so that at about 10pm we stood to. There were sixteen scouts and seventeen others to enter the German trenches. Then there was, in addition, to be a chain of men standing across no man's land, to convey down the prisoners or booty, and there were stretcher bearers also as well as two signallers to carry out a telephone wire to the German line. Captain J McKee was in charge and there were three other officers, including Mr R.V. Drought.

I was carrying a bomb jacket containing twelve bombs; I also had a revolver, twelve rounds of ammunition and an electric torchlight. As we went up to Annscroft Avenue our artillery started the bombardment which eventually became fairly severe. The Germans retaliated and some of their shells came pretty near us; I received a shower of earth and a bit of shrapnel passed very near my head. If I had not ducked I might have had a second wound for I almost thought that my gas helmet had been cut. The officer behind me believed I had been hit also.

One of our fellows, W. Roy, was struck on the foot and I took his place, which was that of carrier of the ammonal tube or Bangalore torpedo. We had two of these, their use being to blow up the German wire. They were each about six feet long and consisted of a tube of zinc, containing ammonal. William Roy had joined the Army when he was seventeen and had been Corporal but relinquished his stripes to become an ordinary ranker. Shortly after the end of the War he told me he had taken part in every action of the Ulster Division, except Cambrai, and had not even been wounded. He had an enthralling account to give of his experiences during the retreat in March, 1918, when he expected to be driven back to the sea. The last time I saw him was in 1922 when I visited a Building Exhibition in London. He was in charge if the stand of Messrs. D. Anderson & Son, Belfast, who manufacture Red Hand Roofing Felt, paint and other supplies. He was then the firm's manager in the North of England and lived in Leeds.

The mine was very fragile and the tube had to be handled carefully. They were pushed into the enemy wire, and one adjusted into the end of the other. Then they were fitted with detonator, fuse and lighter. The explosion acted sideways only and made a wide opening in the wire, absolutely washing it away. The bombardment now ceased, only one of our two guns kept going, so as to screen our movements.

We advanced up to the front line, to the point whence we were to leave. The men with the torpedoes went first leaving a white tape to show the path to the others and the road by which to return. The night was pretty dark and I felt very cool, although I was only a matter of a few yards from the German wire and the longer we stayed the more at ease I got. But we had difficulties with the German wire, which was very strong at that part and had suffered little from our artillery. We had also great doubts about the effectiveness of our gas, although we smelled it on the grass on leaving our own trenches, but out here we perceived no trace of it.

The Germans were very much on the alert apparently; their flares were going up in all directions, as usual. We had cut through a lot of loose stands of the German wire and had advanced about twenty yards in the middle of it. We had pushed in the first tube and were fixing in the second, when all at once, we were challenged in a loud, clear voice from the German trench in front. We could only be quiet and the call was repeated while another challenge came from the left, apparently from a sap. A bomb, one of those with a wooden handle, was thrown and burst quite close. Several shots were fired and two great flares were then thrown up. They lighted the whole ground and a machine gun started but the bullets did not appear to be going in exactly the proper direction for us.

The Germans were absolutely on the alert, their wire was practically uninjured and we had no other choice but to retreat. No-one was hurt, and only one chap was sent away suffering from shell shock. As we marched back to Red Lodge, the dawn was breaking.[57]

In the evening, we scouts were sent to visit the cafés in Romarin to find out if rum was being sold in any of them. The cafes I was in were selling much beer but I saw no rum; however I learned that plenty was always obtainable.[58] The people all spoke English exceedingly well. One woman told of the high price of boots in Belgium, a child's pair of clogs cost eight and a half francs and she said how much cheaper they were in France.

Another day we had a long trail through our subsidiary lines. Heath trench was the most important in this part. It would have been a very useful fire trench in case of retreat and it contained many artillery Observation Posts, yet for one going up it, was continually in view of the enemy. The machine gun emplacements were a disgrace, as any of the Machine Gun Company would relate, but with a little care they could make this hill impregnable.

Most of the positions were in conspicuous ruins, open to German observation and the team occupied them only at night. There they had to remain close as mice all day to avoid observation as no-one could approach a gun post without going across the open.

Sunday 3 September to Tuesday 5 September 1916: Mac's Post
We went into the trenches for four days. I was in the Brigade Post all the time and did one patrol. The weather was broken.

Wednesday 6 September 1916: Red Lodge
We came out to Red Lodge being relieved by a Brigade of the 19th Division.[59]

Thursday 7 September 1916: Dranoutre
We marched to Dranoutre. The weather was warm but the roads were fairly good, if hilly, and a lot of sweat was lost, although the march was not hard. Dranoutre was a grand village with many cafés and possessing a YMCA hut but we went into tents.

---

57 Battalion War Diary, 30.8.16: "Two men were slightly wounded. Party left out trench at 2.50am and returned at 4.10am. During the gassing our guns fired for about 35 minutes. Enemy's retaliation was very light."

58 *Estaminet*, a small café, bistro or bar, especially a shabby one.

59 The 14th Rifles were relieved by the 8th Glosters.

Friday to Monday 8-11 September 1916: Locre

We had a bath at a good hygienic station where not less than sixty-five women were employed in washing our clothes – they were a tough lot. At dinner time I was in one of those beautiful cafés of the country, everything was clean and becoming, including the tiled floor, the marble tables and the comfortable, light chairs. I also looked with pleasure on the old, polished mirrors, the shining glasses, the high ceilings and the tastily-coloured wallpaper. Above all I noticed the charming figure of womanhood who served at the table and spoke English so well.

After dinner we made up our packs again and marched along the Ypres Road where we took possession of our billets, outside Locre, in wooden huts known as Wakefield Huts. There were several camps here, and the huts were very small and gloomy but what would one have? Locre was a well-built, little village with many shops and cafés and also a YMCA hut. Hugh N. Turner and I had chipped potatoes with eggs in one house and enjoyed the meal very well. We paid a visit to Bailleul also. Bailleul was a well-built town with a population of about ten thousand. Its many shops were full of English goods and in all its eating houses, good English was spoken. It had a fine square and a beautiful Hotel de Ville which I believe was smashed to powder in 1918. Bailleul was in France so that we had to cross the frontier to reach it and although we were not stopped, there was a customs hut with a swinging pole to barricade the road.

We were going to take up a new part of the line and I believed, were down for a nasty job. Oh, how sick I was of the whole business. There were no thanks, nor rewards for anything. We were ordinary infantry of the line. Oh, but we got one shilling per day! The motor lorry men however, got two shillings per day, although he ran no more risk than if he were in Donegall Place. He got as much bread as he could eat, also as many blankets as he required and he was never away from the region of civilisation, for there was always the cheery cafés at his hand to guile away the unhappy hour. What an organisation and who would not be proud to be in it? It did not feed one; its system of promotion was absurd and its pay-regulations ridiculous.

Tuesday 12 September to Sunday 17 September 1916: Wytschaete

We took over the line in front of Wytschaete. We left the huts near Locre in the afternoon and marched to Dranoutre along the road towards Messines. We met no Belgian soldiers for certain, but I learned afterwards they were dressed in horizon blue, similar to the French. The whole of the time we were in France we saw remarkably few French soldiers except the guards at railway bridges. These were old soldiers in mixed uniforms, but chiefly in red trousers and dark blue coats. One of their main duties was for the guard to turn out and present arms when a British Battalion passed. There were a few French artillerymen in horizon blue at the Battle of the Somme and occasionally I saw a soldier on leave. I also observed representatives of the French Colonial Forces adorned in their colourful dresses, Zouaves, Turcos and Moroccans.

Our march towards Messines led us past Kemmel Mount, a high hill which no one was allowed to ascend without permission from the Brigadier. I understood a great view could be obtained from it of the fighting region, as far as the Ypres Salient.

We then entered the area where the usual dilapidated farms were first seen and all signs of recent cultivation ceased. The ground was covered with long, withered grass and flourishing hordes of thistles. Barbed wire entanglements were stretching for kilometres, gun emplacements were spotted and a battery was seen in action. Working parties were returning after the day's labour, motor lorries, limbers and water carts were always impeding one's march. A Red Cross collecting station was observed; it was all the same story but in a slightly different setting.

Suddenly we entered a field on the right with a trench alongside, but we kept on the top. After a walk of nearly two miles; partly in a trench called 'King's Way' and partly in the open, we finished up at RE Farm, a ruin about four hundred yards from the German line. We could move about freely in the open here, for the Germans were over the hill and the place was not under observation from any point.

There was a row of dry, small dugouts, or rather houses built with sandbags, and these were our billets. There were few opportunities for patrol here; consequently we were attached to the reserve company. Our duties consisted of supplying several gas-guards, forming small working parties and bringing up rations. We had also to stand-to but altogether we had not a bad time.

About this time I had my only experience of tear gas shelling. The fumes at first were strangely sweet but soon the tears were rolling down my cheeks and I was glad to don my goggles. These were a separate article from the respirator and consisted of a wad of flannel with eyepieces held in position by an elastic band round the head. The troops up in the front trenches, however, had a filthy spell. The German trenches were only a matter of forty to eighty yards away and there was hardly any wire between us. We occupied the top of a long ridge and the Germans were on the eastern slope of it, so that our movements above the parapet, both by day and night had to be very carefully conducted as they showed up against the skyline.[60]

Sniping was very much practised by the Germans and the continual pat of the bullets on the sandbags, just at one's head, was trying on the nerves. The men slept on the fire step at night and indeed almost got blinded with the mud knocked down by these bullets.

The dugouts in the front line, such as they happened to be, were entered only in the daytime and the second line was about fifty yards behind the first. Both were badly destroyed in parts by trench mortars, the holes being huge, some of them were twenty feet across and capable of burying a horse and cart. The very appearance of the landscape was enough to set my nerves tingling: it resembled the German trenches at Thiepval, after the bombardment.

Other names used by the soldiers for different varieties of trench mortars and high explosive shells were flying pigs, footballs, coal-boxes, canisters, sausages, oil-cans, Black Marias, crumps, minnies, Jack Johnstons, woolly-bears, rum-jars and aerial torpedoes. The transport came up a road at night, right to RE Farm where they ran no danger from machine guns and did not seem to be often shelled. The Royal Engineer wagons moved up to the same spot. During the spell here the weather was very unsettled and inclined to be cold.

We bombarded the German trenches with trench mortars and artillery nearly every day and night, also raiding parties went over from the Battalions on our right and left.

---

60 Battalion War Diary 17.9.16: "A certain amount of damage done to our front line by enemy trench mortars, one of which punctured a gas cylinder in our front line, necessitating the removal of the Company holding the sector to the support trench for a few hours. We had no casualties from gas poisoning."

The Germans replied only once, with a number of heavy trench mortars which did a lot of damage. Sharp shooting was common and the strain on the nerves of our men in the front line was very severe. They were constantly on guard against snipers and trench mortars while the dugouts were used only during the day so that the week was a fairly stiff one for them. Near the front line there was a permanent firing-rack with the SOS rockets in position.

Tanks went into action on the Somme for the first time on the 9 September, 1916. Men with a mechanical knowledge were immediately required for the new weapon but I did not offer my services although several of our lads went.

Monday to Friday 18-22 September 1916: Wakefield Huts
We came out of the trenches and entered into billets called the Wakefield Huts, along the Dranoutre Road. We scouts were put into a big dugout and during our stay here we were on working parties for the Royal Engineers, either every day or every night. The weather was very wet and many of these working parties were horrible, fatiguing affairs. After an hour of rain here, the trenches ran like streams which reminded me of the old burn at home, in time of flood. This is a stream about five feet wide which separates the town lands of Ballygowan and Ballyrockard More. On the 25 inch ordnance map it is called the 'McRoberts Burn'.

Saturday 23 September 1916: Neuve Eglise
A party of twenty-nine, which included myself, who had previously been told off and had been fitted out with new clothes, paraded at 12 o'clock to go as Guard of Honour to the King who was to distribute medals to Divisional recipients at Bailleul. I spent a hard morning tidying up for this affair and what a lot of work there was in such a cleanup. First of all the clothes had to be brushed and numerals must be polished. The boots had then to be washed and blackened while the equipment with all its straps and brass buckles must be put in shining appearance. Next there was the rifle and bayonet which had to be cleaned and the cap-badge, strap and puttees required extra attention. Then one also must be well washed and shaved, after this work had been carefully done, one might be presentable. This was what a bit of business of this kind entailed to the ordinary soldier.

After being inspected by the Commanding Officer, Lieutenant F.O. Bowen, the party marches to Dranoutre. From there the Brigade assembly went in motor lorries to a field near Neuve Eglise, not Bailleul, as we had expected. Parties from the other Brigades, from the Army Service Corps, Royal Army Medical Corps, Royal Engineers and Royal Flying Corps also arrived and all, after the usual marching about and dressing by the flank, got into some sort of order.

The recipients were by themselves, the VC on the right, the DSO's next, etc. The VC was a sturdy-looking, middle-aged man with a sandy moustache. Then, instead of the King, there arrived the Corps Commander by motor and the medals, or rather the ribbons, were distributed, each man's performance being read out from the official record. Next we presented arms, making a proper mess of things, and cleared away. We got on the motors again and had a ride back to Dranoutre, then footed it back to the billets, feeling very self-satisfied, of course, and pleased. I spent the night with the Orange Institution of my Battalion who, by my arrangements, met in a Flemish farmhouse. It was strange for an Orange Lodge to meet in a room with Roman Catholic pictures and statuary on the walls. On the Somme, except for the crucifixes along the roadside, there was little evidence of religious piety in the homes.[61]

Sunday 24 September to Saturday 30 September 1916: Wytschaete

We went into the trenches at Wytschaete and the scouts were once more attached to the reserve Company, 'B' this time; six of us, under an NCO, were put on guard for the coming six days. We were chiefly on alert in case of gas, to give warning on the gongs which here were often elaborate affairs, worked with compressed air, or by turning a handle such as was often seen on motor cars.

This garrison, which I had the good luck to be on, had an easy time, for during the night we had two posts, but in the daytime, only one. As a guardroom we had a good, dry cellar containing a lot of stores, including blankets, which could be made into anti-gas sheets, but which we found very useful for their natural purpose.

The weather was quite good, there being no rain and often it was quite warm. We kept a fire going at times and did a lot of extra cooking often. There was a pond of dirty water close at hand and most of us had an open air bath each morning. So altogether we had an agreeable time as were left to ourselves and had a few adventures. Many of the farmhouses here were surrounded by a ditch ten feet or more wide which was practically full of water covered with a green scum. There was a bridge across this moat which added to its appearance as a medieval stronghold.

One day a German kite-balloon broke loose and came drifting across our lines. Our anti-aircraft guns shot at it and then several battle planes came round it and opened fire with their machine guns. The balloon burst into flames and fell out of sight among the trees. I was told afterwards that an officer had escaped, practically unhurt, from it and that his papers were quite untouched.[62]

Although I have looked at scores of German aeroplanes in the air and watched them being shelled by our anti-aircraft guns, yet I never saw a German aeroplane brought to the ground by our shell fire. Indeed I never saw one of our own aeroplanes and a German one in the air at the same time.

Another day a red-kite officer came over with the wind, carrying a message written in German and was captured by the 16th Royal Irish Rifles (Pioneer Battalion).

We always considered that about RE Farm, a person could not be hit by a German bullet. One night I was helping Sergeant Major J.J. Mackey to unload a limber when I heard something coming in contact with his tunic and he said, putting a hand to his stomach, that he had been hit. We led him into the candlelight of our cellar and took off his shirt. There was a German bullet buried about an eighth of an inch in his stomach but there was also a hole drilled right through his right arm made by the same bullet. If he had not stopped the bullet I must have caught it, but about where was the question?

This district was the abode of a legion of ravenous, bold rats that were very easy to kill with a stick at night, when they went food hunting. To prevent our rations being consumed by rats, when the dugout was unoccupied, we would tie our rations in a

---

61   The Orange Lodge of the 14th Rifles was LOL 862.
62   The British aircraft that shot down the German balloon was piloted by Captain D.O. Mulholland, RFC, the brother of the Battalion Adjutant.

sandbag and suspend them from the roof by a string. Although I always found this method successful, yet I have heard of rats descending the string to get at the food.

Outside each dugout there was usually hanging a sandbag into which we put our refuse, such as empty jam-tins, etc. The rats, which had been hiding all day, once it got dark, climbed into the sandbag. At first we thought it would be great fun to tie the mouth of the bag and take them prisoners. But before we had the knot formed the rats had eaten through the bag and were scampering to safety. Then we tried beating the sandbag without entrenching handles, yet we found that a rat was very hard to kill. For half an hour afterwards all would be quiet in the sandbag, then the rustling started again; in fact they seemed to be only shamming death. Once while down for a sleep with a blanket over my face I had the experience of catching one with my hands as it was prowling over my chest, and a pal with an entrenching tool handle finally put it out of all further necessity of procuring its food.

Oh, how many hours did I fester in that old cellar, in full fighting order, with a bundle of blankets under me and several over me as well? On 30th we came out and took up billets in our old Wakefield Huts near Locre.

Sunday 1 October to Thursday 5 October 1916: Wakefield Huts
Sunday was my twenty-first birthday and very uneventful it was with not even a scrap of post from anyone. I was at Church Parade in the morning and the rest of the day was spent loafing about. The time now approached when I should be twelve months in France and Belgium during which I had seen much, learned a great lot, had numerous exciting events and experienced many horrid, hard times. In the matter of health I have been very fortunate having never had, I might say, a day of illness. My standing among the boys has always been highly rated while my judgement and opinion very often sought.

During the time I was at these huts I had an agreeable spell as there were not too many parades. In the evenings I went to Dranoutre or Locre and there, several of us would enjoy a good supper of eggs and chipped potatoes. It was indeed most remarkable how well these Belgians have picked up our language, even to the verbs and all the rest of it.

In Belgium I especially noticed the use of draught dogs. A fairly common sight was a bulky woman, going to market, sitting on top of a mass of agricultural produce contained in a small cart drawn by a pair of dogs of the Great Dane type.

The girls were not as attractive as their French neighbours. They were big and sturdy with robust, ruddy features. They were not so gay and dazzling as the French mademoiselles, but more silent, more thoughtful and probably more intelligent. They were Teutons while the French were Latins, a wonderful difference, more wonderful the more one studied it. The Teuton was dull and undemonstrative in appearance, but with an unerring brain beneath; the Latin was gay, gesticulate, simple and easily pleased.

One night, Hugh W. Turner, of the Transport informed me that at last he had got his commission and that, on the following morning, he would set out for London, so that night there was drinking and singing in the abodes of our Transport.

Friday 6 October to Wednesday 11 October 1916: Wytschaete
We moved into the trenches, the scouts occupying the same old dugout at RE Farm. The first night I was on a listening post. We crawled out, by a hole underneath the parapet,

Company Sergeant Major James Scott, No 14/15892, in his YCV uniform. He was killed on 22 January 1917, age 35 years. The husband of Jane Duffy, Scott, of Finaghy Halt, Balmoral, Belfast, he is buried in La Plus Douve Cemetery, grave IV.B.5. (Nigel Henderson)

and then made our way carefully along an old trench. After having gone twenty yards we stopped, for here the German line was only forty yards from our own. We remained in this place for about two hours, but very little could be heard, as the wind was blowing strongly from our own trenches. Snipers were a nuisance here and one in front of me kept my ears ringing with the report of his shots. A bullet of his struck the ground near me and dashed the earth up into my eyes and face.

The next day we scouts were put on a part of the front line trench where mining was suspected and we had to keep a sentry on there for forty-eight hours in two spells. I can assure you I hated it. It was most trying on the nerves holding this front line – it was enough to drive the sentry mad. There was the appearance of the trench, which was merely a sandbag breast-work, and most of the bays showed signs of having newly been blown in or just recently repaired.

Everywhere there were great shell holes, smashed in dugouts, broken-up rifles, torn clothes and bits of equipment half buried in the sides of the trench. Then no-one could ever know when the trench mortars or rifle grenades might start, when their awful 'swish-swish' might be heard, calling up all kinds of horrible feelings. One stood there, stuck to his position, and looked at his neighbour who also was apparently stuck there. Then the ground underneath was probably mined and there was always the danger of gas, if the wind blew our way.

Oh it was more than flesh, blood and reason could stand, and there was no leave, nor sympathy, only cold and hunger, with an awful end and unknown burial place! Look how many have gone the whole dreadful way, one by one; some day it was almost certain to be my turn, and I did not want to be killed now, once I did not mind particularly. I would just like to see home, see the girls and tell them with my own lips how I suffered awful things and faced death, even as the wonderful heroes in the story books.

When I was awake at night and heard or felt the guns going, my lips ran loose and trembled, my jaws went chattering for I could not help myself. I rose and walked about but the awful feeling was very hard to remove. One night we sent over gas while Fritz retaliated with his trench mortars and there were a number of casualties. A big patrol of ours went out afterwards and although it did not succeed in entering the German trench as it bombed them hard from the outside, for he was standing-to in his front line and made an easy target. One of our fellows was slightly wounded on the leg but I was not on this stunt, being orderly of that day.[63]

The remainder of the spell we spent on observation and patrols: the observation I carried out with a telescope and periscope from the front line. The German trenches have been badly smashed in some places, the parapets have been blown away and trench-boarding scattered about everywhere. The wire was not wide but was pretty strong consisting of steel or huge, wooden knife-edges which were strung together with lots of concertina wire. A view of the land behind the German lines could be seen, with part of the village of Wytschaete, which was still apparently in a moderately erect condition. Patrolling was limited by the good moonlight and I was very thankful when our time came to leave.

Thursday to Wednesday 12-18 October 1916: Daylight Corner

I was engaged on working parties and the weather favoured us very much, being cool and dry for the most part. The first squad was a night one but the others were all in the morning. We did a lot of work on these and it was a fact that we all noticed how much better working parties were managed here than they had been on the River Ancre. We were regularly shelled at our work and there were a number of casualties. I had several narrow shaves from shells but was never hit with anything more serious than the loud detonation and a shower of earth. I was however terribly jumpy now and someday I knew I should collapse with scare.

Volunteers were wanted for another raid and I offered myself, chiefly because we would not be going into the trenches during the following six days and also because it would all come to the same thing eventually, whether we volunteered or not.

These days we spent at Daylight Corner, in newly made huts, were quite comfortable. The place was shelled one day and a woman was killed in her own farmyard; it was probably the batteries roundabout that the Germans were trying to get at. The Battalion went into the trenches on Wednesday.

Thursday 19 October to Monday 23 October 1916: Wakefield Huts

The raiding party moved down to Wakefield Huts in Dranoutre where the 10th Inniskillings were. The weather was very wet at first but afterwards cleared up. During the whole time the Inniskillings did practically no parades of any sort. They played football daily, had sports or went walking leisurely round the country. How different

---

63   Battalion War Diary 8.10.16: "A patrol of ten NCOs' and men under 2nd Lieutenant RV Drought went out at 2.45am to endeavour to see results of the gas, but were unable to approach enemy's front line trench as it was strongly held. One man of patrol slightly wounded."

from the way we were treated when out there. With us it was early morning parade, washed and cleaned at 6.45am, the endless kit inspections, saluting-drill, gas-helmet parades etc.

As for our raiding party; we had a fairly busy time. We laid out dummy German trenches and practised our different parts, day after day, under the supervision of Mr R.V. Drought and Mr J.D. O'Brien. Every night we used to go into a café in Dranoutre where we had a good supper of eggs and chips. This was served up very nicely by a number of attractive young ladies and the resort was a favourite one of the YCV. Félice, Jeanne and the other two were very pleasant girls with curly, frizzy hair who spoke English well and were in all respects quite agreeable companions.

This café in Dranoutre was known to us as 'The Seven Sisters'. It was a fairly big establishment and included a bakery and a shop. It was run by about four sisters while their parents and other sisters were in occupied territory. The first night I dined there I noticed a pleasant looking waitress, but in a few moments she had disappeared and her place was taken by another girl who was obviously her sister. She also soon disappeared and was replaced by a third sister. This happened again and I was slightly amused at this shuffling of waitresses but had no idea that I was the cause of it. Afterwards I got to know Félice who was about fifteen and the youngest. She told me her sisters were just crazy about curly hair and when one of them first spotted me she became excited and immediately withdrew to inform another sister. When she also had a good look at my curly head she retired and another was given the benefit of the view – thus, the succession of sisters which had diverted me. In the evenings Félice was generally attending in the shop and doing her school homework. I was able to help her in some problems in Euclid, and I noticed her school exercises were written in two languages, French and Flemish. Among themselves the girls always conversed in Flemish, but they could talk equally well in French or English. Sometime afterwards I met an old YCV in Belfast who told me that Félice would only be too willing to accept me if I proposed to marry her.

One night (during this time) we did a patrol right up to the German wire.

Thursday 24 October to Sunday 29 October 1916: Bailleul

The Battalion came out of the trenches and we continued our practising for the raid. The weather got colder and wetter and we were served out with strong, leather jerkins, gloves and extra blankets.

One day the Battalion marched into Bailleul; we piled arms in a field and went to the Picture House where the French picture of the Battle of the Somme was demonstrated. We were all delighted with it, for what it showed was the real thing; the surrender of the Germans in their own trenches being portrayed as it could only be done by photographs taken on the spot. Then there was a good performance given by the 'Merry Mauves' after which a short ramble was allowed round the town and then we marched back to Dranoutre. The 'Merry Mauves' was only one of the numerous amateur concert parties organised by the military to entertain the troops when they were 'resting' behind the lines.

Others were called the 'Gaieties', 'The Tri-hards' and the 'B'Hoys'. They had clever, female impersonators among them and their shows were held in barns, schools, tents or hospitals.[64]

Monday 30 October 1916: Dranoutre
We moved out to our dummy trenches while the Battalion went into the real trenches.

Tuesday 31 October 1916: Wytschaete
At the dummy trenches Brigadier Shuter had a few words to say to us and we were informed that we would attempt our raid that night. I met the news with a kind of relief. Personally I disliked one feature about it; that we were to go over in two distinct parties about one hundred yards apart. I heard nothing of the second raiding party that night and I never learned what happened to it.

There was wire to be blown up simultaneously at zero time in two places but I did not see how this could be accomplished in the darkness of no man's land, when there was sure to be some delay or mishap. I went into the affair doggedly, as a true fatalist, caring little what might happen and seeing always a chance of a 'Blighty' wound or a medal. That evening, which was Halloween, we all went to a concert in the YMCA hut contributed by men of a Labour Battalion. It was pretty good and we came back about 8pm.

We made a few preparations for our raid, clearing our pockets of all means of identification and blackening our faces. Blackening our faces was done with a burnt cork. It not only hid our white countenance when the flares went up but it enabled us to distinguish ourselves from the enemy. We carried no equipment, nor steel-helmets, but were armed with revolvers, rifles and bombs. At 11pm we got on to a motor-char-a-banc which conducted the whole party, about ninety, up to Daylight Corner. We marched up the road, through Wulverghem, where one of the party had been wounded in the neck by a bullet. At RE Farm there was hot cocoa for us but I did not take any; then we fell in and moved up to the front line, where we were to go over.

Wednesday 1 November 1916: Wytschaete (Cooker Farm)
I went first, laying down a white tape. It was after 2am and the night was dry and quiet but the ground was very wet. Fritz was throwing up very few lights and it was hard to tell the proper direction to go. Twice Mr J.D. O'Brien told me to keep more to the right and I did not understand why but went on blindly as I was directed. I was perfectly cool, but I knew I was out of my way. Then after a long time Mr O'Brien came up to me excitedly, "McRoberts," he said, "where are you going? You will soon have us back to our own line, there's the German part, we want to enter that way," and he pointed much to the left.

To myself I blamed him for putting me wrong but went as directed. After a little distance there were numerous, big shell-holes and next the German wire appeared right in front. Mr O'Brien came and said, "It is almost 4 o'clock, we are not the proper spot, but put in the tubes." I crawled round the huge shell-holes, the three other chaps coming

---

64 Battalion War Diary 26.10.16: "Damp morning, fine bright afternoon. Battalion, headed by the Divisional Band marched into Bailleul where they were entertained by the 110th Field Ambulance, and attended a performance by the Divisional Follies at the cinema."

up with the three tubes, or Bangalore torpedoes as they were called. All at once there was a flash and shot from the German parapet high up in front.

I knew we were suspected and rushed up to the wire – there was no creeping any longer. I pushed in the first tube and the other chap helped me with the second. We drove the first two home through the wire right up against the parapet; we did not require the third.

My companion, who was a Royal Engineer, quietly fitted the detonator to the fuse and set off the patent lighter. I scrambled back, about fifteen yards and lay down, fingers in ears and mouth open. There was silence for a few seconds, then a terrific explosion, the flame dazzling our eyes.

Our first party rushed the place but I stood by, for I was to enter the trench with the last or search party. Our chaps, however, their eyes dazed by the bright flame and now in complete darkness again, did not rush exactly at the right place and came up against some wire. Bombs were flung and shots fired from the German parapet. I saw our chaps kneeling and feeling their way. "Rush them, Rush them!" I shouted. "Show us the way," said someone. I ran forward to the German parapet, the others beside me, and I tried to fire my revolver but it wouldn't work, it had fallen in the mud when I was laying the tube. I drew out a bomb, and was just about to pull the pin when there was a great flare of light in my eyes and I must have fallen back, although I do not remember doing so. I next found myself in one of the shell-holes, up to the neck in water. There were still shots and the bright explosion of bombs. The water was red and there were bits of flesh floating in it. My mouth was full of blood and shattered flesh, the right side of my head seemed a blank and there were painful places in my right leg. I thought of my first aid bandage but realised it was useless and that the only thing for me to do was to hurry back to my trenches while I could.

I scrambled out of the hole and turning my back to the firing and bomb explosions, I ran across no man's land, got through some wire and scrambled into the trench. No one had observed me and curiously also, I had seen no one. I even thought I had entered some Boche line and was only reassured when I saw an ammunition box of ours with the figures 'VII' on it.

Doctor Garvin was soon found and I had a dressing put on my face. Then I started off, running down King's Way, staggering all the time and accompanied by Alec Flynn, who was also wounded; eventually I reached our First Aid station. My face was again bandaged, also my leg at the knee and I was put on a stretcher and felt myself being carried for a long time. I had frequently pictured myself as being killed and imagined the scene at home when the news arrived. The greatest disability I could conjecture was being blinded in both eyes. I pictured myself with my eyesight gone, typing for a firm to whom I would be particularly valuable because of my knowledge of French! It was getting clear and I could see now, but I was feeling in a bad way, chiefly from the wetting I had got and my knee was paining me a lot.

France

At Daylight Corner I was put into a motor-ambulance and rode to Bailleul where I was handed over to a dressing-station. Here I vomited a quantity of blood and during the dressing I suffered a lot but finally, with bandaging all round my face, my leg in a splint and dry clothes on, I felt much better and looking round, saw several of my companions in adventure who had been slightly wounded but were now watching me eagerly. They smiled and said I had stuck it well. Then they laughingly reminded me of my shouting, 'Rush it, Rush it!' and we wished each other good luck. Some of them had got their wounds inside the German trench.

The raid had been a failure but the following short reference to it from *The History of the 36th (Ulster) Division* by Cyril Falls is interesting: "The raids of October the 31st were held up by showers of bombs from the stout-hearted Swabian peasants of the 26th (Württemberg) Division."

For many years afterwards in the Belfast papers I saw a notice in the 'In Memorial' column to Lance-Corporal William F. Forbes[65] of the 14th Royal Irish Rifles (YCV) who was killed in this raid. I knew him well and he was a Scout in the Permanent Patrol, I was also acquainted with his brother, Alec, who served in our Transport and thankfully survived the War.[66]

Wednesday and Thursday 1-2 November 1916: Bailleul

All Wednesday and Thursday I remained there. I could take liquid food only, through a feeder, for my mouth was sore, as both lips were smashed and I had three, front upper teeth shattered. My right eye was practically blind although apparently untouched. In the past, Jasper Robinson BA, the Methodist Chaplain, had called to meet me on two occasions at least but I had been absent each time. At last he apparently saw me when I was lying unconscious in Bailleul for he wrote to my parents, giving them the first information of my wounds. His letter, and one from me saying I was alright, arrived by the same post.

Friday 3 November 1916: Boulogne

In the morning I was put on an ambulance, carried down to the Railway Station and lifted on to a fine hospital train; I was no longer suffering any pain. The bed in the carriage was lovely and soft and there was a Sister, also lovely and soft, I thought! The Sister paid me special attention for she thought I had been dreadfully wounded. My whole face and head were covered with bandages except one eye and about half the mouth; I had also a splint all along one side. My head had been punctured with dozens of flakes of white metal which had burned into the skin and which I was still picking out even (later) when I was in England. I got more of my liquid food and passed an agreeable time, travelling all day. It was dark when the train stopped and soon afterwards I was taken out and put into an ambulance. There was a short journey and I was again on a stretcher, while rain pattered down. I was carried into the ward of a Field Hospital, a

---

65   Lance Corporal William F. Forbes, No178, killed on 1 November 1916, the son of Sarah and the late Alexander Forbes of Kingsmere Avenue, Belfast, buried in Pond Farm Cemetery, grave G18.

66   Battalion War Diary 1.11.16: "A party of 82 divided into two sections under 2/Lt J.D. O'Brien and 2/Lt R.V. Drought respectively attempted a raid on the Boche trenches. It was unsuccessful, only 2/Lt O'Brien and two men getting into the trenches. Our casualties were one man killed and 2/Lt O'Brien and 11 men wounded. The remainder of the day was quiet. At 5.30pm 2/Lt Ledlie took a patrol of ten men out for the purpose of bringing in the body of the man who had been killed in connection with the raid. It had been impossible to do this at the time owing to dawn breaking, and he had been placed in a shell hole. Unfortunately 2/Lt Ledlie's party were unable to accomplish their objective as the Boche had trained a machine gun on them and killed two of the party. They returned to our trenches bringing in the bodies of the two men."

beautifully finished, wooden hut, with about two dozen beds. It belonged to 13 General Hospital, Boulogne.

Saturday to Monday 4-13 November 1916: Boulogne

I stayed in Boulogne and have no grievances to relate. My leg was still kept in a splint and I had to lie on my back all the time. Hot fomentations were applied to my face and knee three times in the twenty-four hours. The dressing of the face always caused me a lot of pain but the Sister, who came from County Meath, said I was 'awfully good'. She was always very pleasant to me and took great pleasure in my nick-name 'McFuzz'.

I could now eat fairly well, anything that I could push in between my jaws, which had been greatly reduced in their opening capacity. All the cases in the ward were very bad ones. A Canadian in the bed beside me had lost his right leg and eye; he had besides about ten other big wounds. He and I became very friendly. I admired the Sisters greatly for the coolness, kindness and skill with which they carried out all their duties. I also read a couple of books.

England, hospital

Monday 13 November 1916: Dover

I got my labels and by stretcher and ambulance, I was finally removed on board the hospital ship, *Jan Brydel*, once King Albert's yacht, I was told. I have been unable to confirm this and the spelling of the name of the yacht is phonetic. This ship was furnished in the same style as the hospital train, everything being very clean, comfortable and fit for its purpose. We left at 12 (noon) and about 2pm arrived in Dover. I was laid out on my stretcher, on the railway platform, along with many others for a considerable time. On the crossing from France to England, we stretcher cases lay perfectly naked, being rolled in blankets.

On arrival at Dover we were met by kind ladies who handed us out cigarettes and supplied us with a small bag in which we could keep any personal belongings. At last I was put on a hospital train again and had a long, comfortable ride through the darkness.

The Battle of the Somme ended when Beaumont Hamel was captured on 13 November 1916.

England Again

Tuesday to Tuesday 14-28 November 1916: Beckett's Park

I arrived in Leeds in the darkness of the morning and, after another drive in the ambulance and another ride on the stretcher, I was put to bed in the ward Hood 1, 2nd Northern General Hospital, Leeds. The 2nd Northern General Hospital, Leeds, consisted of a brick building to which had been added a long corridor with a succession of wooden wards on each side of it, named after famous British admirals. The permanent building had been erected, I understood, as a school for lady teachers. One day my eye was examined, I was told, by the King's oculist. I was taken out of bed, placed in a bath chair and pushed along the corridor to the permanent building. There I waited my turn along with thirty others who were injured, mostly on the face. Then I learned that I had been placed in the wrong ward, among the 'limbs' cases, for my label had read 'Gunshot wounds on the leg, arm and face'. I should have been assigned to the 'head' ward for my facial wounds were the most serious.

After a convoy of wounded arrived there was 'an operation day' which was an exciting event for the other patients in the ward who were not 'going to the pictures'. The three or four victims would be wheeled out amid a lot of back-chat but in about an hour they returned as silent as corpses. Then gradually they became noisy for a period and often the chaps who were quietest by nature became the loudest shouters. They sang and blasphemed, they wept and they argued.

It was a large wooden hall, dimly lit at that time of the morning, and the numerous beds were occupied by sleeping patients. I was washed by a grand little sister, Miss Scott, from Dublin and then had my dressings attended to, after being relieved of my splint.

James McRoberts laying a wreath at the War Memorial in Armagh. He is accompanied by
Mr. Bennett, a long time friend. Richard Bennett (1871-1970) was, like James, a member
of the Methodist Church and a former member of the UVF. Pre-war he had worked in
the Gillis Factory in Armagh and on 12 June 1889 was one of those who rushed from
work to help rescue survivors of the Armagh railway disaster - among the dead were his
cousin Margaret Mills and her nephew. During the Great War he served in the Royal Irish
Fusiliers and Royal Engineers. On the Somme in July 1916, he was initially listed as being
missing in action. On the battlefield he met up with his friend Johnny Peel in no-man's-
land and as they embraced he said "And are we yet alive to see each other's face", a line
from the hymn by Charles Wesley (1749) and used by Methodists as a greeting and means
of identification. At the War's end he sent a telegram home that read 'Hold the fort for I
am coming, victory is nigh'. He was a long time member of the Royal British Legion and
Orange Order. He claimed that his faith got him through the War. (McRoberts family)

When recovering from his wounds James was lucky enough to be cared for
by some very attractive nurses. (Somme Museum, Newtownards)

The morning came and it was the time to get up for those who could. There was a good deal of noise, joking and laughter, into which the sisters entered in good part and I realised that at least I was free of France. However it was several years before I got rid of my wartime habits. I could not see the quiet fields of County Antrim without planning the most suitable system of trenches to protect them. I often had the feeling that I was exposing myself unnecessarily and expected to hear the whine of a bullet from the adjacent wood. I could not see a hill without imagining there were guns behind it.

Tuesday to Tuesday 14-28 November 1916: Beckett's Park
I remained in this hospital. The food was the best I had enjoyed for a long time past and there was plenty of fun with the chaps. Tuesday and Saturday were visitors' days so that crowds moved into and filled the place, making the scene livelier.

Some of these called to see strangers who might be inclined to appreciate them and it was thus I made the acquaintance of two excellent young ladies, the Bolton sisters, who came from Bramley. I also got to know a Miss Broadbent and two Miss Knoptons who visited me, bringing fruit, cake and cigarettes. The hospital sisters were also very kind and capable and I took particular notice of the young lady from Dublin by the name of Miss Scott, already mentioned.

One night while I was in Beckett's Park a Zeppelin dropped bombs on the hospital in York, about twenty-five miles away; it was brought down off the Durham coast I was told.

I was in bed all the time but the days passed quickly enough. In the bed to the left of me there was a fine-looking, intelligent solider called McCracken, who had been born in the Channel Islands but whose home was now in Leeds. He was visited by his sister who was exceptionally pleasant in appearance and educated in manner.

On the opposite side of the ward there was a Canadian who was now a walking case but who talked a lot and was treated as a joke by the other patients. Now the strangest thing happened, Miss McCracken fell in love with this Canadian, and although her brother was opposed to the wedding, she married him before I left Leeds. Thereafter I have never professed to understand women.

McCracken had been wounded and the doctors were attempting to cure a nerve by opening his thigh for a length of about eighteen inches between the knee and the groin. The appearance of the stitches when the wound was being dressed reminded me of the lacings that used to be at the back of my mother's corsets. The operation was not completely successful for when he got out of bed the toe of his shoe had to be tied to his braces to keep his foot horizontal; he was thus enabled to walk with the help of a stick. He was in the same ward at Gledhow Hall with me and finally he was discharged from the Army.

The dressing of my face-wound was treated with silver nitrate, which was often painful and brought the tears to my eyes, but I could easily stick that. My beard would persist in growing into the bandages and the nurse shaved me using a razor and some colourless liquid.

Wednesday 29 November 1916: Gledhow Hall

On the morning of the 29th November I got out of bed, for the first time for over four weeks, and I felt decidedly unsteady on my feet, dizzy and weak. But I was able to get my outfit at the Quartermaster's store and found myself in khaki, with a kit-bag under my arm. At 2pm I left the 2nd Northern General Hospital by motor ambulance and after a short journey round the outskirts of Leeds, came to a place called Gledhow Hall. Gledhow Hall was at that time owned by Sir James Kitson who later became Lord Airedale. About ten years afterwards the Hall was sold and converted into flats. This was a VAD Hospital, but had been really a fine country mansion and I became one of about eighty patients stationed there. I received a blue uniform, handed in my khaki with kit-bag and go a bed in an upstairs ward with an agreeable number of companions.

Wednesday to Sunday 29 November – 24 December 1916: Gledhow Hall

At Gledhow Hall I had an agreeable time for, from the beginning, I was allowed out of bed with a pass down town. The food was excellent and the sisters were both pretty and very kind, although their nursing skill was somewhat limited. Also at Gledhow Hall, we made our beds and kept the rooms tidy; we also took it in turns to wash up but otherwise had no work to do. It was a pleasant sensation for me to be seated at a dining table for my meals. There were several bookcases, two sitting rooms with fires, free writing paper and envelopes, so I could always find something to do to fill the passing hour. I read *Pip, a Knight on Wheel, The History of David Grieve, Laddie, A Garden of Lies, A Tramp*

Abroad, Tristam Shandy, The Stark Munroe Letters, Lying Lips, In White Raiment and *The Prodigal's Return.* The books of William Le Quex were page-turning as sensational novels, *A Knight on Wheels* was very humorous and *The Stark Munroe Letters* was most interesting. My face was dressed daily by one of the sisters in the large bathroom which was used as the surgery.

On 7th December, David Lloyd-George, after a breach with Asquith, became Prime Minister at the head of a coalition government.

While here I got to know quite a number of people who often invited me out to tea; they were very kind to me, kinder than ever I imagined any strangers could be. The goodness, the generosity, and the sympathy of the Yorkshire people I shall never forget. Nothing that could be done was too good for us and I went to the family of Billows, to Knopton's to Broadbent's and to Boye's. I got to know the mothers and fathers and was surprised at their broad-minded sympathy and generosity.

The girls treated us as if we had been long-standing friends and were delighted to do anything to help us to have a jolly time. We always received the best of food at these houses and the most excellent cigarettes and cigars. We had the best of wishes and always an open invitation to come back again, as often as we liked, while no offence was taken against any irregularities we might be guilty of.

We were often invited out, by the hundred, to have tea and entertainment by some club or wealthy person able to do so. Again everything was done for us in a lavish style while there was no sparing of food, cake, fruits and cigarettes. There were valuable prizes at the whist drives for the more fortunate and the entertainers were indefatigable in their efforts to amuse us. It was thus I visited Harewood House, the residence of Viscount Lascelles who afterwards married Princess Mary, the only daughter of King George V. I won a green-coloured pocket book at the whist drive on that occasion.

This generosity and thoughtfulness was remarkable, considering that there must have been continually about three to four thousand wounded soldiers in Leeds. The same would not be done for us anywhere, except in their city, I was assured. On the trams, if in the blue uniform of a wounded soldier, we always travelled free. Of course, from the tram I often saw Leeds' best-known building, Armley Gaol, where the notorious criminal, Charles Peace, was hanged.[1]

Another busy town I visited by tram was Morley, the birthplace of the First Earl of Oxford and Asquith. In the centre of Leeds there is a square with a mounted statue of the Black Prince, who is supposed to have encouraged the woollen industry. Around him is a circle of female, nude figures, but I never heard a sensible explanation of why they were there.

The VAD nurses at Gledhow Hall were pleasant girls with an abundance of good looks and all were very kind. Although their hours were long and their work often disagreeable, they were always cheerful and smiling. Christmas was now drawing near, my knee was healed and no bad effects remained, so that I walked freely. The bandage was off my face but the scars that remained were not in the way of beauty-marks!

---

1   Charles Frederick Peace (14 May 1832-25 February 1879), came from Sheffield and was a burglar and murderer, who in his time became something of a celebrity. He has been much romanticised in literature and the cinema.

Monday 25 December 1916: Gledhow Hall

On Christmas Day we had to stay inside the Hall. We had turkey for dinner but the potatoes were hard and the pudding was the Daily Mail Christmas gift to the troops, so that the feast could not be pronounced an unqualified success. In the evening there was a whist drive and so ended Christmas 1916.

Tuesday to Thursday 26 December 1916 – 4 January 1917: Gledhow Hall

The remainder of the week was a whirl of concerts and amusements. We were entertained at the Gambie Café, the Albert Hall and at Mrs Knopton's and then we had a night of our own when we could invite any young lady we chose. I brought Miss V. Bolton of Bramley, Leeds; a likeable young lady whom I had met at the 2nd Northern General Hospital.

We had an entertainment given by the nurses and patients, which was a real success, after which we had light refreshments along with our visitors and I saw Violet down to the avenue gates and thus passed the most enjoyable evening of that festive week. Earlier that week another chap and I spent a pleasant day at Bromley with the two Miss Boltons and their parents and had real Yorkshire pudding to our dinner. What spoiled everything was the early hour at which we had to return to the hospital, 7.30pm being the latest extension we could obtain. One night, after a concert, finding myself arm in arm with a girl called Lily, I stayed out in Gledhow Wood until 8pm and expected a rare row when I returned, but my absence had been fortunately overlooked.

I had a really good time and, as I was expecting to leave hospital soon, ignored any consequences. However, when the Medical Officer came round next day I was marked for dental treatment and thus a new chapter opened.

Friday to Wednesday 5-17 January 1917: Gledhow Hall

At that time my cheek was getting massage from a lady visitor at the Hall, to make the flesh fill out and remove the ugly wrinkles round the scars; the treatment seemed likely to achieve good results. So far I had received no word from Belgium since I left the Battalion, although I had written three times.

My letters would seem to have reached their destination for two parcels had arrived from France. One had my pocket book and this diary and bore the postmark Cookstown: the other contained the Battalion Christmas cards, very pretty affairs with a photo of the whole Battalion, taken at Bramshott, and this parcel was stamped by the Field Post Office. I received a letter from my charming, old flame Polly McClellan sympathising with me on my wounds and protesting her old interest in my welfare. I wrote back in just as warm and profuse a manner, for Polly was such a dear girl and such a pal.

I was hoping for my discharge from the Army and would have liked to be back again at Queen's University and my studies. This was an aimless, lazy life and I have had enough of the Army and of the war in France. I was not afraid of my skin but the idea of going out to bear the suspense of that life again was not agreeable.

I had pleasant times often in France and the month spent at Beauval was certainly a happy one. I had no real taste for concerts, house parties, or theatres because I had to attend many and had become bored with them. I wished again to retain my affairs in my own hands and develop my own talents and personality. Firstly I must learn to speak, to

James sits for a photograph after leaving hospital. The scars on his right cheek, caused by the explosion on 1 November 1916, can be plainly seen. (McRoberts family)

argue and debate, for I was too shy at raising my own voice. Above all, I wished to be in a position of truest and authority in my own profession.

During Christmas week there was a lot of snow and frost so that all the roads were in a perilous state for pedestrians. At the end of the week there was a thaw and the weather set in mild at the beginning of the New Year. After the first week there was again more keen frost which lasted until the middle of February. The ponds were all frozen over and there was plenty of skating to be had, if only one had the skates! Our own pond at Gledhow Wood was well frozen over, although the water flowed through it with a strong current.

At night we used to go down in the moonlight with the sisters who skated while we made slides. It was splendid! In Roundhay Public Park, both lakes were frozen over and there were crowds of pleasure seekers enjoying the novelty of skating. I spent a happy Sunday afternoon there. The day was lovely; hard, crisp snow covered the ground and crowds of people were on the ice and on the hillside, watching the tobogganing. I thought, however, I should prefer a climate with an excess of summer weather rather than an abundance of winter, beautiful and invigorating thought it might be.

Thursday to Wednesday 18-24 January 1917: Gledhow Hall

On January 18th, I went to the dentist at East Leeds War Hospital and had five teeth removed, including the roots of the three that Fritz had smashed; cocaine was used and I felt no pain. I returned to the dentist three more times and had all the other decayed teeth stopped.

In the evenings at Gledhow Hall we often had concerts of which I began to be wearied. I remember particularly one audacious, good-looking young lady who, night after night, used to sing: 'On the good ship Yocki Nicky doo!' Other songs were, 'There's a long, long trail a-winding', 'Good-bye-ee, don't cry-ee', 'Everybody's Doing it', 'Somewhere a Voice is Calling' and 'When I told them how wonderful you are', etc.

The talent was generally indifferent although I wished only good to the entertainers who did their best to amuse us. I visited three of the pantomimes in town. *Cinderella* at the Theatre Royal was poor but *Goody Two Shoes* at the Grand was the most magnificent affair of the kind I had ever witnessed; in it were Lupine Lane and Daisy Wood. *Little Bo Peep* at the empire was also very amusing but on the whole I did not find very great enjoyment from theatricals. I also went to various entertainments in town, held for our benefit, and I met lots of different girls, Mabel, Lily, Alice etc.

However, I lived a very hum-drum, blameless life in those days, chiefly no doubt because I had few opportunities to do otherwise! Some 'munitions girls whom I also got to know, were a lively lot who spoke the language of men and were not to be trifled with. It was a fact that on one occasion they took a troublesome railway official into a compartment one day and pushed him back on to the platform again, wearing his boots, that was all! I had several letters from Willie Roy during these months, letter from over yonder, which I read and re-read, and loved the dear fellow for all his past and present kindness.

Willie Roy wrote, surprising me with a great compliment, saying that in times of danger he always admired my coolness which filled him with great confidence. I never thought I merited any such testimonial. He sent a message from Félice enquiring about my welfare. *A la gloire de Mademoiselle Félice*, she loved me, I know, for my curly hair.

Thursday to Wednesday 25 January to 28 January 1917: Gledhow Hall

I now have to tell how I came to know the Watsons of Clarendon Place. One night, about the end of January, a young lady stopped an Irishman, whom she recognised as such by his cap badge. Paddy Norris he was called, of the Royal Irish Regiment and she asked him to come to her home for tea some evening for, as she explained, she was Irish too.

Paddy was going on his furlough to Mullingar in Ireland the next day and said he was sorry he could not accept but promised to send another Irishman in his place and that other Irishman was me.

I went to Clarendon Placed and met Mr. and Mrs. Watson and after a few questions we soon found that not only did I hail from the same corner of County Antrim – but that I was actually a distant relation of Mrs. Watson. We soon became friends and I had the family history.

The conversation went like this:

Myself: "Good evening".

Mr. W: "Good evening – you are from Ireland?"

Myself: "Yes"

Mr. W: "Which part of Ireland?"
Myself: "Near Belfast"
Mr. W: "Whereabouts – near Larne?"
Myself: "Near Kilwaughter"
Mr. W: "What is your name?"
Myself: "McRoberts"
Mr. W: "You are almost certain to be a relation of my wife".

The three eldest sons were in the Army, David had gone to France with the North Irish Horse but had recently been transferred to the 1st Royal Irish Rifles and had been in the trenches, about which his mother was very annoyed. Willie was a Royal Army Medical Corps orderly at York where there had been a Zeppelin raid recently, and Jack was in the cadets, training at Newcastle, County Down. There were two daughters, one at University taking a science course and the younger one in Government work at Dewsbury: there were also two small boys about nine and twelve approximately.

During the month of February, once a week, found me at the Watsons'. I got to know the girls, the elder, Kathleen, was tall and dark, the younger, Dorothy, was shorter and plump with beautiful chestnut-coloured hair, both were considered good-looking and neatly, if plainly dressed. Both had been educated at Methodist College, Belfast, and both hated Leeds, much preferring their grandmother's place at Glenavy, County Antrim.

I got on well with the family and we had pleasant times playing 'Donkey'. The girls went to a dancing class although they were Quakers by religion. Mr. Watson, I always found sitting by the fire, coughing up the chimney and looking forward to Sunday to get a rest. Mr. Watson occupied a small chemical works. I visited it one day and was introduced to the chemist who was a Frenchman, but his laboratory I thought, was not impressive. Mrs. Watson was a healthy, good-looking lady upon whom the years and motherhood had left few marks. I found all delightfully sensible, broad-minded and at the same time homely and fond of home life. The house was large and well furnished; the girls liked piano playing but did not go into ecstasies over picture-houses and music-hall performances in general. They would much rather has lived the quieter, more genial life of the country, so that they seemed to be rather lonely in this great city.

Shortly after the beginning of February we were allowed out from 1 to 6 daily. I was generally back on time but, once or twice, was guilty of being a few minutes late was up against the matron, Miss Edith Cliffe, for my offences. I found her a hard nut to deal with for she took no reasonable excuse. In fact, she would not stand any reasoning but expected the accused to endure a lecture from her. Any interruption of her passionate harangue would draw only sarcastic and probably insulting language.

She was a woman, and of course, one could not deal with a female bully in the same way as the male specimen. A Welshman started whistling to himself, in the middle of one of her lectures, with the result that he did not stay much longer at Gledhow Hall. She was very keen on discipline, so that the hospital was a kind of compulsory reforming school. A few minutes late for roll call was a crime serious enough to send one back to Beckett's Park with a blot on his character sheet.

The fact that this was a new, strange city to us and it was possible to get lost for five minutes, the fact that trams were often crowded and did not always stop for one, the fact that the vehicles often broke down As conditions were, the fact that none of us had watches and a 'good friend's' clock might be slow but none of these excuses carried the least weight with her, they only stirred up her reservoir of intimidating and insulting language.

When a concert was on we must attend it or go to bed and forfeit a packet of Woodbines. We must go to church on Sunday morning and attend a private service at the Hall in the evening, all to please her despotic self. She had an expression that she would doubt her own honour before that of a soldier and yet she was always suspiciously spying on us. Woe to the chap who stood talking to a girl in front of this most respectable house! In appearance the matron was fat with a heavy face and a gradation of chins. In her time she had been a golf champion but now she was middle-aged and unmarried. The Sergeant-Major (or the ward-master), was not a bad sort, considering he was an old, army-provost-sergeant; but he lived in mortal dread of the matron's displeasure.

There was a London chap in my ward, the life and soul of the hospital, who interested me a lot. One evening this Londoner was returning to the convalescent home, during a dense fog, when he felt his knees touching something which he imagined to be a woman.

"Beg pardon Miss!" he exclaimed, and the next moment felt himself prostrated on the wet grass. He had been following the demesne wall when he came to an entrance where it was replaced by a low chain over which he had tripped. This man had no end of Army and family experiences to tell and could relate them in the most animated and amusing manner. When he entered a room, all books were closed and all writing stopped. He was a regular soldier of thirteen years' service; four times wounded, gassed once, married with three children and he did tell some stories.

But even in him I found the traits of a Londoner which made me dislike and shun him more or less. I find Londoners the worst of companions, abominably selfish and with the most rotten idea of humour that I have come across. I never would have anything more to do with them after a little incident that occurred some time ago. In Leeds City I had an encounter with a wounded Londoner which rather exemplified their type of humour that I didn't appreciate. He asked me if I could spare him a few matches. As I had a box half-full, I put a good dozen into his hand. He brought out a box three-quarters full and slipped in my dozen, thanked me, laughed and went away delighted, I suppose, with his joke. I was too much astonished at the time to say what I wanted but I never forgot the incident.

Thursday to Monday 1-12 March 1917: Gledhow Hall
I had asked the civilian doctor who visited us once every week to mark me out for my depot but he would not take upon himself to do so. The dentist said my gums were not ready yet to take the impression for my teeth and he recommended me for further treatment with my unit. On March 9th, Major Neggs from the 2nd Northern General Hospital marked me for a board.

Tuesday to Sunday 13-25 March 1917: Beckett's Park
On Tuesday 13th, I left Gledhow Hall, being much relieved to have reached the end of a period which had become wearisome to me. I was in a party of twenty-three who went by motor ambulance to the 2nd Northern General Hospital and I found myself in my old ward, Hood 1. I changed out of my khaki, in which I had traveled, into the comfortable flannel suit of hospital grey and stayed there the rest of the week.

Post-war reunion of the 14th Battalion. (Royal Ulster Rifles Museum)

On Thursday I went for a walk round Kirskstall Abbey, Guiseley and Hereforth. The day was fine and the old ruined Abbey struck me as noble in its setting of wild and beautiful countryside. The valley of the River Aire was however a great industrial district. I also filled in the papers from my Medical Board. But I still had to wait many days for my board meeting and long days of waiting they were. I had no money and I had practically nothing interesting to help pass the time. After getting out of bed at 6.30am, I helped with the breakfast and washed up afterwards.

In the hospital in Boulogne, where all the patients were bed-ridden, there were orderlies of the Royal Army Medical Corps to attend to our private needs. Screens were put around the bed and a bed-pan was brought. Afterwards the pan still wrapped in the towel was taken away and the screens removed. Here in my ward in Leeds there were very few male orderlies but about one quarter of the patients were on their feet during the day and were able to assist their bed-ridden companions. The pan was taken to the lavatory at the end of the hut and was cleaned in a special sink by a strong spray of water.

Then I swept up and waited from 9 to 12 noon when we had dinner. The time did hang heavily, my only compensation being the respect that I seemed to earn from both patients and nurses. I must indeed be coming into man's estate. I found some employment as a letter writer mainly because the patient had his right arm in a sling, but I suspected in some cases it was because the patient could hardly write. Anyhow I found the experience highly amusing, especially the letters to the wives. On Saturday or Sunday, I always went to the Watsons'. I looked forward to this visit and found myself liking them more and more while I think they all liked me. 'Teddy' was the name they christened me. I stayed out late on several occasions, coming into the hospital by a window at the back of the ward. I was missed one night, reported and given seven days 'confined to barracks'.

Monday to Friday 26-30 March 1917: Beckett's Park

I was 'boarded' by Colonel Barr and marked C111 PT 'Labor of National Importance, Permanently Transferred'. I was well satisfied with the result for, although I was not entirely out of the army, I was practically so. Another week of waiting for my furlough papers this time.

Saturday to Monday 31 March to 2 April 1917: Beckett's Park To Stranraer

I got a weekend pass in order to spend the leave at the Watsons'. I had a most enjoyable time and cannot recollect having had a better one. The girls and I had a lot of fun. They were good enough to tell me how much they liked me and how much they would miss me when I had gone. On Sunday morning there was a heavy snowfall and we scarcely left the house all day.

On Monday morning, the 2nd of April, the weather was worse and trams were stopped by the snow. I had to walk to Beckett's Park Hospital to get my furlough papers and then walk back again. After dinner at the Watsons' I went down town where I met Kathleen coming off her train at 5.15pm, and we both had tea together. Then I met Dorothy at 6.40pm and we all came home together. I took leave of my good friends and was escorted to the station by the girls for the train which left at 8.40pm. I was just in time as I had to enter the carriage by the window. I stopped an hour at Newcastle where there was a YMCA hut, also one and a half hours at Carlisle where there was a restaurant and reached Stranraer at 7am.

In 1922 I called at Clarendon Place, Leeds, to see the Watsons', but on the doorstep was met by a gruff Yorkshire man who believed they had gone to London. Then in 1937, I accidentally got their address and was able to visit them. They lived near London, out the Great West Road, in sight of the demesne of Sir William S. Gilbert (of Gilbert and Sullivan fame). This demesne had recently become part of London's green belt so it was felt that the view from the house was assured for all time. Mrs. Watson and Kathleen were very much alive, but the father was dead. Mrs. Watson told me that he had just perfected his water-softener and now her three sons had a factory in production. I visited one of the sons who with his English wife and family lived in a villa close at hand. I saw Dorothy as well; she had only just married. Kathleen was still single.

Home and remembrance

Tuesday 3 April 1917: Stranraer to Home

I had a rough crossing to Larne but slept most of the time. The weather was cold but there was not so much snow in Ireland as I had left behind. I spent the morning at Mrs Buchanan's in Main Street and went to Kilwaughter Halt by the 2.45pm train, being accompanied home by my brother John from the Grammar School. I received a kind reception at home, where they seemed surprised to see me looking so well.

It was not until January 1918, that I was discharged and after various boards, was classified as eighty per cent disabled for life. Immediately I resumed my work at Queen's University, and in 1919 obtained the degree BSc, in Civil Engineering. For six years I was engaged on various jobs in both the North and South of Ireland but in 1926 I was appointed Assistant County Surveyor of Armagh. In 1931, I was promoted Deputy County Surveyor and in 1947, I became the County Surveyor. I resigned the position, for reasons of health, at the end of 1954.

I married Elizabeth Isabel Emerson of Armagh in 1924 and have two sons. The elder was born in 1931, obtained his LLB, degree at Queen's University, Belfast, in 1953 and is now a solicitor in Armagh. The younger was born in 1939 and is now a student at Dublin University.

James and Isabel on honeymoon at Dunglo, County Killarney. This photograph was taken on Wednesday 3 September 1924, the same day that Civil War broke out in China. (McRoberts family)

The memorial plaque in Ballynure Presbyterian Church. It holds the names of eight local men who died in the Great War, including James' friend Robert Moore, killed in Mesopotamia. (C.H. Mawhinney/Richard Wallace)

Annisgrove, the family home at the Hightown Road, Glengormley, County Antrim, a post-war view. (McRoberts family)

The memorial plaque to Second Lieutenant Allan McClellan in Ballynure Presbyterian Church. (C.H. Mawhinney/Richard Wallace)

Ardmore, the McRoberts family home in Armagh. (McRoberts family)

James McRoberts and his brothers. (McRoberts family)

Lord and Lady Brookeborough, Brian McRoberts, his wife Sylvia
and his mother Jane, nee McMinn. (McRoberts family)

Brother John. (McRoberts family)

Engagement photograph of James and Isobel. (McRoberts family)

Isobel. (McRoberts family)

James laying wreath at the Armagh War Memorial on behalf
of the Methodist Church. (McRoberts family)

Armagh War Memorial, little changed since James McRoberts paid his annual tribute. However, an amount of damage was caused to the Memorial when a bomb exploded directly outside the Courthouse on 3 September 1993, with much greater damage to the Museum of the Royal Irish Fusiliers, seen in the background. (Jonathan Maguire, BA)

Armagh War Memorial today, there is little damage to be seen, unlike Continental memorials, which are not repaired in ensuing conflicts. (Jonathan Maguire, BA)

Remembrance Day Parade, Armagh November 1953. The men have just passed the Orange Hall, about half way along the Mall, James McRoberts in the centre wearing a dark suit carrying a raincoat, to his left is his friend Richard Bennett, behind him, wearing a bowler hat and with glasses, is John Webster JP, while in the centre of the second rank with an impressive array of medals is George McCartney. On the right hand side are two women looking towards the camera - the one wearing the light coloured hat is the late Bessie Blocksidge, the bareheaded woman is Sheila Irwin. On the left-hand side of the parade the first child is Irene McAnlis, the third Brenda Stevenson, while the fourth and fifth are sisters Lynda and Loretta Armstrong.

The 14th Rifles and the remainder of the War

When James McRoberts was evacuated from the Battalion at the beginning of November 1916, his War was, to all intents and purposes, ended. For those Young Citizens who remained the worst was yet to come. The remainder of 1916 was taken up with raids against enemy positions, some more successful than others, while them did their best to deal with the worsening weather conditions.

The beginning of 1917 saw the Battalion, in concert with the remainder of the Division, prepare for the capture of the Messines-Wytschaete Ridge. On 12 January the Battalion Commanding Officer, Lieutenant Colonel Lloyd, was sent to hospital and Captain Mulholland took command – he was the seventh commander since the Battalion had come into service. The 14th Rifles was a very unlucky unit when it came to commanding officers. Throughout February there was severe frost and men suffered due to a lack of proper clothing and equipment. On 9 February a draft of reinforcements arrived, men from the Cavalry, London Irish and the Buffs (Royal East Kent Regiment).

There was much raiding on both sides and the artillery exchanged salvo after salvo. On the night of 27 May Divisional Headquarters, located at Ulster Camp to the west of Dranoutre, was shelled by a German 100mm railway gun. During this month the Battalion sent out patrols on a nightly basis, but due to the bright moonlight little information could be obtained.

On 7 June the Battalion took part in the Battle of Messines, an attack that was a complete success, mainly due to superb planning and the detonation of a series of mines under the German line. The Battalion performed well in this battle and as result the award of nine Military Medals, three Military Crosses, one Distinguished Service Cross and one Distinguished Conduct Medal was made.

In August the Battalion fought in the Battle of Langemarck and at Passchendaele, also known as the Third Battle of Ypres. Between 6am on 16 August and 9am two days later, some 58 officers and 1,278 'other ranks' passed through the 36th Divisional Dressing Station. Due to the torrential rain, which had turned the ground into a sea of clinging mud, it often took eight men to carry a wounded man on a stretcher. One officer recorded, "The Battle of Messines was won at Zero, the Battle of Ypres was lost long before it." The Battalion War Diary for 16 August at 5.30am reads, "Runners could not possibly get through the machine gun fire. The strain on one's nerve is terrific." On 31 August the War Diary records "Owing to the heavy casualties in the 107th Brigade the 8th and 9th Rifles are being amalgamated. The surplus will go to bring the 10th and 15th Rifles up to strength, and the 13th and 14th Rifles will get what remains."

From September to November the Battalion advanced to the Hindenburg Line, a system of trenches described as, "in all probability the most formidable constructed in the course of the War."[1] On 2 September, the supporting artillery was rationed to 30

---

1   Falls, C., *The History of the 36th (Ulster) Division* (Belfast & London, 1922).

shells per day. On 20 September the War Diary records further awards – 15 Military Medals, one DSO, a Bar to the Military Cross and four new awards of the Military Cross. These were for actions fought by the Battalion on 16 August, a 'disastrous day'.[2]

November saw the Battle of Cambrai, and the first major use of tanks by the British. By 11 December the Battalion is almost worn out, sick parades are large, 118 men reported sick on this particular day. A 'working party' of 160 men was required, but only 75 were passed as fit by the Medical Officer.

On 30 January 1918 it was announced to the Battalion that the War Office had ordered a reorganisation of infantry brigades, they would now consist of three battalions as opposed to four. On 17 February the 14th Rifles, after some three and a half years' existence and faithful service, would become No23 Entrenching Battalion, a depressing end to a valiant band of men.

---

2   14th Rifles Battalion War Diary.

Post-war – County Surveyor

Post-war James McRoberts enjoyed a successful career with Armagh County Council as a surveyor. During the Second World War, he had not only served for a time as a Captain in the 8th (Armagh) Battalion of the Ulster Home Guard, but carried out, in addition to his normal duties, the role of an Assistant Surveyor who was away on active service.

His primary responsibilities were in relation to road works, which led to a great improvement in the standard of country roads. Supplementary to this James McRoberts undertook the erection of subsidiary buildings and other works for the Tuberculosis Committee and Mental Health Committee. Added to this was the supervision of maintenance of Court Houses, when all of these services were still a local responsibility. James McRoberts was a relentless worker who constantly rendered invaluable service to the County.

Of particular interest was the work done on the bypass road at Verner's Inn, an excellent piece of construction due entirely to the skilful manner in which James McRoberts carried out the work as Deputy County Surveyor. An application received by the Council to run double-decker buses on some other roads from Armagh was refused as James was of the opinion that in most cases the roads were unsuitable for such vehicles.

"A road improvement scheme which took nearly eight months to carry out and cost about £25,000 will make 'the rough places plain' for thousands of people who travel annually between Belfast and Dublin by road" – so read the *Belfast Telegraph* of Monday 7 November 1949.

The success of this scheme lay in the hands of James McRoberts. Prior to him becoming involved it was felt that any attempt to improve the cross-border road at Newry would meet with too many difficulties. The road was standing on a bog rampart between forty and fifty five feet wide and with almost vertical sides, while a number of outcrops of rock studded the northern side. During frosty and wet weather the sides often experienced landslides. However, when James McRoberts submitted his report he stated, "This was a job that had to be done sometime and it would be better to do it now."

It was decided that due to the narrowness of the route a one-way system would be introduced. All southbound traffic would use the old Dublin Road, while vehicles travelling north would use a side road leading past Aghayalloge Railway Bridge. As double-decker buses were unable to pass under this bridge, the railway company agreed to use only single-deckers on the route. Large vehicles, such as furniture vans, were allowed to use the northern route under strict supervision. Despite the widespread use of road signs there were those drivers who went the wrong way and there was a regular crop of prosecutions at Newry Petty Sessions during that summer. While it had been planned that the road would be closed for a full year, the work was completed in just eight months.

On his retirement, after 28 years of service, James McRoberts was presented with a gift certificate for a new television set. The reception in the area at that time was very poor and it was felt that as this would improve in the future the set could be collected at a more suitable time. Among the guests in Armagh Court House that night was Mr G. Leyburn, MBE, JP and Mr H.W.F. Reid, Secretary to the County Council. Sir Norman Strong sent his apologies and a letter of personal appreciation. Mr Leyburn stated, "His work for the County in his twenty eight years as Assistant and County Surveyor needed no re-telling." Mr J. Black JP, told the gathering that in his opinion they had, in Mr McRoberts, one of the finest County Surveyors in Northern Ireland – "the roads in some parts were once little more than donkey cart tracks and were now capable of carrying heavy traffic."

Casualty list 'D' Company, 14th Battalion Royal Irish Rifles (YCV), 6 May 1916

Names are listed as they appear in the Battalion War Diary. Unless otherwise stated all men are buried in Authuile Military Cemetery.

Second Lieutenant Jerome Lennie Walker, age 27 years, the son, of F. Manderson and Helen Lennie Walker of Mount Royal, Whitehead, County Antrim, also of Helen's Bay and Courtrai, grave D58. The first officer of the Young Citizen Volunteers to fall in action.

No 2907, Private J.H. McBratney, age 24 years, the son of Samuel and Anna B. McBratney of The Toy, Killyleagh, County Down, resided at Brownlow Street, Comber, grave D52.

No 16158, Private E. Adams, age unknown, no family details listed, a former pattern maker in Harland and Wolff, he lived in Cullingtree Street, Belfast, grave D1.

No 17242, Private A. Beattie, age 20 years, the son of the late Mr D.A. and Mrs D. Beattie of Belfast, grave D49.

No 18109, Lance Corporal John Stanley Lowe, age 19 years, the son of Charles and Agnes Lowe, The Station Hotel, Harrogate, Yorkshire. Born at Kidderminster, grave D53.

No 16869, Private Tom Martin, age 22 years, the son of Samuel Alexander and Fanny Martin of Springfield Road, Belfast, grave D55.

No 18780, Private Thomas George Sloane, age 26 years, the son of Benjamin and Harriet E. Sloane of Elswick Street, Belfast, grave D50. His brother, T.G. Sloane, also served and was seriously wounded.

No 6744, Private David T McKeown, age 24 years, the son of George McKeown of Tudyniskay, Dromara, County Down and nephew of David McKeown of McClure Street, Belfast, grave D54.

No 6050, Private G. Tollerton, no other details listed, grave D48. He is listed as J. Tollerton in the Battalion War Diary.

No 4642, Private James Walker, age 24 years, the son of James and Mary A. Walker of Dunadry, County Antrim. Buried in Forceville Communal Cemetery, plot 1, row C, grave 14.

No 15085, Private George Kirkwood, age 22 years, the son of Mary and the late James Kirkwood of Belfast, he was a member of Brantwood Football Club. Served in B Company on attachment to D Company, died of wounds on 9 May 1916 and buried in Forceville Communal Cemetery, plot 1, row C, grave 10.

No 15443, Lance Corporal William McLauchlan, age 19 years. The son of William and Elizabeth Stewart McLauchlan, of Milford, County Armagh, grave D60.

No 14730, Private W.H. Grainger, no age or family detail listed, grave D59.

Bibliography

Belfast Newsletter, various issues

Belfast Telegraph, various issues

Bowman, T., *Irish Regiments in the Great War, Discipline and Morale* (Manchester: University Press, 2003)

Corns, C. & Hughes-Wilson, J., *Blindfold and Alone: British Military Executions in the Great War* (London: Cassell, 2001)

Falls, C., *The History of the 36th (Ulster) Division* (Belfast & London, 1922)

Kipling, R. & Hewitt, J., *Rudyard Kipling: Everyman Poetry* (London: Everyman, 1998)

Orr, P., *The Road to The Somme*: *Men of the Ulster Division Tell Their Story* (Belfast: Blackstaff Press, 2008)

Perry, N. (ed.), *Major General Oliver Nugent and the Ulster Division, 1915-1918* (Stroud, Sutton Publishing, 2007)

Pope, S. & Wheal E-A., *The Macmillan Dictionary of the First World War* (London: Macmillan, 1995)

Sheffield, G. & Bourne, J. (eds.), *Douglas Haig*: *War Diaries & Letters, 1914-1918* (Weidenfeld & Nicolson: London, 2005)

Index